A HISTORY OF
BRITISH RAILWAYS
DOWN TO THE YEAR
1830

Vignette from an old plan. (Author's collection)

A History of
BRITISH RAILWAYS

DOWN TO THE YEAR

1830

---★---

BY

C. F. DENDY MARSHALL

WITH AN INTRODUCTION BY

W. H. CHALONER

---★---

OXFORD UNIVERSITY PRESS

Oxford University Press, Ely House, London W. 1

GLASGOW NEW YORK TORONTO MELBOURNE WELLINGTON
CAPE TOWN SALISBURY IBADAN NAIROBI DAR ES SALAAM LUSAKA ADDIS ABABA
BOMBAY CALCUTTA MADRAS KARACHI LAHORE DACCA
KUALA LUMPUR SINGAPORE HONG KONG TOKYO

FIRST PUBLISHED 1938
REPRINTED LITHOGRAPHICALLY IN GREAT BRITAIN
(WITH NEW INTRODUCTION)
FROM CORRECTED SHEETS OF THE FIRST EDITION
AT THE UNIVERSITY PRESS, OXFORD
BY VIVIAN RIDLER
PRINTER TO THE UNIVERSITY
1971

INTRODUCTION TO THE SECOND IMPRESSION

OVER thirty years have passed since C. F. Dendy Marshall first published *A History of British Railways down to the Year 1830*, and during this period research in this field has gone forward rapidly. A number of corrections have been made to the text from various sources and some of the recent literature is referred to in the new footnotes. The opportunity is now taken to refer to the more important of those books and articles published since 1938 which may be used to supplement the information so diligently collected by the author. No attempt has been made to mention all *post* 1938 articles on every early railway in Great Britain; references to many of these will be found in the bibliographical list printed by Bertram Baxter in his book mentioned below. Attention must also be called to George Ottley, *A Bibliography of British Railway History* (1965), and E. T. Bryant, *Railways: a Reader's Guide* (1968).

A most important addition to the literature is Mr. C. E. Lee's *The Evolution of Railways* (2nd edition, revised and enlarged, 1943).[1] This is indispensable, disposing as it does of a number of hoary legends, such as that which derives the word 'tram' from the surname of Benjamin Outram, the engineer.[2] Mr. C. E. Lee's subsequent paper 'Railway Facts and Fallacies' (*Trans. Newcomen Society*, vol. xxxiii, for 1960–1 (1962), pp. 1–16) should also be noted. R. S. Smith's 'Huntington Beaumont, Adventurer in Coal Mines' (*Renaissance and Modern Studies*, Nottingham, vol. i, 1957, pp. 115–53), suggests that the celebrated Wollaton waggonway for coal was probably constructed in 1605 and not in 1598; see, however, the same author's later article, 'England's First Rails: a Reconsideration' (*Renaissance and Modern Studies*, vol. iv, 1960, pp. 119–34), in which he places the date a little earlier. For the first large-scale use of cast-iron rails, on the Coalbrookdale Company's railway from Ketley to the River Severn, from 1767 onwards, see W. H. Chaloner and A. Birch, 'The First Cast-iron Rails: New Evidence' (*Railway Magazine*, September 1951, pp. 632–3).

Bertram Baxter's *Stone Blocks and Iron Rails* (1966) is a detailed

---

[1] See also M. J. T. Lewis, *Early Wooden Railways* (1970).

[2] The present writer cannot share the doubts of Bertram Baxter, expressed in *Stone Blocks and Iron Rails* (1966), pp. 18–20, about Mr. Lee's conclusions.

study of the rise and fall of the horse railway in Great Britain, based on intensive field-work as well as on research in libraries and archives. It includes a gazetteer of waggonways and tramroads as well as a list, with addendum, of printed and manuscript sources essential for the study of the pre-steam railway (pp. 237–55, 260). It is to this list that researchers should turn to discover whether the line they have in mind has already been investigated. One of the few Mr. Baxter missed was the unincorporated Trevil Rail Road Company in Ebbw Vale (1793), a feeder to the Monmouth Canal Navigation, which is discussed in an anonymous article in *The Railway Gazette* (March 15th, 1940, pp. 380–1).

Mr. C. E. Lee has also written extensively on early British railways in the following sources:

(*a*) 'The World's Oldest Railway: Three Hundred Years of Coal Conveyance to the Tyne Staiths', *Trans. Newcomen Society*, vol. xxv, for 1945–7 (1950), pp. 141–62. This refers to that section of the Tanfield branch of the former L.N.E. Railway between Norwood and Fugar bank in Co. Durham which came into use for coal traffic at least as early as 1671.

(*b*) 'Tyneside Tramroads of Northumberland: Some Notes on the Engineering Background of George Stephenson', *Trans. Newcomen Society*, vol. xxvi, for 1947–9 (1953), pp. 199–229. This article contains three excellent detailed maps.

(*c*) 'The Waggonways of Tyneside', *Archaeologia Aeliana*, 4th ser., vol. 29 (1951), pp. 135–202 (maps and illustrations).

(*d*) 'Early Railways in Surrey', *Trans. Newcomen Society*, vol. xxi, for 1940–1 (1943), pp. 49–79. This deals with the early history, from 1801 onwards, of the Surrey Iron Railway and its continuation, the Croydon, Merstham, & Godstone Iron Railway Company.

Edward Hughes, in his *North Country Life in the Eighteenth Century: the North-East 1700–1750* (1952), has something to say about waggonways (esp. pp. 153–5) in the North-east.

Further light has been shed upon the early history of the first railway for which an Act of Parliament was passed—Charles Brandling's Middleton colliery railway, 1758—in W. Gordon Rimmer's article 'Middleton Colliery near Leeds (1770–1830)' (*Yorkshire Bulletin of Economic and Social Research*, vol. vii, March 1955, pp. 41–57). Mr. V. A. Hatley has chronicled Northamptonshire's first railway, although a temporary one, in his pamphlet *The Blisworth Hill Railway, 1800–1805* (3rd printing,

1966; originally appeared in *Reports and Papers* of the Northamptonshire Antiquarian Society, 1962–6).[1] C. E. Lee's *The Swansea and Mumbles Railway* (2nd revised edn., 1954) deals with the earliest passenger line in the world, which was incorporated by Act of Parliament in 1804; the transport of passengers on it began on March 25th, 1807. Mr. C. R. Clinker's *The Hay Railway* (1960) is the first history of an early railway company to be written largely from the original records of the line, constructed by virtue of an Act of 1811.

Miss Lois Basnett's 'The History of the Bolton and Leigh Railway, based on the Hulton Papers (1824–8)' explores the early years of the first public railway in Lancashire which was opened throughout two years before the line from Liverpool to Manchester (*Trans. Lancs. and Ches. Antiquarian Society*, vol. lxii, 1950–1, pp. 157–76). The first volume of J. I. C. Boyd's *The Festiniog Railway . . . 1800–1889* (1956) contains details about the origins of this interesting line, and its historical connexion with the Nantlle Railway, the first Act for which was passed in 1825. Further details about early railways in North Wales will be found in A. H. Dodd, *The Industrial Revolution in North Wales* (2nd revised edn., 1951, pp. 110–19).

R. E. Carlson's *The Liverpool and Manchester Railway Project, 1821–1831* (1969) is an exhaustive history of the early stages in the history of this celebrated company, with an excellent bibliography (pp. 246–64). Also to be noted is the translation and editing by E. A. Forward of the 'Report on Railways in England, 1826–27' by two Prussian engineers, Carl von Oeynhausen and Heinrich von Dechen (*Trans. Newcomen Society*, vol. xxix, for 1953–5 (1959), pp. 1–12).[2] Mr F. C. Mather's *After the Canal Duke* (1970) contains new material on canal–railway relations in the 1820s.

On the early railway engineers themselves less has been published. Chapter X, 'The Coming of the Railways', of L. T. C. Rolt's *Thomas Telford* (1958) will be found useful. Sir Alexander Gibb's *The Story of Telford: the Rise of Civil Engineering* (1935) contains (pp. 320–1) a list of early railway projects with which the great engineer was concerned. The first 200 pages of L. T. C. Rolt's *George and Robert Stephenson* (1960) are particularly relevant. The same author has also written

---

[1] See, however, Kenneth Brown's article in *The Railway Gazette* on 'Northampton's First Railway: was it Britain's one and only "Railway Road?"' (March 24th, 1939, pp. 502–3) and his letter in the issue of May 12th, 1939.

[2] An edition by C. E. Lee of Forward's complete translation of this report is to be published by the Newcomen Society during 1971.

an introduction (pp. iii–vi) to the centenary reprint of Mrs. E. M. S. Paine's *The Two James's and the Two Stephensons, or the Earliest History of Passenger Transit on Railways* (1st edn., 1861; 2nd edn., 1961). This concerns the relationship between William James (1771–1837), the pioneer railway projector and surveyor, and his son W. H. James on the one hand, and the Stephensons on the other. Mrs. Paine was the elder James's daughter, and as Mr. Rolt remarks: 'Mrs. Paine . . . believed passionately that her father and her brother . . . had been the victims of grave injustice. Unfortunately strong emotion of this kind, however justifiable, seldom goes hand in hand with objective truth.'

A note on the author will be found on the following page. But before concluding, I wish to express my gratitude to Mr. Charles E. Lee for the long loan of the late C. F. Dendy Marshall's annotated file copy of the original edition of the present work, and for other unstinted help.

W. H. CHALONER

The University of Manchester
September 1970

A NOTE ON THE AUTHOR

CHAPMAN FREDERICK DENDY MARSHALL, born in 1872, received his education at Hurstpierpoint and Trinity College, Cambridge, from which he graduated M.A. Although called to the Bar at the Inner Temple in 1898 he did not practise, and preferred to devote himself to railway engineering and to the writing of engineering history. On the practical side he evolved a realignment of four cylinders in locomotive compounding so as to control steam entry by two valve spindles and derived motion, thus saving two sets of valve gears (W. A. Tuplin, *North Western Steam*, pp. 125–7). This was applied to the L.N.W.R. Company's locomotive no. 1361, *Prospero* (*The Locomotive*, vol. xxi, p. 219). During the First World War he became a technical examiner at the Munitions Inventions Department and managed the Ministry of Munitions *Journal*. His paper on 'The Motion of Railway Vehicles on a Curved Line' was awarded the George Stephenson Research Prize by the Council of the Institution of Mechanical Engineers in 1930, and another paper on 'The Resistance of Express Trains' was the first extensive study of aerodynamics as affecting railway trains.

The four works for which he will be best remembered are his *Centenary History of the Liverpool and Manchester Railway* (1930), *A History of the Southern Railway* (1936), the present work (1938), and *A History of Railway Locomotives down to the End of the Year 1831*, which was published posthumously in 1953. In this last work will be found (p. ix) a list of his published books. His railway books were conceived on the grand scale and his scholarship was of a high order. Possessed of comfortable private means, he was described at the time of his death in 1945 as 'a kindly gentleman ever ready to discuss engineering history with those interested and to show them his magnificent collection of railroadiana'. He was a member of numerous learned and professional societies, and assisted in the foundation of the Newcomen Society for the study of the history of engineering and technology in 1920. He held the office of President in 1934–6. He was also an outstanding philatelist (see *The Railway Gazette*, June 22nd, 1945; *The Locomotive*, July 14th, 1945).

PREFACE

A PROMINENT feature of this book is the large proportion of quotations; in fact an unkind critic might liken it to a collection of newspaper cuttings.

If it had been written in the old-fashioned way, all the information would have been paraphrased and cast into a continuous narrative, interspersed with the author's own ideas and comments; without any references to authorities. By that method a book might have been produced which would have ranked higher as literature; but it would have been impossible for a reader to know whether any particular passage was merely a guess of the author's, or was based on a contemporary source; and, if the latter, still impossible to assess its reliability, without knowing the origin.

I have thought it best to lay all the cards which I have been able to collect on the table, thereby allowing every one to form his own opinion of the value to be attached to each. As some further justification, it may be added that most of the books from which quotations have been made are now of considerable rarity.

All peculiarities and mistakes of spelling, &c., have been reproduced. Matter in square brackets has been interpolated for the purpose of amplification or elucidation.

The Index has a character of its own, as it contains a good deal of information not given in the text, such as notes on railways which just entered the period under investigation, without developing materially therein, and on others which have come to the author's knowledge too late for inclusion in their appropriate chapters; it also includes a glossary of terms and some biographical notes. Consequently, any one in search of information on a particular point, who consults the Index, will (it is hoped) either find what he wants on the spot, or obtain a direction to the page required.

The arrangement adopted is by geographical groups rather than chronologically.

It may be well to mention that where the word 'Newcastle' is used, Newcastle-on-Tyne is meant.

I have received valuable assistance from many kind friends—in fact, without them the book would have been a feeble shadow of itself. Among those who have been so good as to search their records, to permit me to make use of material in their possession, or to help in other ways, are:

The Earl of Crawford and Balcarres.

The Earl of Elgin.

Miss Lily Arbuthnot.

Messrs. Edgar Allen & Co., Kenneth Brown, Lewis I. Cadell, Stanley Davies, H. W. Dickinson, Arthur Elton, Thomas Hornsby, Rhys Jenkins, J. A. Kay, T. E. R. Morris, George Pate, John Phillimore, M. C. Pottinger, J. Harling Turner, and Professor George S. Veitch.

CONTENTS

ILLUSTRATIONS

CHAPTER I

THE BEGINNINGS OF THE RAILWAY

THE conception 'railway' contains three elements: (1) the wheel, (2) a prepared track, (3) means for lateral constraint of the motion. The origins of (1) and (2) are lost in antiquity. The Romans laid stone tracks for their chariot wheels. It is possible that (2) may have preceded (1), as sledges on runners may have been used on prepared tracks before the invention of wheels, which were probably evolved from rollers. The result of modern research is that the date of the introduction of element (3) goes farther and farther back in the past.

The earliest known illustration of a truck which appears to be running on some kind of rails is given in Fig. 1. It occurs in a book entitled 'Der Ursprung gemeynner Berckrecht wie die lange zeit von den alten erhalten worde darauss . . . über alle Bergrecht geflossen' . . . in English, 'The origin of Common Mining Law, as it has come down long ago from the Ancients whence the Royal and Princely mining regulations for all mining law have come'. This book was printed for Johan Haselberger of Reichenau. Whether he was the author or not is uncertain. He was a publisher who had various books printed for him during the years 1515 to 1538. This one is unfortunately not dated, but may be put down as about 1530. There is some indication in the dedication that it was based on a previous work which had been for a long time in obscurity, but this cannot be taken as certain. The illustration reproduced in Fig. 1 appears twice in the original book, on the title-page and in the text. The latter, which is difficult to translate, is not very enlightening; it merely says: 'Haulage path: is that which is constructed of boards laid along the gallery . . . and on which one goes in and out, and on which material is hauled in and out of the mine.'

A more or less similar illustration occurs in Sebastian Münster's 'Cosmographia Universalis' (1550);[1] which is reproduced here (Fig. 2), from Professor Wolf's 'History of Science, Technology and Philosophy in the 16th and 17th centuries' (1935).

Another illustration belonging to the same period is shown in Fig. 3, from Agricola's 'De Re Metallica' (1556). It is of great interest, as the

[1] The first edition of this work was published in 1544, but it did not contain the illustration of the truck.

lateral constraint is produced on a peculiar principle; namely, an iron pin
—marked F—which ran in a groove formed in longitudinal planks. This
system was used as late as about 1870, on a horse tramway at Geneva.
The rails were flush with the surface of the road, and a wheel, carried on

FIG. 2.   A German railway of 1550

an arm projecting downwards from the car, ran in a central slot. When
two tramcars met, one of the drivers raised his guide wheel by depressing
a pedal, and drove round the other car.[1]

[1] Another illustration in Agricola's book shows a truck travelling on what is called in
America a 'corduroy road', with what at first sight appear to be wooden rails stretching
behind it; but the text indicates that they are meant for baulks of timber drawn behind the
truck to act as a brake and retard its progress downhill.

Fig. 1.   A German mine railway (?) of about 1530

Fig. 3.   A German mining truck of 1556

The honour of the introduction of railways, therefore, for the present appears to rest with Germany. But this state of affairs may be merely due to the industry of that nation in producing books dealing with mining and kindred subjects. And it seems rather significant that Jars' 'Voyages Métallurgiques', published in three volumes 1774–81, which contains a description of a great number of mines all over Europe, occupying 1,674 pages, only mentions railways at Newcastle and Whitehaven (the latter underground), and none outside England.

At various times vague statements have been made that railways were introduced into this country from Germany, but there is nothing in the way of definite evidence on the subject. Francis, in his 'History of the English Railway' (1851) gives (on p. 89) a quotation, without mentioning the source, but presumably from some German book, which begins by claiming the original invention of the railroad system for a Mr. Friederichs, a mining engineer in the Hercynian district of Hanover, who laid down iron rails and, what is more, was said to have employed a locomotive.

There is a reference to this railway in Beck, 'Geschichte des Eisens', Bd. 3, p. 757, as follows (translated):

> In Germany the first to use iron rails was Friedrichs zu Klausthal in the 1770s—for the transport of ore from the Dorothea mine to the stamping mills.

There is a similar reference in a German translation of Ritchie's 'Railways, their rise, progress and construction' (1846), but it does not occur in the original.

According to the *Verein Deutscher Ingenieure*, the date of the line was 1775, and it was a horse-railway.

In the absence of any further evidence, therefore, we can only allow Friedrichs the credit for laying down the first iron railway *in Germany*, and not for the locomotive.

Ritchie, in the book mentioned above, gives a note (on p. 8) which apparently refers to another German claim (of course for a wooden railway this time).

> It has been claimed for Germany that a railway was formed in the mountainous district of Hartz, and that the principle was brought to England in the year 1676 by some miners who came to this country, but this is not much credited.

Tomlinson, in his 'History of the North Eastern Railway' (1914), says:

> The small four-wheeled tram used in the metalliferous mines of Germany may have been brought into this country by the German

adventurers who opened out copper mines at Keswick in the reign of Queen Elizabeth.

Another vague remark on the subject of early railways abroad may be mentioned: Wood, in his 'Treatise on Railroads' (1825), says that wooden railways appear to be 'as ancient as civilization in Russia', but gives no authority for the statement, nor any idea of the date he had in mind for the introduction of civilization there. That the Russians took an interest in railways at a fairly early period is shown by the existence of an elaborate description of the Surrey Iron Railway which was published at St. Petersburg in 1805, and by the fact that the Tsar had asked for a model locomotive by 1824, which is recorded in the first prospectus of the Liverpool and Manchester Railway.

Evidence pointing to the Russians' having derived their knowledge from us is contained in a letter from William Vaughan[1] to Vice-Admiral Chichagoff, Minister of marine at St. Petersburg. The letter is dated 'London, June 14th, 1804', and was accompanied by models of trucks and both models and full-sized samples of rails.

Vaughan describes a plate-rail, flat at the bottom, a grooved rail for use in the crossing of public roads, and a plate-rail with a lower web to strengthen it. He says, speaking of sleepers, that in England old ship timber comes the cheapest and is as durable as any.[2]

This document has only been recently brought to the author's notice. The covering letter, from the Academy of Sciences of the U.S.S.R., dated in 1935, says:

We have no information of the Russian government having undertaken any measures for the adoption of railways by state or private enterprises. What must mainly be explained by the great economic backwardness of the country. Nevertheless, it must be recognized that Vaughan's letter, with its detailed description of the construction and exploitation of the railways then used in England, casts some light on the question of the introduction of these railways into Russia, where according to available data such railways of local importance already existed at some works at the very beginning of the 19th century.

Altogether, the claim of Russia to be considered a pioneer seems weak.

The earliest mention of a railway in our own country may be a passage

[1] William Vaughan (1752–1850) in 1791 endeavoured to form a society for the promotion of English canals, and afterwards became one of the first authorities on the subject of docks, in connexion with which he published a series of pamphlets, 1793–7. 'The great development of London as a port must be regarded as partly due to his unceasing exertions.' 'Dictionary of National Biography'.

[2] Blocks made from old ships' timber were extensively used on the Stockton and Darlington Railway. See Tomlinson, 'Hist. N.E.R.', p. 91.

in the will of Ambrose Middleton of Barnard Castle, dated August 5th, 1555. The will is given in the *Publications of the Surtees Society*, vol. 38 (1860), p. 37. The relevant paragraph runs:

> To the amendinge of the highway or tram, from the Weste ende of Bridgegait in Barnard Castle 20s.

It is doubtful, however, whether this passage has anything to do with a railway. Probably 'tram' meant a straight piece of road. Cf. Latin *trames*, a path or road.[1]

We now come to something quite definite.

A report on the manuscripts of Lord Middleton at Wollaton Hall, Notts., (issued by the Historical MSS. Commission) gives an instance of the use of rails in that county before the end of the sixteenth century. In the reign of Queen Elizabeth coal was being worked on quite a considerable scale on the estates of Sir Francis Willoughby of Wollaton. In a statement of weekly deliveries from October 1597 to October 1598, the following passage occurs: 'The whole gettes this yere 13,204 rookes[2] 1 quarter. The whole sale and deliverie to all persons, railes and bridges: 13,271 rookes 2 quarters.'

The meaning of the word 'railes' is made quite clear by a letter in the same collection, of 1610: 'I beseeche you to take order with Sir Thomas[3] that we maie have libertie to bring coales down the railes by wagen, for our cariadges onely, and we will bring them down by raile ourselves, for Strelley cartway is so fowle as few cariadges can passe.'

Railways were introduced into the north of England early in the seventeenth century. It appears by the order of the Hostmen's[4] Company 'at a courte holden the thirde day of February, anno Reginae Elizabethae, &c. 43, annoque Domini 1600' that waggons and waggonways had not then been invented, but that the coals were at that time brought down from the pits in wains (holding eight bolls[5] each; all measured and marked) to the staiths by the side of the river Tyne.[6]

In an interesting paper on the 'Archaeology of the Coal Trade' by

---

[1] As late as 1838, 'tram road' was used for a road with stone sills for the wheels of carts. (Simms, 'Public Works of Great Britain', plate 115.)

[2] A 'rooke' measured '2 yeardes one quarter hye, and one yearde square, close stacked'.

[3] Sir Thomas Beaumont. His brother, Huntington, is believed to have been the 'Master Beaumont' mentioned in 'Chorographia'. See p. 7, *post*.

[4] Elizabeth in 1600 incorporated the Society of Hoastmen, who had, however, existed as a guild or fraternity in Newcastle from time immemorial. They were incorporated for the better loading and disposing of pit coals and stones upon the Tyne. 'Stones' probably means grindstones, which were an important local product.

[5] A boll was equal to 35 or 36 gallons, weighing about 276 lb.

[6] Brand's 'History and Antiquities of Newcastle-on-Tyne' (1789), vol ii, p. 272.

T. John Taylor,[1] a 'bargain and sale' of 1660 is mentioned, from Sir Richard Tempest and others to Wm. Carr. and others, of ten keels or lighters, and a quarter part of the wood or timber laid upon trenches, bridges, and waggonways, or unlaid upon the same. Taylor concluded, from a comparison of all the statements he had found, that wooden railways were introduced in the Newcastle area between 1632 and 1649, but were not in general use till 1670 or 1680, and adds 'Even within the last dozen years [i.e. as late as 1846] the wooden railway was still to be seen in full operation in this neighbourhood'.

With regard to Shropshire, R. L. Galloway, in his 'Annals of Coal-mining' (1898), says:

> It contests with the north of England the honour of being the first to employ railways at its mines. At what date these were introduced we have no record. Professor Pepper (*Playbook of Metals* [1861], p. 23) speaks of Coalbrookdale, in this county, being celebrated as the place where railways of wood were first used in the years 1620 and 1650, though without adducing any authority in support of the statement. There seems, however, to be no reason to doubt the fact, inasmuch as we have independent evidence that this method of conveying coal was in common use in various parts of the coalfield about the end of the seventeenth century. The railways appear also to have been thus early carried into the underground workings; and the same small wagons conveyed the coals direct from the working-places of the colliers to the point of shipment on the Severn.

Evidence from Coalbrookdale itself points to the railways there having been imitated from the North Country.[2] But there is definite evidence of the existence of railways in Shropshire by 1705, and probably before 1695.[3]

There are references to 'tylting railes' at Broseley in 1606 (*Star Chamber Proc.*, James I, 109/8, 310/16); which appear to indicate a waggon-way down to the river.

An often quoted passage from Gray's 'Chorographia, or a Survey of Newcastle-upon-Tyne' (1649) records that 'Master Beaumont . . . adventured into our mines with his thirty thousand pounds;[4] who brought with him many rare engines, not known then in these parts; as the art to boore with iron rodds to try the deepnesse and the thicknesse of the coale: rare engines to draw water out of the pits; waggons[5] with one

---

[1] *Proceedings, Archaeological Institute of Great Britain and Ireland*, vol. i (1858).
[2] See p. 54, *post*.   [3] See p. 81, *post*.
[4] Corrected to £20,000 in Gray's own copy, which is in the Gateshead Public Library.
[5] Taylor, in the paper mentioned above, remarks that Gray could not have been alluding to common wains, which had long been in use.

horse to carry down coales, from the pits to the staithes, to the river', &c. It has been usually inferred that the waggons ran on rails, as the hero of the episode was almost certainly Huntington Beaumont, brother to the Sir Thomas previously mentioned in connexion with Wollaton, where we know there was a railway by this time. Beaumont's venture in the north was not a success, as the 'Chorographia' goes on to say 'within few yeares, he consumed all his money, and rode home upon his light horse'.

Whether Beaumont really did introduce railways into the neighbour-hood of Newcastle when he went there, which was about 1602, cannot be determined with certainty. Nicholas Wood, in his 'Practical Treatise on Railroads' (1825) favours Beaumont's claim, on the grounds that the coal-carts used on ordinary roads were called wains or waynes in the seventeenth century.[1] Wood assumes that the date of the substitution of railways for the common roads at Newcastle was between 1602 and 1649. In his 'Address on the Stephensons' (1860), he is more definite, saying: 'The colliery "wagon-ways", as they were called, dated back as far as 1602, as "wooden railways".'

The late Fred Bland, in 'A Century of Permanent Way' (1925), quotes (giving a photograph) an extract from a Counsel's opinion upon a con-veyance dated 1672, as follows:

Some short time before this conveyance a new method was invented for carrying Coals to the River in large machines called Waggons made to run on Frames of Timber fixt in the Ground for that purpose and since called a Waggon Way which frames must of necessity lye very near, if not altogether upon a level from the Colliery to the River and therefore when there are any Hills or Vales between the Colliery and the River and the same cannot be avoided, it is necessary in order to the laying such waggon ways, then to make cutts through the Hill or level the same, and to raise or fill up the Vales so that such Waggon Way may lye upon a level as near as possible.

By 1676 they are spoken of as being common in the district, in another very favourite passage for quotation, from the 'Life of Lord Keeper North' (1740), wherein they are described as consisting of rails of timber laid from the colliery to the river; on which ran bulky carts, with four 'rowlets' fitting the rails 'whereby the carriage is so easy that one horse will draw down four or five chaldrons of coal'. Owners of the inter-mediate ground received way-leaves for the passage of the railway, 'so dear that the owner of a rood of ground will expect 20*l.* per annum for this leave'.

[1] There are, however, instances of the word 'waggon' being used for a road vehicle in the sixteenth and seventeenth centuries. See O.E.D., s.v. Wagon.

Robert Stevenson, in a 'Report on a proposed railway from the coal-field of Midlothian to Edinburgh and Leith', written in 1818, says: 'Wagon ways constructed entirely of square wooden frames or rails, laid in two right lines on wooden sleepers, appear to have been in use at Newcastle so far back as the year 1671.'

Tredgold, in 'A Practical Treatise on Rail-roads and Carriages' (1825), says: 'The first rail-ways appear to have been used in the neighbourhood of Newcastle-upon-Tyne, about 1680. The rails were of wood, resting upon wooden sleepers, and in some places near the Tyne the same species are still in use.'

There is a very interesting paper by T. V. Simpson on 'Old Mining Records and Plans in the possession of the North of England Institute of Mining and Mechanical Engineers at Newcastle', dated 1931.[1]

He quotes Watson (one of several well-known mining engineers of that name), whose collection of papers 1745–1832 is among those examined, as saying that waggon-ways came into use soon after the Revolution; they were laid with wooden rails and worked by a horse. Mr. Allan of Flatts, near Chester-le-Street, was the first to use them, and next on the Tyne, Mr. Montague of Stella.

John Buddle (the most celebrated mining engineer of his day) supports Stevenson's date of 1671 for the introduction of wooden railways at Newcastle, writing in 1807 (vol. 15, p. 202 of his papers). Cumming, in 'Illustrations of the origin and progress of Rail and Tram roads' &c. (1824), puts it one year earlier, 1670. He says wooden railways were first introduced at Whitehaven in 1738.

Rees' 'Cyclopaedia' (1819) says:

> The necessity of an expeditious and cheap mode of conveyance from the pits to the keels or ships had as early as the year 1680 intro-duced the use of wooden railways for the waggons to move upon, between the Tyne river and some of the principal pits, and these by degrees became extended to a great number of other coal-works.

The following passage occurs in Hutchinson's 'History of Durham' (1794), vol. iii, p. 497:

> It has been alleged, that waggonways were first used on the river Wear soon after the revolution, by Mr. Allan of Flats near Chester,[2] but that was subsequent considerably to the waggonways on the Tyne, made by Colonel Liddel, which extended from Dunstal to Ravenswath,[3] to this time called the Old Way; he was joined in the coal by Charles

---

[1] *Trans. Inst. Mining Engineers*, vol. 81, p. 75.   [2] Chester-le-Street.
[3] Dunston (on the Tyne, about 2 miles west of Gateshead) to Ravensworth.

Montague Esq. of Stella, and from that copartnership originated the combination called the Grand Allies.[1]

There is a comment on the above passage, in Bailey's 'General View of the Agriculture of the County of Durham' (1810), as follows:

Mr. Hutchinson in his History of Durham says, that waggon ways were first made and used in this county by Colonel Liddell at Ravensworth, but upon examining the books at Ravensworth Castle, Mr. Robson (the present agent) informs me that the first staith bills are in 1671, in the time of Sir Thomas Liddell, Col. Liddell's grand-father ... Joshua French was then staithman, and from his bills, beginning with that year, it appears that coals were then led by waggons to Team Staith.

It is a little unfortunate that the passages quoted above do not contain any definite reference to rails, but the writers probably considered that they were implied by the word 'waggon'. Team Staith is no doubt another name for Dunston Staith, as the latter was close to the point where the River Team flows into the Tyne. Team itself, where a colliery with a waggon-way is shown on Gibson's map of 1788, is 4 miles south of the Tyne.

Matthias Dunn, 'View of the Coal Trade of the North of England' (1844), gives 1671 as the date of the Ravensworth Colliery waggon-way, and 'about 1693' for the line running to the Wear at Allan's Flatts Colliery.[2] In Sykes's 'Local Records of Northumberland and Durham' (2nd edition, 1833), under date 1693, the introduction of waggon-ways on the Wear is mentioned; by Thomas Allan, 'who amassed a large fortune in the collieries and purchased estates, a part of which still retains the name of *Allan's Flatts*, near Chester-le-Street'. Allan died in 1740. In 1789 General Lambton succeeded to the Flatts estate and colliery.

The only other possible rival to Northumberland and Shropshire for the possession of the earliest British railway after Nottinghamshire is South Wales. A good deal of literature exists, which is dealt with in Chapter V, on the subject of a railway made by Sir Humphry Mackworth between Neath and Aberavon about 1695.

In conclusion it may be remarked that antagonism between canals and railways did not exist in the early days. In fact, many of the latter were made as feeders to the canals; quite a large number of Canal Acts embodying powers to make railways.

[1] There was a third partner, George Bowes of Gibside. The partnership deed was dated June 27th, 1726. (Galloway, 'Annals of Coal Mining', 1898, p. 248.) Bowes died in 1760.

[2] The following prices given by Dunn are interesting: 'In 1745 the cost of a yard of wooden way was 4s. 2d., viz.—Two yards of oak rails, 1s. 2d.; three sleepers, 2s. 6d.; pins, 1d.; laying, 3d.; filling and ballasting, 2d.'

CHAPTER II

EARLY RAILWAYS IN THE NORTH OF ENGLAND

Evidence of the importance of the Newcastle coal trade at a very early period is widespread. A licence was granted by Edward III in 1351 to burgesses to work the coal in two portions of the town lands, the Castle Field and the Frith.[1] In the latter end of Queen Elizabeth's reign, a duty of fourpence per chaldron upon coals produced £10,000 a year.

In 1800, no less than 69 out of 71 vessels laden with coal, from Shields to London, were wrecked. On May 11th of that year 144 vessels sailed from Shields under convoy for the Baltic, having on board, besides other commodities, 11,600 chaldrons of coal.

The result of the rather conflicting and somewhat vague evidence as to the establishment of railways in this neighbourhood given in the previous chapter is that the two earliest waggon-ways which can be definitely located are one from Ravensworth to Dunston Staith on the Tyne in 1671, and one from near Chester-le-Street to the Wear in 1693, but there were possibly earlier ones which are now forgotten. Tomlinson, in his 'History of the North Eastern Railway' (1914) says: 'From about 1620 to 1820 the northern coal-field was the theatre of experiments which culminated in the formation of the Stockton and Darlington Railway.'

If we are unable to point to the earliest line, we do know the most important one of its day, namely the Tanfield Waggon-way. Part of it was laid over Tanfield Moor, which lay about 7 miles SW. of Gateshead, by Sir John Clavering and Thomas Brumell from their Lintz and Buck's Nook collieries, in 1712. About then, or shortly after, George Pitt of Strathfieldsaye opened the Tanfield coal-field, using the above line, and constructing others. Disputes over the question of way-leaves arose, turning on the point as to whether a right of conveying coals in waggons over the ground in the ordinary manner covered the use of railroads, culminating in a Chancery case. The following passage occurs in Barnadiston's Reports, vol. i, p. 318:

Pit and Lady Claverinth [i.e. Clavering] 2 Geo. II (1729):

One Wray was seized of a Manor in the North, in which there was a great Waste called Tanfield-Moor, and sold it about thirty years ago,

---

[1] Many authors quote a similar charter of 1239, but this has been proved to be a myth. See (*inter alia*) Galloway's 'History of Coal Mining', p. 14, footnote.

reserving to himself and his Heirs a convenient Way-leave, such as he and his Heirs should think proper, for the carriage of Coals thro' this Waste, from certain Coal-Works of his to the River Tyne. There was an Invention found out about Twenty years before [i.e. 1679] which was used pretty much in the North at the time this Manor was sold, of making Waggon-ways for the more easy Carriage of Coals which was done by levelling Ground from one Place to another, and then laying Planks into it, for making a more easy and short Conveyance of it. The Defendant was Lessee of some Coal-Works under the heirs of Wray, and by virtue of the Power in the Reservation she made a Waggon-Way for her Coals, upon which the Plaintiff preferred his Bill against her.

It was referred to the Barons of Exchequer, who gave their opinions that a waggon-way was not reserved. The case had been dragging on at least since October 1721, at which date there is a 'Plea and Demurrer of Dame Jane Clavering, Widow . . . and her answer to . . . the bill of complaint of George Pitt Esq.'.

The grounds for the decision were that a waggon-way was not contemplated when the original agreement was made about 1700, but one's sympathies are distinctly with Lady Clavering, because Pitt was obviously not actuated by any dislike of the waggon-ways, but wished to keep her coal off the market. That she, or her family, came to some working arrangement, is shown by a manuscript which has survived, containing 'An Account of Coals Ledd to Dunston Staith and Delivered there on account of Sir Thomas Clavering, Bart. March to December 1767 and December 1779 to December 1780'. Details of the amount of coal carried each week with running charges and other expenses in connexion with the waggon-way are given.

The Grand Allies (Montagues, Liddells, and George Bowes, as mentioned in the last chapter) came on the scene in 1726—a number of their collieries being in this neighbourhood—and set about the extension of the waggon-ways, and the formation of one formidable one, comprising a huge embankment across the valley of the Beckley Burn, and a fine bridge known as the Causey Bridge, or Tanfield Arch. Sykes ('Local Records') describes it thus, under date 1727:

Tanfield Arch, in the county of Durham, a remarkable structure, was built by Colonel Liddell and the Hon. Charles Montague, the founders of the partnership now vulgarly called *the Grand Allies*, to obtain a level for the passage of coal waggons. It is frequently called Cawsey Bridge, from its being built over the deep and romantic dell of Cawsey burn, near Tanfield. The span of the arch is 103 feet; it springs from abutments about nine feet high, and being semicircular, the entire elevation is above 60 feet; it cost £12,000. The architect was Ralph

Wood, a common mason, who, having built a former arch of wood, that fell for want of weight, committed suicide from a fear of this beautiful structure experiencing a similar fate. On a sundial, on one of the piers, is the following: "Ra. Wood, mason, 1727". This arch was built for a waggon-way to a colliery, which was set on fire, and has long been unwrought. It has been many years neglected, and is falling to ruins [writing in 1834].

The arch, which has recently been scheduled by H.M. Office of Works as an 'ancient monument', is shown in Fig. 4.

The Tanfield waggon-way was extended later to Shield Row colliery, a distance of eight miles from the river. Part of it was afterwards taken into the Brandling Junction Railway.

Before dealing with any more of the railways in detail, some descriptions by travellers and historians will be given.

Pennant, 'Tour in Scotland', (1769), speaking of Newcastle, says:

The collieries lie at different distances, from 5 to 18 miles from the river, and the coal is brought down in waggons along rail roads.

Arthur Young, in his 'Six Months Tour through the North of England' (1770), vol. iii, p. 12, says (also in connexion with Newcastle):

The coal waggon roads, from the pits to the water, are great works, carried over all sorts of inequalities of ground, so far as the distance of 8 or 10 miles. The track of the wheels are marked with pieces of timber let into the road, for the wheels of the waggons to run on, by which means one horse is enabled to draw, and that with ease, 50 or 60 bushels of coal.

Hutchinson, 'A View of Northumberland' (1778), vol. ii, p. 417, speaking of the export of coal from the Newcastle neighbourhood:

The collieries which supply this exportation, about 24 in number, lie at considerable distances from the river. From the mines, the coals are sent to the places of lading in large unwieldy carriages or waggons, of the form of a common mill-hopper, carried on wheels of iron, the fellies or rims of which are hollow, so as to run on strings of wood adapted thereto, with which the roads are laid. By this means, these carriages on an easy descent run without horses, and sometimes with that rapidity, that a piece of wood, called a tiller, is obliged to be applied to one wheel, and pressed thereon by the weight of the attendant who sits on it, to retard the motion: by the friction of which frequently the tiller and sometimes the carriage is set on fire.

The frontispiece of the second volume of John Brand's 'History and Antiquities of the town of Newcastle-on-Tyne' (1789) consists of a fine view of Newcastle, engraved by James Fittler in 1783, the right-hand

Fig. 4. A recent view of Causey Arch. (*Railway Gazette*)

Fig. 5. View of Newcastle-on-Tyne in 1783, showing the 'Parkmoor Waggon-way'

part of which is reproduced here (Fig. 5). It shows the termination of one of the old waggon-ways on the banks of the Tyne. A loaded truck has just made the descent, with the driver sitting on the 'tiller', and a dejected horse walking behind, no doubt contemplating the return journey uphill. The print was also published separately, with the title 'A run on the Parkmoor Waggon-way, Gateshead'. The south end of the high-level bridge is just about where the horse is.

Hutchinson, in his 'History of Durham' (1794), after the passage which has been quoted on p. 8, goes on thus:

> Not far from Chester[-le-Street] are those [waggon-ways] erected by Mr. Jollif[1] at an immense expense, and several more are to be seen in this county. Darwenthaugh waggon-way, extending from Burnopfield and Brian's Leap to the river Derwent, was the most difficult and expensive work of the kind hitherto executed in the coal trade.[2]

> Where the descents are easy, the carriages run without horses, and sometimes with that rapidity, that a piece of wood, called a *convoy*, is obliged to be applied to one wheel, and pressed thereon by the attendant who sits on it to retard the motion; by the friction of which the carriage is hindered from running amain. The waggons proceed to the staiths or repositories at the water side, where a platform of timber is constructed to receive them, and the bottom of the vehicle, which is fitted as a door, with hinges on one side, and a hasp on the other, to fasten it to the sole of the waggon, being opened or let down, the load is instantly discharged, either into keels below, or into the staith, where they lie under cover, and are ready to be cast into the keels, when the tide or the trade does not suit the arrival of waggons from the remoter collieries.

A more detailed account occurs in a 'General view of the Agriculture of the county of Northumberland', by J. Bailey and G. Culley, second edition, 1797.[3] It is as follows:

> Many of the collieries are situated at a considerable distance from the river to which the coals are conveyed from the pits in a peculiar kind of carriage, called a *Newcastle coal-waggon*, . . . it has four small wheels about 34 inches diameter, *fixed to the axles*, with which they turn round,

[1] Though there is no longer any male representative of the Joliffe family, the royalties from a number of collieries in the district still belong to descendants, and are administered by the 'Joliffe Trust'.

[2] Tomlinson, 'Hist. N.E.R.' (p. 11), described this line thus:

This waggon-way, which in length and cost of construction equalled, if it did not surpass, the Tanfield line, ran from the Pontop, Pontop Pike, Bushblades, and afterwards Tanfield Moor Edge collieries by way of Bryan's Leap, Rowland's Gill, and Swalwell to Derwentshaugh. It was formed by Lords Windsor and Dunkerron, Matthew Ridley and John Simpson, who worked the coals demised by Anthony Meaburne—previous to 1729—to Lady Clavering, Richard Ridley and others. A mile and a half of it is retained in the Hare Law branch of the L. and N.E.R.

[3] The first edition (1794) does not mention railways.

and move on a road (called the waggon-way) made on purpose *with wood*, which is formed by long pieces of wood (rails) about four inches square, laid lengthwise on sleepers of wood, and the thickness of the rail above the plane of the rest of the road, and at the exact distance of the waggon wheels from each other, as it is upon these rails the wheels run. A new waggon-way (including timber, levelling, gravelling and workmanship) will cost about 5s. per yard, or 440l. per mile, and the expense of keeping it in repair is generally about 1½d. per chaldron on a quantity of 15,000 chaldrons, annually, or 93l. 15s. per mile.

Upon levels, or easy ascents, a single horse draws the waggon: on such parts of the way where the declination is sufficient for the waggon to move by the power of gravity, the horse is taken out, and follows behind; and where the descents are such that the waggon would move with too great rapidity by its own weight (or *"run amain"*), the motion is regulated by a crooked piece of wood (called a *convoy*), coming over the top of one of the hind wheels, upon which the waggon man presses with such force as he finds requisite, to regulate the motion of the waggon. This mode of conveyance has been used here upwards of 120 years [taking us back to 1677].

An illustration is given of a 'Newcastle coal-waggon' as used by John Buddle about 1764. A similar print appeared in the *London Magazine, or Gentleman's Monthly Intelligencer*, vol. xxxiii, with a letter signed 'T. S. Polyhistor, Chester-le-Street, Dec. 21, 1763'. The identity of 'Poly-histor' appears to be revealed by the following passage in Rees' 'Cyclo-paedia' (1819), in the article Canal:

Mr. *John Buddle* in the *General Magazine* for 1764, p. 285, has given a view and description of the coal waggon which had been then long in use on the wooden railways in the neighbourhood of Newcastle-on-Tyne. This waggon moved on four wheels of cast-iron or of wood with iron rims, having an edge standing up on the rim of each wheel, in order to guide and keep them upon the wooden rails. The waggon is in shape of an inverted prismoid, having a door or false bottom hung with hinges, and fastened by a hasp, that can be let go to let out the coals when the waggon has arrived at the staith.

The waggon carried upwards of 19 'bowls' of coal. The persistence of the type is shown by the accompanying illustration from a photograph taken during the Newcomen Society's Summer Meeting in 1935 (Fig. 7).

For many years it was the custom to use cast-iron wheels in front and wooden ones behind (on which the brakes were applied). The following extract from *Archaeologia Aeliana*, vol. xxiv (1903), p. 226, is of interest.

May 1731. A grant from His Majesty unto Elias Thornhill of Sunderland . . . whitesmith . . . of the sole use and benefit of his new invention for making the rim or edge of coal waggon wheels with iron

FIG. 6.   A 'Newcastle Coal-waggon' of about 1764

FIG. 7.   Newcastle coal-waggons being
contemplated by the author in 1935

or steel and with iron ribs or tabbs[1] and iron bolts, rivets and screws for the fastening the same, which will preserve the said wheels and make them last many years longer than those now used and thereby prevent the destruction of many thousands of timber trees in the year to the great advantage of all persons concerned in the coal trade and by preserving the timber trees for ships and other vessels to the benefit of the nation in general.

(Extracts from Privy Seal Dockets, relating principally to the North of England. By F. W. Dendy.)

With regard to the latter part of the above quotation, it may be remarked that there was at one time a considerable importation into Newcastle and Sunderland of rails, planks, and waggon wheels from various parts of the south of England, particularly from Sussex and the New Forest.

The most valuable guide to the waggon-ways of Northumberland and Durham which the author has discovered is a fine map published by John Gibson in 1787, and re-issued, with the date altered, in 1788. An interesting vignette in the corner is reproduced as the frontispiece to this book.

The map begins just above the river Blyth, in the neighbourhood of which two lines are shown. One runs from Bedlington Colliery $1\frac{3}{4}$ miles ESE. to the bank of the river about $3\frac{1}{2}$ miles from its mouth. The other goes from Blyth Colliery $4\frac{1}{4}$ miles ENE. to the sea at Blythe, just below the mouth of the river. The next is one of a mile in length from Hartley Colliery NNE. to 'Hartley New Harbour, or Seaton Sluice'.

We then come to the Tyne system. The first is the line from Wylam 5 miles east to Lemington Staiths on the north side of the river. It runs SE. for half a mile, and more or less follows the course of the river. About half-way along it is joined by a short branch from Heddon Colliery. When within three-quarters of a mile from the staiths, a line comes down from the north, starting from Holywell Main ($3\frac{3}{4}$ miles), with branches from Greenwick Moor (3 miles), and Walbottle Moor ($2\frac{1}{2}$ miles), which appears to cross it.

The Wylam line is described thus by Oswald Dodd Hedley,[2] son of William Hedley, who (i.e. William) was appointed engineer at Wylam in 1805:

The railway was a wooden one, subject to great undulations. It was worked by the old method, one horse being employed for each

[1] Probably spokes. The O.E.D. gives as one of the meanings of tab 'one of the revolving arms which lift the beaters of a fulling-mill', quoting from Knight, 'Dict. Mech.', 1877.
[2] 'Who invented the Locomotive Engine' (1858), p. 1.

waggon. But about the year 1808 the wooden rails were taken up and cast-iron plate rails substituted. These were adopted by Mr. Blackett [the owner] on the recommendation of the late Mr. Thomas, of Newcastle,[1] and subject to some slight modification in the line of traction. The horses now took two waggons each, but the daily exertion consequent on this increased weight being too great, it became necessary to keep spare horses.

Hedley records that in 1811 traction by oxen was tried, but given up, as they were slower than horses.

The plate-rails, which were quite an exception for the north of England, were taken up, and replaced by edge-rails, about 1830.

Smiles, in early editions of his 'Life of George Stephenson', said that there was a rack-rail at Wylam, but the statement was incorrect.

The Walbottle line has been given a very prominent niche in history by Wood, as he says malleable iron rails were first tried there, in 1805.[2]

Returning to the map, a little farther east there are more staiths, with a short line from Baker's Main and one of 2 miles from Montague Main. For the next 6 miles along the river, past Newcastle, there are no lines, nor are any shown in the area north of this stretch. There is no Heaton railway, nor Kenton and Coxlodge, nor Killingworth, all of which are shown in the map of 1812 which is reproduced here (Fig. 10), from R. J. Galloway's 'The Steam Engine and its Inventors'.[3] There is a short one from Walker Hill running south to the river, with a branch from Byker St. Anthonys; Walker Hill being at the spot marked 'Walker' on the 1812 map. On the older one there is a separate Walker, half a mile to the NE., from which an independent line of three-quarters of a mile runs to the river. The lay-out of the lines round here is quite different in the two maps. One of these pits, probably the one marked Byker St. Anthonys, was also known as Lawson Main. At all events, a colliery of the latter name in the township of Byker, adjacent to the old Walker colliery, was leased in 1793 for a period of twenty-one years (extended from time to time). It was owned by Sir John Lawson, and we have here, as elsewhere, confusion caused by the colliery sometimes being called by the name of the place, and at others by that of the owner. The interesting point about it is that Wood ('Treatise on Railroads', 1st edn., p. 46) states that stone supports were first used on this railway 'in forming the first iron Railroad, which was laid down in the neighbourhood of Newcastle-upon-Tyne, viz. from Lawson Main Colliery to the river, in 1797'. He says by 'the late Mr. Barns', really Thomas Barnes. The stone supports were not

---

[1] No doubt William Thomas, of Denton Hall. See p. 175, post.
[2] See p. 150, post.   [3] By permission of Messrs. Macmillan & Co.

FIG. 8. 'Rail head' at Lemington Staith (1935). The terminus
of the railway from Wylam

FIG. 9. Walbottle Colliery. Foot of the shaft

square blocks, as one would have expected from Wood's remark, but long slabs forming transverse sleepers.[1]

In a 'Practical Treatise on the Construction and Formation of Railways', by James Day (1839), it is stated that stone blocks were introduced by Mr. Barnes in 1797 when forming the railway from Walker Colliery to the river.

In Gibson's map, we next come to a system forming, with the river as base, a bulging rectangle, with sides of about a mile and a half, the upper angles being at Bigges Main and Willington.[2] Near the latter place, a line comes down south from Long Benton $2\frac{1}{2}$ miles to the staiths. It will be seen that by 1812 the connexion between Bigges Main and Willington had disappeared, while the Kenton and Coxlodge (with a branch from Fawdon) came in near the former, and the Killingworth line joined up just below Long Benton, the line then passing west of Willington, instead of east, as before. In the old map, the line from Wallsend is shown, inside the rectangle, but more to the west than in 1812.

Of the last-mentioned group of lines, Kenton and Coxlodge, and Killingworth are both famous in connexion with locomotive history. George Stephenson was appointed engineer at the latter in 1813, where there was a cast-iron edge railway. Eleven years before, he went to Willington Quay, where his occupation was that of working a stationary engine which dragged waggons full of ballast taken out of the ships up a wooden railway from the wharf to the top of the ballast heap.

There is a letter in the *Franklin Journal* (vol. iii, 1827) which mentions the Fawdon line, where there were cast-iron rails. It was partly worked by stationary engines (the owner being Benjamin Thompson):

> The rope is placed in the jaws of a vice attached to the waggon, where it is secured. . . . Where the railway crossed a public road, the rope was bent down by friction rollers and carried under a plank bridge, to the other side of the road, where it again rose above ground. When the waggon comes to the public road, the boy who rides on it releases the rope from the vice; the velocity of the waggon carries it over the road, and the boy again hooks up the rope into the vice, while the waggon continues its motion.

William Chapman, in a 'Report on the cost and separate advantages of a Ship Canal and of a Rail-way from Newcastle to Carlisle' (1824),

---

[1] For drawings see Figs. 70 and 71. Separate stone blocks had been used before this, in the Midlands, probably also in Scotland (see p. 149, *post*).

[2] Tomlinson ('Hist. N.E.R.', p. 82) says the line from Willington Square to Willington Quay was laid in 1762; and considers that this line (afterwards part of the Killingworth Ry.) inaugurated the 4 feet 8 inch or 4 feet $8\frac{1}{2}$ inch gauge.

spoke of the reciprocating system[1] at Fawdon and at Ouston. The latter is shown on the map of 1812, $2\frac{1}{2}$ miles NW. of Chester-le-Street, but it is not on that of 1788, nor on one of 1801, in J. R. Fletcher's address to the Newcastle-on-Tyne Association of Students of the Institution of Civil Engineers (1901).

Only one more railway remains to be mentioned on the north side of the river: one 3 miles long, from High Flatworth, afterwards extended northwards to Shiremoor on the left and Murton Main on the right. This line appears to represent what was afterwards known as the Brunton and Shields Railway, of which presently.

Now to take the lines south of the Tyne, where we are in Durham. Those from Ryton ($2\frac{1}{2}$ miles) and Whitefield (5 miles) are as given in 1812; the latter without branches. Near where the Derwent flows in, there is a line of one mile from Blaydon Main. The differences now shown are interesting; the line from Pontop ('to the staith, 8 m.') does not connect with the Tanfield line, but passes three-quarters of a mile to the west of Tanfield Moor, throwing off two short branches to the right; then swings round to the NNE. and crosses the Derwent, evidently by a bridge which carried a road. It then bends round and runs up the west bank of the Derwent; this last stretch being turned to account in 1812 for Thornley Colliery, which is not shown by Gibson.

The line from Tanfield Moor (the south terminus being 7 miles from the river) and that from South Moor are as shown in 1812; also from Team (4 miles) and Low Moor (Eighton not shown). Three-quarters of a mile east of Low Moor there is a colliery called Sheriff Hill, with a line running 2 miles NNE. to the river which does not appear in 1812. Except for two very short lines from Gateshead Park and Brandling Main, the only remaining one south of the Tyne is one of 4 miles running up from 'Usworth Main or Russell's Main', which also has a line to the Wear.

The other lines communicating with the latter river are, firstly, two running nearly due east, and parallel to one another, from Beamish South Moor ($6\frac{3}{4}$ miles) and from Pelton Moor, which is less than a mile from the South Moor just mentioned, due south of it. About half-way along the Beamish line, one comes in, crossing the Pelton line, from Deanry Moor, which is 2 miles SW. of Chester-le-Street; this has disappeared by 1801. The Lee Field branch is shown. Urpeth does not appear, nor the line curving upwards to the Tyne.

The Pelton line corresponds more or less with the line on the 1812

---

[1] For descriptions of Thompson's 'reciprocating system', which consisted of fixed engines and ropes, see pp. 27, 160, *post*.

map starting from 'Allan's Main' and passing Flatts. This doubtless represents the line of 1693 mentioned on p. 9, but the routes of these old waggon-ways were evidently much altered as time went on. A house is indicated in 1788, marked 'Flats, General Lambton', but no collieries corresponding to Bedford Main or Allan's Main; Pelton Moor, the terminus, being $2\frac{3}{4}$ miles west of 'Flats'. It is curious that the Allan line is marked more satisfactorily in 1812 than it was in 1788; possibly it was abandoned for a time and reconstructed.

There was a railway in this neighbourhood at Shield Row Colliery (about 5 miles west of Chester-le-Street) which does not appear under that name on either of the maps. O. D. Hedley, in 'A Descriptive Account of the means used on the Tyne and Wear for effecting the safe transit of Railway Carriages . . .' (1834), states that brake-blocks acting on the fore as well as the hind wheels were introduced there in 1790. The colliery belonged to William Bell & Co. Tomlinson mentions it as being of 4 feet 4 inches gauge.

From the 'Inventions, etc. of Benjamin Thompson', it is clear that Urpeth was also called Bewicke Main. On this subject, Sykes's 'Remarkable Events' gives some interesting details:

1809 (May 17).—The opening of the waggon-way from Bewicke main to the river Tyne took place, on which occasion every road leading to it was crowded with passengers at an early hour, and before eleven o'clock, about 10,000 people were assembled. About this time four waggons of small coals were brought up the first plane by the steam engine,[1] to the great admiration of the spectators, but owing to some little difficulties which often occur in new machinery, the four waggons of best coals, intended for the Tyne, did not start till a much later hour. As soon as the waggons reached the summit of the second and highest plane, up which they went with surprising velocity and regularity, the British flag was hoisted at Ayton cottage, and announced by a discharge of six pieces of cannon, which were answered by an equal number from the Ann and Isabella, his majesty's armed ship on the Tyne, and from Deptford-house, the residence of Mr. Cooke. Immediately on the waggons reaching the first plane, about 400 gentlemen sat down to dinner, in a tent fitted up for the occasion. An excellent military band attended. In the evening, in order to prove the excellence of the level railway, six men, without horses, took with the greatest ease four laden waggons, with each ten men on the top, from Ayton cottage to the Tyne; and the first coals being put on board the Ann and Isabella, the same was announced by discharges of artillery as before.

---

[1] According to Tomlinson ('Hist. N.E.R.', p. 18), this was the first fixed engine ever used for hauling waggons, which would account for the enormous crowd. The hill was called Birtley Fell.

1810 (March 15).—A self-acting plane of a wonderful construction, was put in motion, for the purpose of conveying coals from Bewicke-main colliery, to the Tyne. It was constructed and executed under the direction of Samuel Cooke esq., of Ayton-house, one of the owners of the colliery. The length of the rope on this incline was 1,600 yards, and it was made to convey fifty chaldron waggons of coal, at the astonishing speed of ten miles in one hour.

This plane is mentioned in the *Transactions of the Highland Society* (1824), thus:

The Whitehouse inclined plane on the Urpeth waggonway is 1,600 yards in length; from 6 to 9 laden waggons bring up as many empty ones.

In 1788 there were lines from Birtley, Blackfell, and Harraton or Boundary Moor, converging to a point on the Wear at the east end of the same staith as the Beamish and Pelton lines. By 1812 the names were all altered, owing, no doubt, to the opening of new pits. There is also an independent one of a mile and a half from 'Harratton' (not the same place as that just mentioned). Besides a very short one from Errington's Main, there are only two more on the north of the river; one from Mount Moor ($2\frac{1}{2}$ miles), which is three-quarters of a mile west of Usworth, with a branch coming in half-way down from Washington Colliery, which is a little way from the village, just to the SW. of Usworth. The line from the latter then comes down close to, and parallel with, the one from Washington. These do not appear in the 1812 map.

From Simpson's 'Old Mining Records', which was quoted from in Chapter I, it appears that about 1820 Washington Colliery had two waggon-ways, one to the Tyne and one to the Wear, so that coals could be shipped on either river. Buddle records that when the wooden rails were replaced by metals (4 feet long, cast iron) the waggonman made four trips to the Wear instead of six under the old system, but he took two waggons per trip instead of one, so that his day's work was increased from six to eight waggons.

In 1826 the coals from Mount Moor were diverted to the Tyne. It is recorded in Messrs. R. Stephenson & Co.'s books that two locomotives were supplied in April of that year to Mount Moor, subsequent entries relating to them appearing under the name Springwell. In the map of 1788 Mount Moor is shown 4 miles SSE. of Gateshead. The modern village of Springwell is given in a gazetteer as 3 miles SE. of the same, so the pits were evidently quite near one another.

There is a long description of the opening of the line to the Tyne in Sykes:

1826 (Jan. 17).—The first coals from the new colliery on the Spring-well estate, belonging to the Right Hon. Lord Ravensworth, and part-ners,[1] were conveyed down the new railway (about five and a half miles in length) to the river Tyne, and put on board the Ship Industry, at the improved new drop, erected on the Jarrow Grange estate of Cuthbert Ellison, esq. About half-past eight o'clock on the morning, the excellent band composed of his lordship and partners' colliers at Mount Moor, in their new uniforms, with cockades at their caps, marched to the pit playing several pleasing airs, and followed by a great concourse of spectators, amongst whom was an individual nearly 100 years old, (who had ex-pressed a wish to see the first coals go from the pit, having when a girl, on the like occasion, seen the first coals sent from the old colliery to the Wear), for the accommodation of whom the agents sent a carriage to convey her thither, and gave her a cockade which she displayed at her bonnet. The procession left the pit at 9 o'clock in four waggons, fitted up for the accommodation of the band, the agents of the colliery, and several ladies and gentlemen visitors, with a numerous concourse of per-sons on foot, and with eight chaldron waggons of coal, descended down the inclined plane, and preceded by the band, passed onwards towards the Tyne. On the coal waggons crossing the turnpike road from Sunderland to Newcastle, the company gave three cheers, the band playing *"God save the King"*. On the procession arriving at Monkton, it was joined by some of the agents of the other collieries of his lordship and partners, and other gentlemen, and finally arrived at the top of the inclined plane, near the river, about half-past eleven o'clock, where numbers had assembled to join the procession, and view the operation of shipping the coals, which are called Lord Ravensworth and Partners' Peareth's Wallsend. After placing the band in front of the cottages built on the spot, the coal waggons descended down the plane, one at a time, and landing upon the platform of the drop, were lowered on to the deck of the ship. The emptying of the first waggon was announced by a discharge of cannon, returned by a like discharge from the opposite shore. After the emptying of the coal waggons, the agents with a few select friends proceeded to Newcastle, and partook of an excellent dinner provided on the occasion by Mr. Richardson, of The Three Indian Kings, on the Quayside. Many local toasts were given, with songs; one composed for the occasion, and sung by Captain Welsh, gave much satisfaction.

There are only a few lines running up to the south bank of the Wear, all near together, and all quite different from those of 1812. First comes one from Lambton's Main, which runs due north, striking the river just at the B of Biddick on the 1812 map. Biddick itself is served by a short line running due west to the river.

---

[1] The 'Grand Allies'. About this time they consisted of Lord Ravensworth (created a baron in 1821; formerly Sir Thomas Henry Liddell), James Archibald Stuart-Wortley, and the trustees of the Earl of Strathmore (10th earl, died 1820).

The Phillimore collection contains a letter, from Wm. Brown to Hy. Wilkinson, dated Durham, January 28th, 1770, referring to the Lambton line, in which the writer says: 'Last Friday I got the waggon way sett out, much to my satisfaction, it will really be an Eligible Way.'

There is a line of 4 miles from Ducks (called 'Rainton or Old Ducks' in 1812), to which a short branch comes in from Primrose Moor, and another, higher up, from Burn Moor Colliery, which is three-quarters of a mile NW. of the village. When within a mile and a quarter of the river, it bifurcates into two parallel lines, somewhere about 200 yards apart. The line from Newbottle, instead of joining the Ducks line as in 1812, crosses it and the branch from Burn Moor, and runs up to the river independently; this arrangement is the same in Fletcher's map of 1801.

One of Brunton's walking engines was used there in 1813, and exploded in 1815. In 1818 there was a new line, running to staiths at Bishopwear-mouth, which enabled the coals to be delivered straight into the ships, instead of having to be taken down the river in lighters.[1]

Turning now to the map of 1812, Heddon and Greenwich Moor have disappeared from the north side of the Tyne. A dotted line shows a 'subterraneous tunnel', also given in Fletcher's map, there called a 'sub-terraneous Waggon Way', running from East Kenton down to the river. It is described thus in Rees' 'Cyclopaedia' (1819), article Coal. On arrival at the staith, about four miles above Newcastle, you were taken in

a set of small empty coal waggons capable of containing two persons each, seven of which were drawn along a rail-way by one horse. As soon as you are placed, with your candles lighted, you set off at full speed, with a boy on the first waggon for a charioteer, into a tunnel, or subterranean passage six feet high, about the same breadth and three miles in length. . . . The water from the pit runs down the side of the railway to the Tyne. At intervals there are double railways; and where you come to one of these your driver stops his horse, and a dead silence ensues; he then calls aloud, and listens to hear if any loaded waggons are coming down, that they may pass each other.

The account just quoted mentions that the owners of the East Kenton Colliery were Messrs. Knowsley & Chapman. In Galloway's 'Annals of Coal Mining' (1898) the tunnel is said to have been made about 1770, by Christopher Bedlington, an eminent 'viewer' of the period, after whom it was called 'Kitty's Drift'.

In the 1812 map the Fawdon, Kenton, and Coxlodge line appears, part of which was laid with a rack in 1813.

[1] Tomlinson, 'Hist N.E.R.', p. 51.

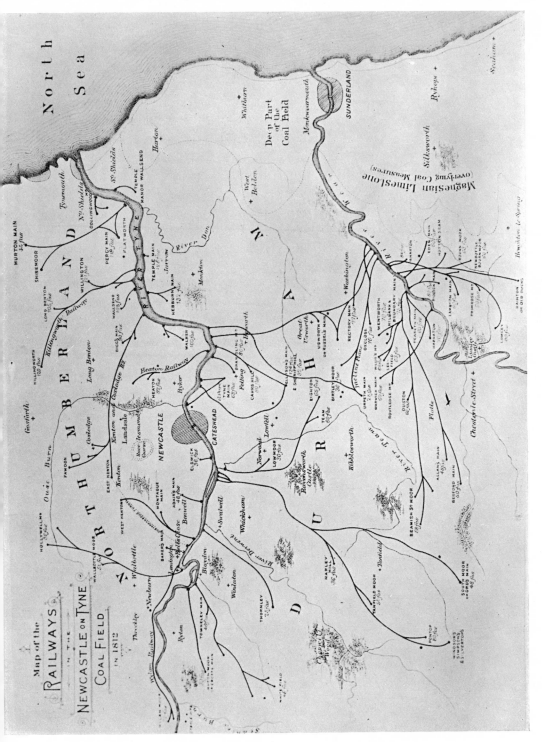

Fig. 10. Map of 1812

Fig. 11. Staiths at Wallsend

Fig. 12. The Jubilee Pit, Coxlodge Colliery. (From Hair's 'Sketches of the Coal Mines in Northumberland and Durham', 1839)

It will be noticed that the line from Willington joins into the Killingworth line and has no connexion with the Kenton railway. This arrangement appears either to be incorrect, or to have been altered, according to a memorandum dated May 16th, 1813:[1]

Expense of keeping and working one of the Travelling engines is estimated at £5. 10. 0 per week including wear and tear of the same, and will take down the way from the pits to where the Kenton way joins Willington waggon-way a distance of 3¾ miles.

The distance from Coxlodge to the staith was about 5 miles, so the junction must have been about a mile and a quarter from the river. The point is of some importance in connexion with locomotive history. Moreover in 1813 the Willington line, like the Kenton, was a rack railway. It may, of course, have run alongside the Killingworth line.

The pit at Coxlodge was called the 'Jubilee', so was opened in either 1809 or 1810. It was about a mile north of the Town Moor, Newcastle, and three-quarters of a mile west of the main road to the north.

It is strange that in neither map is there a line from Throckley. The village is shown on the 1812 map, just north-west of Newburn. Probably the line was a branch from the Wylam railway. From a letter in the possession of the North of England Institute of Mining and Mechanical Engineers, quoted in Chapter VIII, in connexion with brakes, it is clear that there was a waggon-way there in 1754. There is quite a little history of this line in a footnote on p. 83 of Tomlinson's 'North Eastern Railway'. After quoting O. D. Hedley ('Who invented the Locomotive Engine') to the effect that the gauge of the Wylam line was 5 feet,[2] he goes on:

This, according to Mr. J. B. Simpson, was the gauge of the cast-iron railway which replaced, in 1830, the cast-iron plate-way of 1808, altered about the year 1868 to the standard gauge by the Throckley Coal Company.

The Heaton line is a new-comer. Here Chapman's chain engine was tried in 1813, and there was a Stephenson locomotive by 1821.

In connexion with the little curved line shown in 1812 running from Temple to South Shields, Sykes records even more than the usual jollification, thus:

1810 (April 23).—This being the day appointed by Simon Temple, esq., for opening his new colliery, at South Shields, the morning was ushered in by the ringing of bells, &c. &c. Eight waggons being loaded with the coals, were about one o'clock drawn by one horse from the pit

[1] *The Engineer*, January 31st, 1930, p. 128.
[2] The reference should be to p. 23, not 33.

to the staith, preceded by the band of the East York militia, and followed by Mr. Temple, and a long procession of his friends, and two associations of shipwrights under their banners. Seven of the waggons in succession were let down by a new inclined plane to the deck of the ship Maida, belonging to Mr. Temple, which was decorated with colours. The delivery of each was succeeded by a general discharge of cannon, and three times three cheers from the surrounding multitude. The eighth waggon was given to the families of the unfortunate men belonging to South Shields, who were prisoners in France. The company then proceeded to Hylton castle, where one hundred and fifty gentlemen sat down to dinner. The high sheriff of Northumberland, the mayor of Newcastle, several of the chapter of Durham, and most of the magistrates of the district, were at the table. At eight o'clock the ball commenced. At one o'clock, near four hundred ladies and gentlemen sat down to supper; after which dancing recommenced and continued till near six, when all retired highly pleased with the entertainment and respectful attention paid to them.

There are a number of railways which call for mention, but do not appear on the maps which we have been using, for various reasons, usually because they were constructed subsequently to 1812. Firstly, there is one well to the north, recorded by Sykes:

1809 (May 15).—The inhabitants of Alnwick and its vicinity were gratified by the completion of an undertaking hitherto unattempted in that quarter, viz. the delivering of coals at Alnwick, from Shilbottle Colliery, by waggons conveyed along a metal rail-road.

An interesting point about the above is that it seems to have been the first line laid down specially for the supply of coals direct to the consumers; all those previously mentioned having been intended for the purpose of shipment.

There remains one small line still further to the north, namely a tram-road at Berwick-on-Tweed, a view of which, in 1822, is given from a block used in Bland's 'Century of Permanent Way'. Priestley shows it in his map of 1830, as in the annexed sketch, but does not mention it in the book he wrote to accompany the map.

The Hetton Colliery Railway, which ran from the colliery at Hetton-le-Hole to Sunderland, was the first entirely new line laid down by George Stephenson. It was begun in March 1821, and opened on November 18th, 1822. Sykes's record of the proceedings is given in the author's 'Two Essays in Early Locomotive History', on p. 42. The best short description of the line is that of Wood, in his 'Address on the Stephensons':

This line was about eight miles in length, over a very undulating district of country, and Stephenson . . . laid it out with about one and-a-

FIG. 13. Old tram-road, Berwick-on-Tweed, 1822

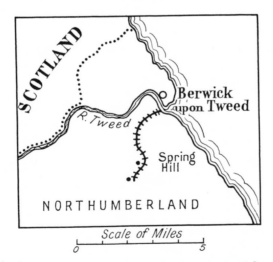

FIG. 14. Sketch showing position of Berwick
tramway. (From Priestley's map of 1830)

half mile locomotive, then one and-a-half mile with fixed engines, ascending a summit of about 250 feet, then self-acting planes for about two and-a-half miles, and ultimately locomotive engines two miles, ending with half-a-mile self-acting plane; there being no less than three fixed engines, five self-acting planes, and three and-a-half miles locomotive.

A most elaborate description of the Hetton line is given by the German engineers C. von Oeynhausen and H. von Dechen in 'Ueber Schienenwege in England . . . 1826 und 1827' (Berlin, 1829).[1]

They devote 22 pages to the railway. With German thoroughness, they not only state the length of each section as given them by the engineer, but also add their own estimate, obtained by pacing it out!

They call the Hetton coal-mines the largest in England. The main part of the pits was a quarter of a mile from Hetton, and was called the Lion pit; there was a smaller one a mile to the south, called the Elmore pit.

The rails were made of cast iron and were 4 feet 7 inches apart.[2]

The following passage is translated:

Partly by the help of stationary steam engines, and partly by steam carriages and self-acting planes, the coal is conveyed in trucks containing one Newcastle chaldron . . . which are similar to those on the Darlington railway. Their speed is such that, were it not for the unnecessary waste of time at the stations, if necessary the whole distance of 8 English miles could be covered in one hour, whereas it takes from $1\frac{1}{2}$ to 2 hours for the empty trucks to do the distance.

This railway, which next to the . . . Darlington Railway is the most beautiful in England, has aroused much admiration on account of its great technical display. In a distance of 8 English miles 3 steam engines, 6 stationary engines, and 5 brake contrivances work on the same number of inclined planes.

The usual speed of the locomotives was '4 or $4\frac{1}{2}$ to 5 English miles per hour', drawing 16 chaldron waggons.

On the self-acting planes 8 loaded waggons descended at 10 miles an hour and pulled up the same number of empty ones.

[1] Also published previously (the same year) in *Archiv für Bergbau*. A French translation came out in 1830. It deserves to be published in English. It is extremely rare, the author's copy being the only one known to him.

[2] It is probable that they made a slight mistake here. No definite contemporary statement of the gauge at Hetton has been found elsewhere, but Wood ('Treatise', 3rd ed., p. 138) says: 'The width between the rails of that railway [Stockton and Darlington] was made four feet eight inches and a half, taking the Killingworth Colliery railway as a standard'; which settles the gauge of the latter, and it is unlikely that Stephenson would have departed from it, especially as he made locomotives for all three lines. Tomlinson says, 'For the Stockton and Darlington Railway, as for the Hetton Colliery Railway, George Stephenson had adopted the gauge of the Killingworth waggonway.' It was 4 feet 8 inches as a matter of fact. He gives evidence to that effect in a footnote on p. 81.

They suggest that if a tunnel had been made under the mountain, 3 stationary engines and 5 self-acting planes would have been saved.

They mention that locomotives had been given up at the Sunderland end on account of the deterioration of the track.

In a note-book of Rastrick's,[1] under date 1829, 22nd January, he mentions that the stationary engines were by Boulton and Watt. He found two locomotives with 3-foot wheels working from the last plane to the pits, a distance of about 1½ miles. 'These engines are the same in all respects as the three engines that were formerly at Work upon the lower Part of the Road towards Sunderland when we tried our Experiments in 1825.'

The following account of the arrangements at Sunderland is taken from the *Transactions of the Highland Society* (1824):

At Sunderland, the sea-vessels pass under the great iron-bridge over the river Wear, which is 236 ft. span and 100 ft. high.[2] On the south side of the river, a short distance above the bridge, a steep ravine branches towards the south-east; on one side of the ravine, a series of warehouses have been erected, in which large quantities of coal are deposited, and from them a waggon-way is erected, supported on long wooden pillars, which descends at an angle of about 30 degrees, through an arch cut in the opposite rocks, and then continues to run on a level but elevated platform along the side of the river. This waggon-way is so constructed, that when a waggon, loaded with coals, descends one side, it pulls an empty one up on the other. The ship to be loaded is placed immediately under the elevated platform, when a trap door is opened, and the bottom of the waggon being let down, the coals descend through a trough into the ship; in some cases, the waggons themselves are lowered altogether by machinery from the platform.

The Rastrick note-book mentioned just previously, five days after the reference to Hetton, i.e. on January 27th, 1829, refers to the Brunton and Shields Railway. The exact course of this line is not easy to trace. Rastrick says it started from the coal pit at Brunton, about 3½ miles west of Newcastle. But it included the 'Backworth plane' (down which, he says, the waggons had to be pulled when the wind was against them), and according to the map of 1788 Backworth is about a mile north-east of Killingworth. That it was somewhere in that direction is borne out by the fact that another plane on it was called the Killingworth plane (down which Rastrick rode at 10 miles an hour). The gauge was 3 feet 6 inches. The whole length was 9¾ miles and 193 yards, of which 3 miles were worked by horses. The engineer was Benjamin Thompson, the patentee of the stationary-engine system.

[1] In the library of the University of London.
[2] The third iron bridge in the world. Finished in 1796 and superseded in 1930.

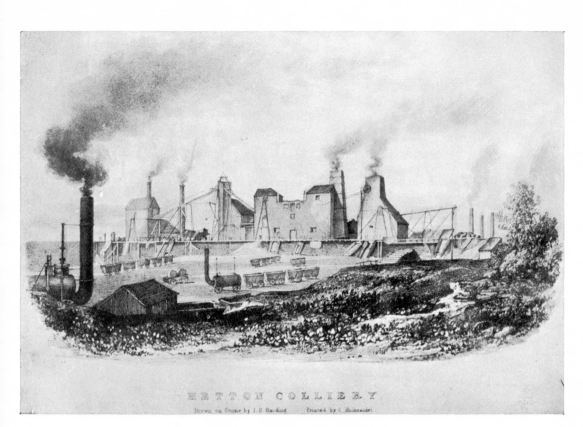

FIG. 15.   Hetton Colliery, 1822
(From a contemporary engraving)

FIGS. 16 & 17.   A Boon Wood Colliery token
(Author's collection)

In Stephenson and Locke's 'Observations . . .', being a reply to Walker and Rastrick's report, Thompson's system is described thus:

> The plan consists in placing Steam Engines at intervals of one or one and a half mile along the whole line of Railway, and having ropes running on rollers, placed between the rails, to extend from one Engine to the other, by which the waggons are drawn forward. When a train of waggons leaves a station, it takes along with it another rope, technically called the *"tail-rope"*, which serves to bring back the next train which is moving in the contrary direction; the rope which drew the first train then becomes the *"tail-rope"*, and is drawn back by the former, which then becomes the *"head-rope"*. This is called the reciprocating system. . . .
>
> The Brunton and Shields Railway has five continuous planes worked by Fixed Engines, only one of which may be said to be on the reciprocating plan; for on three of the planes the loaded waggons run of themselves, and the rope is merely used to draw back the empty ones; and on the other the full waggons are drawn up, and the empty ones run back with the rope: from which it appears, that on four of the planes it is only necessary to use one rope, the gravity of the waggons dispensing with the other.

For Thompson's own description of his system, see p. 160, *post*.

The satisfactory working of this railway induced both Walker and Rastrick to recommend stationary engines in their reports to the directors of the Liverpool and Manchester Railway.

We must return farther north for a moment to mention a line laid with malleable iron rails in 1820 from Bedlington Colliery to Bedlington Iron Works, a distance of about 3 miles, which was spoken of as the best they had seen by both William James and Robert Stevenson. It was the first to be laid with rails rolled under Birkinshaw's patent.[1]

The Stockton and Darlington Railway has been given a chapter to itself (X).

RAILWAYS IN CUMBERLAND AND THE LAKE DISTRICT

The Whitehaven coal-field was the scene of many very interesting developments in mining practice. The town and harbour owe their existence entirely to the coal trade. To quote from Galloway's 'History of Coal Mining in Great Britain' (1882):

> In the time of Queen Elizabeth Whitehaven consisted of six fishing cabins, and possessed only one small boat (of nine tons), called the *Bee of Whitehaven*, which carried herrings to Liverpool and Chester and brought back cattle. The working of coal for local requirements, in the

---

[1] For an account of the line and the circumstances under which it came into existence, see p. 154, *post*. For Birkinshaw's patent, see p. 152.

land which had previously belonged to the dissolved monastery of St. Bees, was already going on during this reign; but it was not until Whitehaven came into the possession of the Lowther family . . . that the systematic development of the mines and the exportation of coal commenced.

In the *Transactions of the Royal Irish Academy* (vol. v, p. 266) there is a paper by Joseph Fisher, entitled 'Observations and Enquiries made upon and concerning the coal-works at Whitehaven in the County of Cumberland in the year 1793'. The following is a quotation therefrom:

It was from this pit (Parker's) that the first waggon-way (as it is called) was laid in this country. . . . It is made with wood laid down fast on each side of the road at a proper distance for the solid iron wheels of the waggon to move upon; the wheels are confined from running off from the wood by a protuberant rim of iron on the interior side of each wheel. The road is made so as to have a gentle descent along its whole length, so that the loaden waggon runs without any horse to draw it; where the descent is such that the motion would be too quick, a man, who is mounted behind the waggon, by pressing down upon one wheel a piece of wood, called the convoy, which is fixed to the waggon for that purpose, can restrain the too rapid motion. . . . A horse is used to draw the empty waggon back to the pit from the staith by an easy ascent along another similar waggon-way laid along the side of the first at about three feet distance.

The staith is a large wooden building on the west side of the town adjoining to the harbour and covered in. In this staith are fixed three hurries or spouts, at such a distance from each other that a ship of three hundred tons burden can lie under each hurry and receive a loading at one time. The staith is about thirty-seven feet above the level of the quay, and when the waggons arrive there, the bottom of each waggon is drawn out and the coals drop from thence into the hurry or spout under it, through which they run down into the ship. . . . The hurries or spouts lie with an inclining slope of about forty-five degrees.

When there are no ships ready to receive coals they are deposited in the staith, which will contain about six thousand tons, Dublin measure.

A shorter, but generally similar, description of the early wooden railways occurs in 'The Literary Life of William Brownrigg, M.D., F.R.S., to which are added an account of the Coal Mines near Whitehaven', &c., by Joshua Dixon (1801). He says the Howgill Colliery (to which Parker's Pit belonged) very much exceeded any colliery in the kingdom in extent.

There is an interesting passage in 'A Voyage round Great Britain', by Richard Ayton, vol. ii (1815), on the subject of Whitehaven. There were at that time 20 miles of iron railway underground (he does not say how much there was on the surface):

Some of the pits lie at a considerable distance from the town, and the coals are conveyed from them to the vessels in waggons containing 45 cwt. each, and running upon railroads. The "staithes" were called "Hurries".[1] The loaded waggons pulled up 3 empty ones, which were not enough to check their descent, so they were made to give motion to some machinery which required considerable power, working a huge pair of bellows that forced air through a valve into a receiver.

Horses were used for traction underground, driven by girls.

From a report of 1817, or thereabouts, by the French engineer de Gallois, it is clear that the apparatus described above was not intended for the storage of compressed air, but was simply a brake. According to him, an air-pump had its piston driven by a crank on the shaft of the drum round which the rope worked, compressing the air into a reservoir. The speed was controlled by opening or closing a cock which allowed the air to escape. As he mentions a reciprocating pump, and Ayton, bellows, it is possible that there was more than one apparatus of the kind. It must have given admirable control, subject to the disadvantage that the speed had to be regulated from the top of the hill, instead of on the vehicles themselves.

Two very good descriptions of the Whitehaven mines have been written in later years, the first being 'Archaeology of the West Cumberland Coal Trade', by Isaac Fletcher, M.P., F.R.S.; reprinted at Kendal in 1878 from the *Transactions of the Cumberland and Westmorland Antiquarian and Archaeological Society* (Old Series, vol. iii, 1876–7). The other consists of the article 'Coal Mining' in the 'Victoria History of Cumberland', vol. ii (1905), which was written by R. W. Moore, a former 'viewer'.

The following is an extract from Fletcher:

Early in the seventeenth century, Sir John Lowther, of Lowther,[2] purchased and presented to his second son Christopher, the lands belonging to the dissolved monastery of St. Bees, at Whitehaven. This gentleman (who afterwards was created a baronet) settled at Whitehaven, where he built a house under the cliff and close to the harbour. He died in 1644. . . . He also converted the little creek at Whitehaven into a harbour by protecting it from the south-west winds by means of a small pier.

Christopher was succeeded by his son John, who developed the mines considerably. He died in 1706 and was followed by his son, Sir James.

---

[1] In view of the previous quotation, Ayton seems to have made a mistake in applying the word 'hurry' to the whole staith. O.E.D. says a 'spout'.

[2] The village and castle are in Westmorland, about 4 miles south of Penrith.

The Speddings, who belonged to a family which is still an important one in the Lake District, now come into the picture:

In 1685 Edward Spedding settled at Whitehaven as principal steward of the Lowther estates. His eldest son, (afterwards John Spedding, Esq., of Armathwaite Hall, and sheriff of Cumberland), succeeded in that important office, and his fourth son, Carlisle Spedding, a man of great eminence from his scientific attainments, was appointed engineer to the Whitehaven collieries about the year 1718.

He invented the Steel Mill,—a machine by which a disk of steel is made to revolve with great rapidity against a piece of flint—by which a constant shower of sparks is produced, and until the Davy lamp[1] was invented, in 1816, it was the only means of obtaining an artificial light with safety in an explosive atmosphere.

We now turn to Galloway for a moment:

Tradition records that previous to entering on his duties at Whitehaven, Spedding was sent *incognito* to Newcastle-on-Tyne by Sir James, to acquire a knowledge of the methods of mining possessed in that district. Here . . . he obtained employment in the pits as a hewer, or haggar, of coal, making in the meanwhile all the inquiries and discoveries he could . . . After continuing in this capacity for a considerable time, Spedding, who was then known by the name of "Dan", had the misfortune to be burnt by the fire-damp, whereupon a message was sent to Newcastle to procure the best medical assistance. . . . The extraordinary attention paid to a person in the apparent situation of Spedding . . . led to the discovery of his true character and motives; accordingly after his recovery, having already accomplished to a large extent the object of his mission, he returned to Whitehaven and set about the improvement of the collieries.

Only three years after the erection of the first Newcomen 'fire-engine' for pumping (near Dudley Castle in 1712), one was erected at Stone Pit Ginns, Whitehaven. The date is fixed by a deed of 1726, quoted by Moore. It is said by more than one authority that this innovation was due to Spedding, who doubtless saw one when in Northumberland, where there were two or three by that time; therefore Fletcher's date 'about 1718' for his appointment is perhaps a little too late. A second 'fire-engine' was erected later, at the Ginns, and both are said to have lasted till 1780.

Sir James Lowther and Carlisle Spedding died in 1755; the latter being killed by an explosion of fire-damp.

The former—who never married—was succeeded by his kinsman and namesake, who was created Earl of Lonsdale in 1784. He was a most

[1] He might have added the Stephenson lamp, which was used concurrently with that of Davy. Both were invented in 1815. There was also another, the Clanny.

extraordinary character, of whom an interesting account is given in Chapter IX (headed 'The Tyrant of the North') of 'Annals of a Yorkshire House', by A. M. W. Stirling (1911).

Carlisle Spedding was succeeded in office by his son James, who introduced great improvements in the ventilation of the mines.

Returning to the subject of railways, according to the 'Victoria History' the first seems to have been a 'coal-way' constructed in 1683, from the Woodagreen pit (sunk near the Ginns in 1679), at the suggestion of a Mr. Gale. It is described as a 'causeway', bounded on each side with wood 'balks' on which the cart wheels would run.

Quoting Fletcher again:

The Whitehaven Coal Field is divided into two distinct and separate portions. One embraces the vast tract laying between the St. Bees' Valley and the sea, and under the sea, and the other lays to the north-east of the same valley. The former is called Howgill Colliery, and the latter Whingill Colliery. . . .

At Saltom [where coal was reached August 1st, 1733] the coals were raised by a horse-gin to the surface near the shore; they were then run into a drift some distance into the hill side and lifted by another gin to the summit of the cliff (twenty-seven fathoms higher) by a vertical shaft, when they were put into waggons of 44 cwts. each, and conveyed by means of a wooden railway to the harbour, where they were either shipped or deposited in an immense staith or store-house built along the quay, at the south side of the harbour. About the same time, or possibly a little earlier, a similar railway was laid down from Parker Pit to the harbour,[1] and all the arrangements connected with them, especially the inclined plane from Ravenhill (where the Saltom Coals were lifted), were of the most complete and ingenious character.

Before the completion of the Saltom winning, Sir James Lowther seems to have turned his attention to the development of the Whingill Colliery to the east of Whitehaven. . . .

Wooden railways were laid from all the Whingill Pits[2] to the Arch at the north entrance to Whitehaven, where they were deposited in a large staith, and carted from thence to the ships. The Arch was built with the intention of carrying the railway over it by an inclined plane to the harbour, but the plan was never executed.

The 'Bransty Arch', as it was called, was opened with great éclat on August 9th, 1803.

Evidence as to the date of the introduction of railways at Whitehaven is rather confused. There is, however, no doubt that the original ones were of wood. Rees' 'Cyclopaedia' (1819), after speaking of the intro-

---

[1] See quotation from Galloway, below.
[2] See Index, s.v. Whitehaven.

duction of 'waggon-roads or wooden rail-ways' about 1680 in the neigh-bourhood of Newcastle-on-Tyne, goes on to say:

It was not until the year 1738 that this important improvement was introduced at the White-haven collieries on the western coast, and it is surprising to observe how slow the introduction of them was in other parts.

As was remarked in Chapter I, Cumming (1824) said wooden rail-ways were first introduced at Whitehaven in 1738 (possibly following Rees).

Galloway ('Annals of Coal Mining', 1898) speaks as follows:

Wooden railways were also first constructed by Spedding at White-haven, though the exact date of their introduction, as well as the name of the pit first provided with this method of conveyance, are somewhat uncertain. According to Hutchinson (*Cumberland*, ii. 66) the earliest was constructed between the Parker Pit[1] and the staith, a distance of half-a-mile. This railway is shown in a print entitled, *A Bird's eye View of Whitehaven* (*Trans. Fed. Inst.*, vii. 625), engraved from a painting made in 1738.

We now come to an episode of surpassing interest, but concerning which the evidence is sadly unsatisfactory. As the Whitehaven Collieries had been so early in the field with a Newcomen engine—the one of 1715 must have been only about the fourth or fifth made—it is only to be expected that they would have done some pioneer work with a locomotive, and sufficient evidence has now come to light to prove that they did so. One can now say definitely that a locomotive was built by Taylor Swainson, the engineer, in the year 1812, which failed owing to the usual trouble, namely breaking the rails by its weight, and that it was nick-named the 'Iron Horse'.

Moore gives the following interesting account of the methods of under-ground haulage:

Corves were probably introduced at Whitehaven about 1675. They were circular baskets made of hazel rods, provided with an iron bow for attachment to the hook at the end of the winding rope. At first they con-tained $2\frac{1}{2}$ cwt. of coal each, but were enlarged as larger pits were sunk, and when the horse-gins were superseded by steam winding engines. Eventually some held as much as 12 cwt. (used till 1875 at William pit, when they were superseded by steel tubs). The corves were undoubtedly in the earliest days placed on ashen runners resembling a sledge, and conveyed along the corf-way, constructed of two parallel lines of wooden rails. These old wooden roads continued to be used for the conveyance

[1] As quoted earlier in this chapter, Fisher (1793) said the Parker's Pit line was the first 'in this country', probably meaning neighbourhood, or perhaps county.

of coal underground until the end of the XVIII century, when cast iron tram rails (of the angle iron pattern) and edge rails were adopted. After the introduction of tram plates the corves were placed on low trams fitted with small plain wheels without flanges and conveyed to the sidings at the rolley-roads, which were laid with edge rails. At these sidings there were hand cranes for lifting the full corves off the small trams on to larger trams with flanged wheels, which were drawn by horses along the rolley-roads to the shaft bottom. Later light wooden bogies with small plain wheels were used on tram-plate roads for bringing the rise coals down from the working to "stears", which were tips erected at the sidings, and at which the bogies were emptied into the corves or baskets for conveyance to the shafts. These baskets were made up into trains or "rollies", which were drawn by horses to the pit bottom. Later a steam engine hauled them by ropes. It is difficult to say when mechanical haulage was first introduced in the Cumberland coalfield, but probably it was in the year 1816, when a H.P. engine was erected underground at William pit, Whitehaven.

Among other mines mentioned by Fletcher there is Harrington, 4½ miles north of Whitehaven (Workington being 2 miles farther north still). Here there were upwards of a dozen pits, mostly sunk between 1750 and 1790; the produce being shipped at Harrington, where a harbour was built about 1750. To this wooden railways were laid, somewhere about 1800, from the mines, along which the coals were conveyed to the ships, and a large export trade was carried on for upwards of a century. These mines were worked by the Curwen family.

There was also apparently some kind of local tramway at Boon Wood Colliery, at Distington, about 4 miles north of Whitehaven, judging by the copper token illustrated in Figs. 16 and 17. The colliery has been disused for sixty or seventy years.

Some time before 1750 Sir James Lowther began to work coal on an extensive scale in Clifton, and laid down a wooden railway from his quay on the north side of Workington Harbour to a point near the village of Great Clifton, 2½ miles to the eastward, to which the produce of the various mines was taken in carts.

Another 5 miles up the coast we come to Maryport, the harbour of which, originally called 'Elnefoot', was made about 1750. About this time Broughton Colliery, 2½ miles in a south-easterly direction, was developed by a Mr. Christian, who constructed a wooden railway from the pits to the 'Arches' as they were called, near the present (Maryport) railway station; whence the coal was carted to the harbour.

In 1775 Smeaton reported[1] on the feasibility of exporting coals from

[1] *Reports*, vol. iii, p. 396.

the estates of Bransty, Birkby, and Aspatria, belonging to the Earl of Egremont, proposing certain railroads, but nothing further is known about them.

A railway of 5½ miles in length was made in 1775, from the Earl of Carlisle's colliery at Tindale Fell to Brampton. It was the scene of an early experiment with wrought-iron rails, in about the year 1808.[1] It was originally laid with cast-iron fish-bellied rails. Moore says that boring for coal on Tindale Fell, which is about 14 miles east of Carlisle, and 6 east of Brampton, was in progress in 1628. In 1769 the Earl of Carlisle was carrying on Tarnhouse or Tindale Fell Colliery, besides the Talkin and Midgeholme Collieries. The railway, along which the coals were conveyed by horses in chaldron waggons, did not take the same route exactly, nor was it so long, as the existing railway, which begins at Brampton and terminates at Lambley station on the Alston branch of the N.E.R. Priestley mentions that the Newcastle and Carlisle Railway crossed it at 13 miles from the latter place. ('Navigable Rivers, Canals and Railways of Great Britain', 1831.)

Midgeholme was a mile and a half farther to the east than Tindale Fell, and no doubt the line was extended there at an early period. The first locomotive to be used was the celebrated Rocket, which was purchased from the Liverpool and Manchester Railway in 1837.

Nenthead village, 4 miles south-east of Alston, in Cumberland, lay in an extensive lead-mining district. Near it was the aqueduct of 'Nentforce Level'. T. Sopwith, in 'An Account of the Mining Districts of Alston Moor', &c. (Alnwick, 1833), says: 'Nentforce Level set the example of cast-iron railways, which, in the London Lead Company's[2] works and numerous other mines, were speedily adopted in the place of wooden rails.'

Unfortunately he does not give any date, nor does he say whether the example was merely being set to the neighbourhood. Later on, he mentions an interesting method of signalling below ground, thus:

When a signal is to be made to some distance, it is done by beating on the rails or posts, five beats, the first two slow, the other three quick, and this is repeated several times. The same signal is used in the Newcastle coal-mines, where it is denominated 'jowling'.

[1] See p. 153, post.
[2] An interesting paper on this company, by Dr. A. Raistrick, is contained in vol. xiv of the *Newcomen Society's Transactions*. It was incorporated by charter in 1692. The books are preserved in the library of the North of England Institute of Mining Engineers, Newcastle-on-Tyne.

RAILWAYS IN LANCASHIRE

In the *Transactions of the Highland Society* (1824), a paper by Alexander Scott of Ormiston contains the following information with regard to Lancashire:

> In the county of Lancaster there are a great many iron-railways for the convenience, accommodation and advantage of the different collieries, manufactories and other works. The coal-works near St. Helens in the vicinity of Liverpool, have a double railway, some miles in length; and at the works of Lord Balcarras, near Wigan, as well as his canal coal-pits near the same place, there are double railways of very considerable length. To the southward of the town of Preston there is a double railway, and of great length.

No other mention has been found of this railway at St. Helens. Priestley gives the well-known St. Helens and Runcorn Gap Railway, the Act for which received the Royal Assent on May 29th, 1830, but says nothing of any earlier line. The same applies to lines at Wigan; he only mentions the Wigan Branch Railway, which received its Act on the same day. Under the head 'Leeds and Liverpool Canal', he cites an Act (obtained by that company in 1819) for making a 'navigable Cut, and also a collateral Branch or Railway, from their said Canal at Hennis Bridge near Wigan, to join the Duke of Bridgewater's canal at Leigh'. The 'collateral Branch or Railway' appears to have been only about a mile in length, branching off northwards 'at the road leading from Ashton to Platt Bridge'.

The 'Lord Balcarras' was Alexander, 23rd Earl of Crawford and 6th Earl of Balcarres; great-great-grandfather of the present Earl, who has kindly searched for information among the records at Haigh Hall. The only reference to railways which came to light was that the waggon-way for the collieries was surveyed in 1788. Lord Crawford has given the author a copy of a most interesting presidential address which he delivered before the Manchester Statistical Society in 1933, entitled 'Haigh Cannel'. It is a fascinating account of the early history of his family's cannel-mines—one must not say 'coal'—which have been in operation for four centuries. Unfortunately for the present purpose, there is nothing on the subject of railways.

The Haigh Foundry was another of the family enterprises, dating from 1810. They built a good many steam-engines for winding and pumping, also made sugar-refining machinery for export. On one parcel of the latter, which went to New Orleans, the buyers defaulted, to the tune of £3,000. The Foundry was far from being as profitable as the mines. In 1835 it was taken on a 21 years' lease by the 'Haigh Foundry

Company', who went in for locomotives, and built 109 between 1835 and 1856. For part of the time, J. W. Melling was manager. There is an article in the *Locomotive Engineer* for September 1899 by C. E. Stretton which enumerates all their engines. Three of them, nos. 60–2, were four-wheel tanks for the son of Lord Alexander, the original founder, to carry coals from his collieries to the town and docks at Preston, delivered in 1842. They supplied engines to all the leading railways of the day, including two of the original freaks on the Great Western, in 1838, named Viper and Snake.

It has been possible to discover something about the last railway mentioned by Scott, namely the Preston Railway; Priestley does not fail us this time. It was a plate-railway, otherwise known as the Preston and Walton Summit, and formed a link in the Lancaster Canal.[1] The latter, which is described by Priestley as a stupendous undertaking, was authorized by an Act of 1792, to be made from 'Kirkby Kendal in the county of Westmoreland to West Houghton in the county palatine of Lancaster'. Other Acts followed, for the purpose of modifying the route or raising more money, in 1793, 1796, and 1800, and in 1807 a further one empowered them to make a railway part of the way. The latter started from Preston, crossed the Ribble, and ascended some high ground, joining the second piece of the canal at the summit level, at a place called Thorpe Green, rising 222 feet in the process. It was about $4\frac{1}{2}$ miles long, and was opened June 1st, 1803. It was acquired by the Bolton and Preston Railway, under its Act, in 1837.

The Bolton and Leigh Railway calls for mention. It received its first Act March 31st, 1825, entitled 'An Act for making and maintaining a Railway or Tramroad from or from near the Manchester, Bolton and Bury Canal, in the parish of Bolton-le-Moors, to or near the Leeds and Liverpool Canal, in the parish of Leigh, all in the county palatine of Lancaster'. Stationary engines were to be used on the inclined planes, and locomotives on the other parts—both burning their own smoke. It was opened August 1st, 1828.

There was a railway from Orrell Colliery[2] (about 3 miles WSW. of Wigan), running for about 2 miles northwards to the Leeds and Liverpool Canal. Details are difficult to obtain, but there was a steep gradient at each end, on which rack-locomotives were used as early as 1822. Tradition has it that the middle section was worked by horses.

---

[1] Eventually became the property of the L. & N.W.R. Co.

[2] Coal from Orrell was exported in large quantities to America, and the word 'Orrell' over there held the same place, as regards reputation, as 'Wallsend' did for many years in this country.

At the east end of Chat Moss, the Liverpool and Manchester line passed through land belonging to John George Legh, who is mentioned in clause XVI of the Act of 1826. He had a railway, as a directors' minute of January 30th, 1832, mentions 'Mr. Legh's new engine, the "Newcastle"'. The following evidence given by Thomas Lee, architect and surveyor, on the London and Birmingham Bill (1832) probably refers to him:

> Previous to the railway [Liverpool and Manchester] being made, Colonel Lee's coal was sent from Newton to Liverpool by canal [Sankey Navigation], he had a railway about $\frac{3}{4}$ of a mile long to it.

An account has been handed down of a temporary railway which is of interest. It occurs in the 'General View of the Agriculture of the County of Lancaster', by John Holt (1795). On pp. 97 and 98 he describes the operations then in progress of draining Trafford Moss (3 miles west of Manchester), and possibly also Chat Moss; which included the use of a plate-railway with rails cast in 6-foot lengths and jointed together by 'dove-tailed steps', resting upon wooden sleepers. This road was laid down temporarily, and moved when required; 'a single person will with ease take up, remove, and lay down 200 yards of it in one day'. There is an illustration showing the rails and a peculiarly shaped truck. For a later railway on Chat Moss, see Index.

RAILWAYS IN YORKSHIRE

Passing southwards to Leeds, we come on something much more important, namely, the Middleton Colliery Railway.

Previously to the year 1758, all railways had been made either on the property of those interested or by negotiation with the owners of land over which they had to pass. But when Charles Brandling, the owner of the Middleton Collieries, $3\frac{1}{2}$ miles south of Leeds, wished to construct one to convey his coals thither, it was found impossible to arrange the matter by private agreement, and he applied for an Act of Parliament, which received the Royal Assent on June 9th, 1758 (31 Geo. II, cap. 22). This was the first Railway Act ever passed. Its title was 'An Act for Establishing Agreements made between Charles Brandling, Esquire, and other Persons, Proprietors of Lands, for laying down a Waggon-Way, such as is used for and about the Coal Works and Coal Mines in the counties of Durham and Northumberland, in order for the better supplying the Town and Neighbourhood of Leeds, in the County of York, with Coals'.

In return for the privilege, he had to guarantee a supply of 240,000 corves of coal of 210 lb. each per annum, delivered at the terminus at Leeds at $4\frac{3}{4}d.$ per corf—equivalent to 22,500 tons at 4s. $2\frac{2}{3}d.$ per ton.

The reasons for having an Act of Parliament, although all the property-owners appear to have been agreeable, are set out thus:

As some of the owners and properties . . . may happen to have only a limited and not an absolute interest and property therein, and may be under other disabilities to assure to the said Charles Brandling and his assigns the enjoyment of the said Powers Liberties and Privileges necessary to render the said Agreement effectual . . . without . . . an Act of Parliament.

Further Acts were passed in 1779, 1793, and 1803, increasing the supply and the price, the latter being eventually made 8*d*. per corf.

The line ran across Hunslet Moor, being more or less level, though on the whole downhill towards Leeds, with one fairly steep drop about half-way. It was about $3\frac{1}{2}$ miles long. Fig. 18 shows the Leeds end of it.

According to an article in *The Locomotive* for March 1910, by W. B. Paley, the rails were of wood, with renewable pieces on the top, of 4 feet 1 inch gauge. Very small and broad wheels of beech, with deep sharp flanges, were used.

The rack-rails he described as follows:

Two early specimens of the rails were shown at the 'Old Leeds' Exhibition in 1908, the oldest 3 feet long, parabolic, or 'fish-bellied' on its lower edge, with six half-round cogs projecting $2\frac{1}{4}$ in. on one side, 3 in. diameter and 3 in. apart. The metal of these teeth was $\frac{1}{2}$ in. thick, but the hollow form was evidently not strong enough, for the next rail, which was 6 ft. long, parallel on the base, with a small foot midway without plug-holes, had solid teeth, 12 per rail. The tread of both rails was 2 in. wide.

In 1811 John Blenkinsop, coal viewer, of Middleton, took out a patent (no. 3431 of that year) for a 'tramway for conveying coals', with a rack or toothed rail laid down on one side of the railway from end to end. Power was to be obtained by any suitable method, a steam-engine being preferred. The first commercially successful employment of locomotives followed.

At some time previous to 1826 a gravity arrangement was put in, to haul the empty trucks up to the pit head, shown in Fig. 19, which is taken from Strickland's 'Report on Canals, Railways', &c., published in that year. Fig. 20, which is from another part of the same plate, shows what is probably the first railway signal in the world.

The Middleton collieries are still working, though not to the same extent as formerly, and a railway still runs over the route. A piece of an old rail and one of the stone sleepers are in the Leeds Museum.

Drawn by N. Whitrock.   Engraved on Steel by T. Owe

CHRIST CHURCH AND COAL STAITH, LEEDS.

F<small>IG</small>. 18.   The Middleton Colliery Railway.   (From an engraving published in 1829)

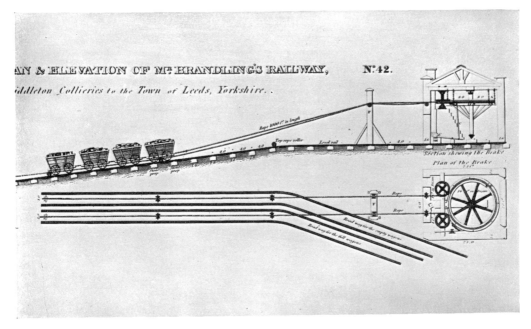

F<small>IG</small>. 19.   Part of the inclined plane, Middleton Colliery Railway

There do not seem to have been many very early railways in Yorkshire. Smeaton stated that the first waggon-way in that county had
been laid within his remembrance. He was born in 1724.

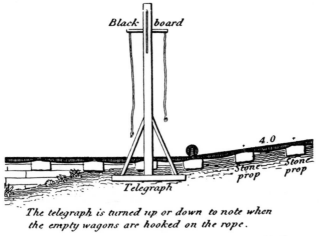

The telegraph is turned up or down to note when
the empty wagons are hooked on the rope.

FIG. 20. Early signal on the Middleton Colliery Railway

The only line given by Priestley under a heading of its own is the
Heck and Wentbridge (Acts 1826 and 1827). He describes it thus:

> This work commences at a place called Wentbridge, adjoining the
> turnpike road from Doncaster to Ferrybridge; and, pursuing a circuitous
> course in a north-east direction, arrives at its termination in the basin
> communicating with that part of the Aire and Calder Navigation called
> the Knottingley and Goole Canal, in the township of Heck, after having
> completed a distance of seven miles and thirty-five chains.

Under the heading 'Aire and Calder Navigation' he gives the following:

> From Mr. Haxby's canal a short railway is carried to the lime-
> quarries, north of Brotherton; near to the west end of Crier Cut, close
> to the Leeds Race Course, there is a railway and staith for conveying
> and shipping the coal from Lord Stourton's collieries on Rothwell Haigh;
> near Knowstrop there is a railway from the Marchioness of Hertford's
> collieries, at Waterloo, for the supply of Leeds: there are also railroads
> at Crier Cut and opposite the Leeds Race Course, for the delivery of
> coals from this colliery going eastward; near to Methley, a staith and
> railway from Sir John Lowther's collieries at Astley; and in the township
> of Methley, there is a railway for conveying to the river the coals from
> the Earl of Mexbro's works. . . .
>
> A little above Wakefield Bridge are the Calder and Hebble Naviga-
> tion Warehouses, and, on the opposite side of the river, the Earl of
> Cardigan's railway, which conveys the coal from his collieries at New
> Park, two miles from Wakefield. . . .

At Bottom Boat, about five and a half miles from Wakefield by the course of the navigation, the Lake Lock Railroad communicates with the river. This road, which was constructed about thirty years ago by a company without application to parliament, extends to the East Ardsley Coal-field, a distance of four miles from its junction with the navigation. When it was at first constructed, as its name imports, it joined the river at Lake Lock; it was however, in 1804, removed to Bottom Boat, a mile lower down the river, to which place about seventy to one hundred thousand tons of coal are now annually brought down by this railroad; and another belonging to the Duke of Leeds, communicating with his collieries on Wakefield Outwood, terminates within a short distance of the former, from which forty or fifty thousand tons of coal are shipped annually.

Under 'Calder and Hebble Navigation':

From the collieries at Flockton, a railway extends to the river at Horbury Bridge; from the Storr's Hill Colliery there is also a railway, terminating at the Calder, a little above the same bridge; within a few years there was a railway from the White Lee Colliery, above Heckmondwike, which terminated at this navigation a short distance above Dewsbury, but the colliery is now worked out, and the railway taken up. At Kirklees a railway is laid to this navigation, from Sir George Armytage's Collieries; and the Earl of Cardigan has also a railway from his valuable collieries at New Park, to the Calder, at Wakefield, where are convenient staiths for shipment.

Under 'Bradford Canal', he mentions that 'iron railways approach the town of Bradford' from Bowling Iron Works and Wibsey Low Moor.

The following passage occurs in Rees' 'Cyclopaedia', article Canal:

In the year 1783 we remember seeing an inclined plane . . . on which the coal waggons descend down the hill from Wibseyslack to . . . Bradford, which is on a branch of the Leeds and Liverpool Canal.

A line was made in 1809 from a branch of the Barnsley Canal at Barnby Bridge, past the celebrated Silkstone Colliery, to what was known as House Carr Colliery, a distance of about $3\frac{1}{4}$ miles. Two sections of rail from this line are preserved in the York Railway Museum. They are channel-shaped, more like gutters than rails, and are very thick and substantial. They rested in chairs, keeping in position merely by their own weight; the chairs being spiked down to stone blocks. Whether these rails are typical of the whole line is not known; they may have been merely used in some special place, such as crossing a road, or, as in the case of the Hay Railway, going over a bridge. The line was not finally closed until 1860. The northern entrance of the 'Black Horse' tunnel still remains visible, under the present railway at Silkstone station.

Railways at Sheffield are described in the next chapter.

CHAPTER III

EARLY RAILWAYS IN THE MIDLANDS

As has been shown in Chapter I, the first railway in the whole country of which any definite evidence has so far been found was that of Sir Francis Willoughby at Wollaton in Nottinghamshire, which can safely be put as early as 1597. Fairly good authority was given for wooden railways at Coalbrookdale from about 1620 to 1650, but, as will be seen later, they are perhaps rather mythical, and for really detailed information with respect to railways in the Midland area we have to leap over a couple of centuries.

To begin at the most northerly part of the district, a railway made about 1775 from the Sheffield Colliery to the town, a distance of about 2 miles, will be first mentioned. It was laid by John Curr, the manager of the Duke of Norfolk's collieries, and appears to have been made at first of wood. Curr, to whom further reference is made in Chapter VII, says in the Preface to his book 'The Coal Viewer', writing at least as early as 1796, that he introduced railroads at the Sheffield Colliery 'about twenty-one years ago'. They were not received with favour. His son in 'Railway Locomotion and Steam Navigation' (1847) says, 'a riot ensued,— the railway was torn up,—the coal staith burnt, and the inventor, my father, reduced to the necessity of concealment in a wood, for three days and nights, to escape the fury of the populace'.

When matters had calmed down, the line was relaid with plate-rails cast at Butterley.

In the 'Repertory of Arts and Manufactures' for 1800 (vol. xiii, 1st series, p. 167) the following interesting article appears, entitled 'On the Utility of Iron Rail-ways. By Joseph Wilkes, Esq. of Measham'[1] (from the 2nd volume of *Communications to the Board of Agriculture*):

> On the 14th of August 1799, a party deputed from the committee for conducting the concerns of the Grand Junction Canal, with other gentlemen, attended at my colliery at Measham, in Derbyshire, for the purpose of obtaining ocular and satisfactory proof of the utility of the iron rail-ways, previous to that company adopting them (which they have now done) in lieu of some portion of their line of canal. The result of the experiments was nearly thus: one horse of the value of 20*l*. on a declivity

---

[1] Measham is 3½ miles SW. of Ashby de la Zouch. The railway was originally a wooden one.

of an iron road $\frac{5}{16}$ of an inch at a yard [1 in 115], drew 21 carriages or waggons, laden with coals and timber, amounting, in the whole, to 35 tons, overcoming the *vis inertiae*, repeatedly, with great ease. The same horse, up this acclivity, drew 5 tons with ease; he also drew up the road, where the acclivity is $1\frac{3}{4}$ of an inch at a yard [1 in 21], three tons. But on this declivity it is necessary to slipper or lock the wheels, the horse not being able to resist the increased momentum of more than three or four tons.

The same gentlemen proceeded the next day to another colliery I have at Brinsley[1] in Nottinghamshire, where one horse, value 30*l*. drew, on a road of the same construction, where the declivity was $\frac{1}{3}$ of an inch at a yard [1 in 108], 21 waggons, of 5 cwt. each, which with their loading of coals, amounted to 43 tons 8 cwt.; the same horse drew seven tons up the road. It must be observed, that in both the foregoing statements, the cwt. is 120 lb. On this road the rails are three feet long, 33 lb. weight, and calculated to carry two tons on each waggon, laid four feet two inches wide, on stone or wood sleepers, placed on a bed of sleck,[2] so as to fix it solid and firm. The expence of compleating one mile of such a road, where materials of all descriptions lie convenient, and where the land lies tolerably favourable for the descent, will be about 900*l*. or 1000*l*. *per* mile, single road, fenced, &c. exclusive of bridges, culverts, or any extra expence in deep cutting or high embankments. Rails are made from 20 to 40 lb. *per* yard, agreeable to the weight they have to bear.

He goes on to mention the 'railway of the Peak Forest in Derbyshire which joins the Ashton canal, the road from Denbigh [i.e. Denby] to near the town of Derby, and a great many others'. As to Shropshire, he says:

Iron rail-ways have been used for some years in Shropshire, and other places, but, for want of proper system in the forming and laying of such roads they have been found of little or no more service than wood railway, which, from the late improvement in iron roads, are now in disrepute.

Some interesting old plate-rails at Denby Colliery are shown in Fig. 21. This line remained in use, in its original state, for about a hundred years.

There is much detailed information given in 'A General View of the Agriculture of Derbyshire' (1817) by John Farey, father of the author of the fine 'Treatise on the Steam Engine' published in 1827. Under the head IRON RAIL-WAYS, he writes as below (in places it is slightly condensed):

Within the County of Derby, or near it, I believe, there is not any Public Rail-way under Act of Parliament separate and distinct from the Canals, as there are in several other parts of England . . .

[1] Eight miles NW. of Nottingham.
[2] An old form of 'slack', i.e. small or refuse coal.

Some few of the earlier Rail-ways laid in or near this county were of wood; there were such wooden railways formerly to Greasley Colliery, Notts., Measham, Pinxton lower pit (which alone remained in use at the time of my survey) and Shipley, from the old wharf above Newmanleys Mill, disused and removed in 1796.

In the use of these wooden Rail-ways, the flanch or projecting rib for keeping the Waggon on the Railway, was on the wheel; but now the flanches of iron Rail-ways are almost universally cast on the bars, and the wheels are plain, by which they are fitted for being occasionally drawn off the Rails on common Roads. I have heard it said, that the earliest use of these flanched Rails above ground (for they were first introduced in the underground Gates of Mines, it is said) was on the South of Winger-worth Furnace; leading to the Ironstone Pits, by Mr. Joseph Butler, about the year 1788.[1]

I observed, however, three instances in the district of flanched wheels being used on Iron Rails; viz. on a Rail-way branch of the Ashby de la Zouche Canal, from Ilot Wharf in Measham,[2] constructed about 1799, wherein pulley wheels ran on metal ribs, cast on the bars; another was on a separate railway near Congleton . . . wherein the bars were oval or egg-shaped, according to Mr. Benjamin Wyatt's plan.[3]

There are in the district I am speaking of, two instances of very considerable *inclined planes* for Rail-way waggons, viz. on the east side of Chapel-en-le-Frith, belonging to the Peak Forest Canal, and on the north and north-west sides of Whiston in Staffordshire, belonging to the Caldon branch of the Trent and Mersey Canal, and in other situations.

Ankerbold and Lings Rail-way.

Private, constructed by Mr. Joseph Butler as an appendage to his Lings Colliery on the north side of North Winfield Town, about 1¾ miles. Bars 4 ft. long, 32 lb.; only 20 inches gauge, wooden sleepers. Trucks had detachable bodies, lifted by cranes into barges or on to road wheels as desired.

Ashby de la Zouche Canal.

From the Tunnel House[4] near Old-Park, one mile north of Ashby, a Rail-way branch proceeds 3¾ miles north-eastward, past Lount Col-lieries to Clouds-hill Lime-works: and from Ilot Wharf on the east side of Measham there is another Rail-way branch northward of about 1000 yards long, past Meashamfield Colliery to the Coal-yard near Jewsbury Farm by the Hinckley Road.

---

[1] For a discussion of this remark, see p. 145, *post*. The railway is mentioned again on p. 46, *post*.

[2] No doubt he is referring to Wilkes's railway, just previously described.

[3] See p. 108, *post*.

[4] The tunnel appears to have been not on the canal, but 4 miles away, on a railway. The lay-out is described more clearly by Priestley; see p. 47, *post*.

From the Tunnel House at the north-east end of Tunnel to Ticknall Quarries 4⅛ miles of single railway. Bars flanched, 3 ft. long, weigh 38 lb., on blocks of stone.

Belper and Morley Park Rail-way.

Laid in the valley from Belper to Morley Park Collieries and thence to Denby-Hall Colliery (which also has a Rail-way to the Derby Canal),[1] a distance of near 4 miles, for better supplying that large and increasing Town with Coals.

Chesterfield Canal.

No powers to make Rail-ways, but several private ones have been made on the proprietors' own Lands, or by consent of their neighbours, viz. from near Renishaw Furnace a Rail-way north-east to their Ironstone and Coal-Pits at Spinkhill; a cut [i.e. canal] south to Norbrigs Wharf and a Rail-way thence east to Norbrigs Colliery [1½ miles ENE. of Staveley]; on the south-east side of Staveley two Rail-ways south to Inkersall Collieries; near Brimington a Rail-way branch north, to Glass-house Colliery and the Glass-works. . . .

The Spinkhill Rail-way is about one mile in length, and rises considerably above the Canal: the Rail-way from Norbrigs near one mile rises considerably at its eastern end: the eastern Inkersall Rail-way is more than one third of a mile with a considerable rise, and the western one, near one mile passing the Commonspot Coke-yard, is also much elevated above the Canal.

The Glass-house Common Rail-way is near two miles long, and considerably elevated at its northern end.

Congleton Rail-way.

On the south-east of Congleton in Cheshire, about 2 miles at the north-west corner of Congleton Moss, a coal-yard was established about the year 1807, for the supply of this town and a Rail-way was laid there-from south, about 2 miles to Stone-trough Colliery in Woolstanton. It was laid with oval bars of iron, on the top of which the pulley-formed wheels of the tram ran; but when I saw this Rail-way in July 1809, it seemed to be almost or quite disused.

Coventry Canal.

Rail-way N.W. to Bedworth Colliery—W. to Griff Colliery—from near Atherstone Rail-way branch S.W. to Oldbury Colliery: near Grendon a Rail-way S.W. to Badesley Colliery, etc. All these branches rise from the canal.

Cromford Canal.

From near Langley Mill E. 1¾ m. to Beggarlee Colliery, with a branch therefrom N.E. 3/8 m. to the Pumping Engine; this is a very neat

[1] See p. 42, *ante*.

and perfect Rail-way belonging to Thomas Walker Esq.;[1] it crosses a Rail-way branch from the Nottingham Canal to Old Brinsley Colliery.

From Brinsley Wharf, N.E. 1 m. to New Brinsley Colliery:[2] from Brinsley aqueduct, N.W., $\frac{3}{4}$ m. to Benty-field Colliery: from Codnor Wharf, N.W., $\frac{3}{4}$ m. to Codnor Nether Park Collieries and Ironstone Pits: from Codnor Lower Park Wharf $\frac{1}{4}$ m. S. to Codnor Nether Park Colliery: from Golden Valley, S., $\frac{3}{4}$ m. to Codnor Upper Park Collieries and Ironstone Pits: from Golden Valley, N.N.W., $1\frac{1}{2}$ m. to Greenhill-lane Colliery; from Butterley Furnace (on the Tunnel) S., 3/8 m. to Butterley-car Colliery: from near Padley Hall S.E., 1 m. to Greenwich Colliery: from Padley Hall N.E., $\frac{1}{4}$ m., to Pentrich Colliery: from near Pentrich Mill S.E., $\frac{1}{2}$ m. to Harts-hay Colliery: from Bullbridge Wharf N., $1\frac{1}{8}$ m. to the Crich S.E. or great Limestone Quarries. Also, from branches of the canal, rail-ways to Riddings Collieries and Ironstone Pits: to Somercotes Colliery: to Nether Birchwood Colliery: from Pinxton Wharf N.E., $\frac{1}{4}$ m. to Pinxton Lower or South Colliery, on which Wooden Rails remained in use in 1808: and from Pinxton Wharf N.E., $\frac{3}{4}$ m., to Pinxton Upper Colliery.

Erewash Canal.

Rail-way from Cotmanhay $\frac{3}{4}$ m. N.W. to Cotmanhay-wood Colliery: a little south of this is another short cut, whence a Rail-way led across the Erewash to Newthorpe Common Colliery formerly. From Shipley Old Wharf near Newmanleys Mill there ran a wooden Rail-way branch W. for $1\frac{1}{2}$ m. to Shipley Colliery, discontinued about 1796.

Leicester Navigation.

From the Loughborough Basin to Forest-Lane Wharf is $2\frac{3}{4}$ m. of Rail-way with one ascent of 185 ft., thence to the foot of Barrow-Hill, N.W. of the village of Osgathorp is $8\frac{5}{8}$ m., and level: and thence there is a Rail-way extension of 130 yds. rising into the Barrow-hill Limestone Quarries Rail-way, Thringstone-bridge Wharf $\frac{3}{4}$ m. S.S.W. to Swanning-ton-common Colliery, and another S.W., $\frac{3}{4}$ m. to Cole-Orton Colliery. The descent is so considerable from Cole Orton that the Trams of Coals descended without Horses, regulated by means of a clamp or logger, acting on the wheels by a man who rode on each, and the empty Trams were drawn up by Horses. Rail-ways belonging to this Company are single, and have bars flat on top and the wheels are cast with flanches, inside. Detachable bodies to trams.

Nutbrook Canal.

Rail-way, Shipley Wharf, $\frac{1}{2}$ m. N.N.W. to Shipley Colliery: from north of Lewcote Gate $\frac{3}{4}$ m. W. to West Hallam Colliery; formerly others to Ferneyford and to Dale-Abby Iron Furnace (Earl Stanhope).

Peak Forest Canal.

From near Jow-hole Old Furnace a Rail-way branch proceeds under

---

[1] The colliery has been closed down for forty or fifty years, but the Beggarlee sidings are still in existence and are situated in the neighbourhood of Langley Mill, Eastwood.

[2] See p. 42, *ante*.

F

the Turnpike-road nearly S.W., 1 m. to Diglee (or Whaley Moor) Colliery: and on the N.E. of Yeardley there is a short Railway branch passing under the Turnpike-road into a Quarry of 3rd Grit Building Stone. A large Inclined-plane for Trams $\frac{1}{2}$ m. E. of Chapel-en-le-Frith has a double Rail-way varying from 3 inches to 6 inches in a yard. Large inclined pulley with brake so loaded trucks draw empty ones up, by a chain with 5 inch links, cost at Birmingham £500. Short inclined plane at Disley Wharf, $\frac{3}{4}$ m. N.E. of the town.

Trent and Mersey Canal.

Rail-way, Dale-hall to Burslem Potteries.
      „   Red-Bull Wharf E. to Trubshaw Colliery, etc.
      „   Etruria, N.E. to Handley-Green.
      „   Stoke S., 1$\frac{1}{2}$ m. to Lane-End.
      „   Armitage Wharf, S.W. about $\frac{1}{2}$ m. to Bruerton Colliery.
      „   Froghall, about $\frac{1}{4}$ m. to Cupola Flint-Mill.

The first Rail-way laid from Froghall to Caldon Low in 1777 was composed of Cast iron Bars, spiked down on wooden sleepers, but this line appears to have been set out, before the true principles of this branch of Engineering was well understood and was very crooked, steep and uneven. A few years after, a new line was chosen and the old one abandoned, but the second was also very defective in the above particulars. The inconveniences of these steep and imperfect Rail-ways occasioned the application in 1802 for the Act[1] for a new double line on stone blocks, with moderate slopes and intervening Inclined planes, and in the following year the same was carried into effect under Mr. Rennie and are among the most complete works of the kind in Britain.[2]

Wingerworth and Woodthorp Rail-way.

A private one constructed about 1788 by Mr. Joseph Butler, for the use of his Iron Furnace in Wingerworth, about 1 m. from the Bridge-loft of the Furnace to Woodthorp end Ironstone Pits. Bars 4 ft., about 32 lb. Wooden sleepers, 20 inches gauge.[3]

Wyrley and Essington Canal.

Three small branches $\frac{1}{4}$ to $\frac{1}{2}$ m., to Butts Lime Quarries near N.E. end of Walsall: to Birch-hill new Iron Furnace Colliery, etc. (made 1806): and to Brownhill Colliery.

Before leaving this part of the country, some short notes on the canals mentioned, together with some further developments of the railways, will be given, from Priestley's 'Historical Account of the Navigable Rivers, Canals, and Railways of Great Britain' (1831). The dates in brackets are those of the first Acts.

---

[1] This was a second Act. There had been a previous one, 16 Geo. III, cap. 33 (1776).
[2] An interesting article on 'The Caldon Low Tramways', by J. R. Hollick, appeared in the *Railway Magazine* for June 1937.
[3] See p. 43, *ante*.

ASHBY DE LA ZOUCHE CANAL (1794)

Commenced at Marston Bridge, on the Coventry Canal, 3 miles south of Nuneaton; terminated at Oakthorpe Fire Engine, on Ashby Wolds, 1 mile NW. of the Moira Baths, in the parish of Ashby de la Zouche. Length $26\frac{1}{2}$ miles, level throughout. Quoting:

When authority was first obtained, for the making of this canal, it was the intention of the company to have continued the canal to the places mentioned in the title of the Act, which would have made the total length of canal about fifty miles, with 252 feet of lockage. They, however, adopted railways for all the branches where lockage was necessary.

Evidently fairly considerable alterations had been made after Farey had seen the railways connected with this canal. Priestley describes them thus (again slightly condensed):

The railway to Ticknall Lime Works commences at the Ashby de la Zouche Canal, $\frac{3}{4}$ m. S.W. of the village of Willesley, co. Derby; and at the distance of $2\frac{1}{2}$ m., passes through Ashby de la Zouche. $1\frac{1}{2}$ m. further, it passes under a tunnel, at the end of which the Cloudhill Branch commences, and $1\frac{3}{4}$ m. further it enters Derby sluice; whence it is rather more than $2\frac{1}{2}$ m. to Ticknall Lime Works, making the whole distance from the canal $8\frac{1}{2}$ m.

The Cloudhill Branch Railway, commencing from the tunnel on the Ticknall Railway, runs W. for $1\frac{1}{4}$ m., where a railway, more than $\frac{1}{2}$ m. long, branches to a colliery. Another branch, $\frac{1}{4}$ m. further on, runs S. about 300 yds. to a colliery near Park Wood. From hence it takes a northerly course, passing W. of the village of Worthington, to the Cloudhill Lime Works, a distance of $2\frac{3}{4}$ m., the total length being $4\frac{1}{4}$ m.

There is also a railway, $\frac{1}{2}$ m. long from a colliery near Moira, to the canal, opposite the Moira Baths.

An earlier reference to an 'Ashby-de-la-Zouch Railway' appears in Anderson's 'Recreations in Agriculture' (November 1800): 'four miles of double and eight miles single rails, not yet completed, but will be finished about Midsummer next'.

Returning to Priestley:

CHESTERFIELD CANAL (1771)[1]

Commenced in the tideway of the Trent, at Stockwith, Notts., about 4 miles below Gainsborough, proceeding with 65 locks and a long tunnel[2] to Chesterfield; length 46 miles.

---

[1] Became the property of the Great Central Ry. Co.
[2] The Norwood Tunnel, 3,102 yards long. Owing to colliery subsidences it has now partly fallen in.

COVENTRY CANAL (1768)

Started from the Trent and Mersey Canal, on Fradley Heath, and eventually terminated at Coventry, but not till 1790; length 37¾ miles. Priestley does not mention any railways.

CROMFORD CANAL (1789)

Designed by William Jessop, this canal commenced in the Erewash Canal, near Langley Bridge, Notts., and went 18 miles to Cromford. At Butterley Park it entered a tunnel 2,966 yards in length, which terminated a short distance west of Butterley Iron Works, under which it passed. It crossed the Derwent by an aqueduct 200 yards long and 30 feet high. Within half a mile of Cromford it was joined by the Cromford and High Peak Railway, of which presently. Near Codnor Park Iron Works a branch from the Mansfield and Pinxton Railway communicated with it; the main line of which started from its termination. This railway obtained its Act in 1817 and was opened in 1819. Length 8 miles 2 furlongs 4 chains. It was an independent company, and was purchased by the Midland in 1848, being reconstructed to form part of their Nottingham and Mansfield branch.

DERBY CANAL (1793)

Commenced on the north bank of the Trent, near the village of Swarkstone, and entered the Trent and Mersey Canal at a distance of 3 furlongs to the northward. It left the latter a quarter of a mile to the east of the junction, and terminated at Little Eaton (3 miles north of Derby), a distance of about 8½ miles. There was a branch from near Derby to the Erewash Canal, also 8½ miles long.

As we have seen, Farey mentions that there was a railway to Denby Colliery; more details are given by Priestley, thus:

From the northern end of the main line at Eaton, a railway proceeds by Horsley and Kilbourn, to Smithy House, which is nearly 4¾ m. in length. From Smithy House there is a branch of 1¾ m. to the collieries at Henmoor, 1¾ m. E. of Belper; another, 1½ m. long by the potteries to the extensive coal works near Denby Hall; with a collateral branch out of the last-mentioned branch, ¾ m. long, to other collieries N. of Salterswood.

The railways were made by the Canal company, under powers contained in their Act. The expression 'main line' refers to the canal.

The first of the railways mentioned by Priestley in the above extract seems to be the subject of a remark by Stevenson, in his notes on the Highland Society essays, as being laid with plate-rails and stone blocks.[1]

[1] See p.145, *post.*

FIG. 21.   Old rails at Denby Colliery

FIG. 22.   Track of the Ashby and Ticknall Tram-road
(Block lent by the Editor, *L.M.S. Magazine*)

Brewster's 'Edinburgh Encyclopaedia' (1830), s.v. Navigation, Inland, says the Derby Canal crossed the Derwent by a 'tumbling bay', and gives a railway from it to Smolley Mills, $1\frac{1}{2}$ miles, which is also mentioned in Scott's 'Highland' paper (1824).

EREWASH CANAL (1777)

Commenced in the Trent, about 1 mile east of the village of Sauley, and terminated near Langley Bridge in the Cromford Canal; length $11\frac{3}{4}$ miles. Brewster mentions a railway to Brinsley Ironworks.

LEICESTER NAVIGATION (1791)

From Loughborough to the Soar at the West Bridge in Leicester, 11 miles; designed by William Jessop. Priestley adds a railway from the west end of the Great Level (in Charnwood Forest) to the Clouds Hill Lime Works, effecting by these means a communication with the Ashby-de-la-Zouch Canal.[1]

NUTBROOK OR SHIPLEY CANAL (1793)

From the collieries at Shipley and West Hallam to the Erewash Canal in the parish of Stanton-by-Dale, $4\frac{1}{2}$ miles. Priestley remarks: 'Railroads are laid from various parts of this canal to the coal mines near, but as the situation and number of these are changed as circumstances require, it would be impossible to describe them fully or correctly.'

PEAK FOREST CANAL (1794)[2]

Commenced in the Manchester, Ashton-under-Lyne, and Oldham Canal, to the west of Ashton-under-Lyne, to Bugsworth (3 miles WNW. of Chapel-en-le-Frith), with a short branch to Whaley Bridge; executed under the direction of Benjamin Outram, and opened May 1st, 1800. Anderson and Brewster both mention a railway of $1\frac{1}{2}$ miles to Marple.

Two other references to Peak Forest railways possibly relating to the same line; one which does not seem to have been given by the writers cited so far, are:

Peak Forest Railway from the lime-works near Boston to the canal near Whaley bridge—six miles. (Anderson, 'Recreations in Agriculture', November 1800.)

From the Peake Forest Canal, a railway proceeds six miles from Chapel Milton to Loads Knowle Lime-quarries. (Scott's 'Highland' paper, 1824.)

[1] See p. 47, *ante.*   [2] Became the property of the G.C.R.

TRENT AND MERSEY CANAL (1766)[1]

From a place called Wilden Ferry, co. Derby, where the Derwent joins the Trent, to Preston Brook on the Bridgewater Canal, a distance of 93 miles. It included the celebrated Harecastle Tunnel, 2,880 yards long.

WYRLEY AND ESSINGTON CANAL (1792)

From Wyrley Bank, Staffs., to the Birmingham Canal near Wolverhampton, 24 miles.

A little more information remains to be added with regard to the Ashby-de-la-Zouch Canal and railways. This system was bought by the Midland Railway Company in 1846. The lines were plate-lines, on Outram's principle. Part of the Cloudhill tramway was converted to a modern railway, from Ashby to Worthington. The Ticknall line, laid by Outram in 1799, remained in its original state for more than a century, and was not officially closed until September 1914. Fig. 22 shows a recent photograph of a piece of the track near Ticknall.

LOUGHBOROUGH AND NANPANTAN RAILWAY

Scott's 'Highland' paper contains the following reference:

The first Public Railway Company seems to have been established at Loughborough in the year 1789 under the direction of the late Mr. William Jessop. Here this eminent engineer introduced the Edge-rail, the upper part of which was of an elliptical figure, with flanges upon the wheels to guide them upon the tracks of the road; for hitherto the Plate or broad rail, under various forms, is understood to have been solely in use.

Stretton gives the following account:

The Loughborough and Nanpantan Railway was to have been a plate-way on the system of Mr. Outram of the Ripley Iron Works, Derby. It had to cross the main Derby and London road on the level. Opposition to the plate line crossing the road led Jessop to suggest edge rails, with the top level with the road surface, and grooves for the flanges of the wheels. Opened June 1789. The rails were laid with their outsides 5 feet apart, which made about 4 feet 8½ inches inside.

Elsewhere he says the rails were cast iron, 3 feet long, on wooden sleepers, 'the only edge-railway then in existence'.

This line has been frequently spoken of as the prototype of the modern

---

[1] Became the property of the North Staffordshire Ry. Co.

WILLIAM JESSOP,
CIVIL ENGINEER.

Fig. 23

railway, but there is little to be found in contemporary literature relating to it.

At one time Jessop was a partner in the Butterley Iron Works (Outram, Jessop, Wright, and Beresford), but he and Benjamin Outram (who between them laid out a large number of the railways made about the end of the eighteenth century) were not agreed as to the best system; Outram always using the plate-rails, with which his name has been so closely associated that it has, quite falsely, been often considered to be the derivation of the word 'tramway'. He founded the Butterley Iron Works and was the father of Sir James Outram, the distinguished general.

A memoir of William Jessop in Weale's *Quarterly Papers*, vol. i, part 2 (1844), from which the portrait has been taken, says that the active period of his career was comprised between the years 1788 and 1805, and goes on: 'During this and the following years of his life, he was consulted on almost every canal, railroad, and harbour that was projected in any part of the kingdom.' He died in 1814.

Beyond describing the Surrey Iron Railway, of which he was the engineer, the memoir is almost entirely taken up with his work in connexion with canals. It does mention, however, that in 1803 he surveyed a line of railroad from Portsmouth to London; the proposed terminus being on the side of the river Thames at Stamford Street—in other words, at Waterloo.

BELVOIR CASTLE RAILWAY

This was a private line, described by Stretton thus:

In the winter of 1790–1 William Jessop was surveying the Nottingham and Grantham Canal. The Duke of Rutland was interested and wanted a branch made to Belvoir, 'leading into the coal-cellars of the Castle'. Owing to the elevated situation this was not feasible, and Jessop concluded his report on the subject thus: 'I advise your Grace to abandon the idea of a branch canal, and to have one of my edge-railways laid down from Muston Gorse to the Castle, and to be in every way similar to the Loughborough and Nanpantan Edge-rail-way which I laid down in 1789, and which has been working nearly two years.'

In an article published in the *Railway Magazine* for June 1938, Mr. C. E. Lee has shown that Stretton's account is utterly inaccurate. Documents in the Belvoir Castle Estate Office show that this two-mile private railway was built in 1815 by the Butterley Ironworks Company and opened in two portions in June and September of that year. It was used regularly until May 1918, lay derelict for many years, and was dismantled for scrap metal early in 1941. There is a rail from it in the Science Museum.

CROMFORD AND HIGH PEAK RAILWAY

The Act authorizing the construction of this very remarkable line received the Royal Assent on May 2nd, 1825. It was 'for making and maintaining a Railway or Tramroad, from the Cromford Canal at or near Cromford . . . to the Peak Forest Canal, at or near Whaley' (Cheshire). Josias Jessop was the engineer. It was 33 miles and 7 furlongs in length, and attained an elevation of 990 feet above the Cromford Canal, and 1,271 feet above the level of the sea at low water, by means of inclined planes. The summit level was maintained for about 12 miles, including a tunnel 638 yards long. It had 740 feet to descend to the Peak Forest Canal.

F. S. Williams in 'Our Iron Roads' speaks of it as having been at one time one of the thoroughfares of England, and gives a very amusing account of a journey upon it in the year 1877.

The following extracts from a report by Jessop (the second, dated November 29th, 1824) are of interest:

> Having completed the survey of the proposed Railway from Cromford to the Peak Forest Canal at Whaley, and prepared the Plans necessary to enable you to proceed to Parliament in the next Session; I now submit to you the Estimate for a double line . . . £149,206. 16. 8.[1]
>
> I have made the Railway ascend an eleventh of an Inch in a Yard [1 in 396] after passing the Embankment near Pike Hall, and continued that ascent for 3½ miles which leaves a deep cutting of 24 feet at the brow of the hill; this slight rise will not be attended by any inconvenience, as its obstruction to carriages will not be greater than is caused by the curves of the Railway: it will only require the precaution of laying the curves in this part perfectly level. . . .
>
> The comparatively small expence of forming Railways will be a cause of extending our resources and finding new channels for capital and industry, that would for ever have been neglected, if there were only the more expensive modes of Roads or Canals to resort to; the first being expensive in the carriage,—the latter in the execution:—but a Railway can, according to circumstances, be made at from a half, to a fourth of the expence of a Canal (a Canal to form the same connexion as is proposed by the Railway, was estimated in October, 1810, by the late Mr. Rennie, to cost £650,000) and convey goods more cheaply, which would render them lucrative when any other mode would be ruinous.

He then speaks of what he considered to be an improvement in the formation of railways, namely to have more or less level stretches to be

---

[1] Of this £20,000 was for 'Steam Engines, &c. for the Inclined Planes'.

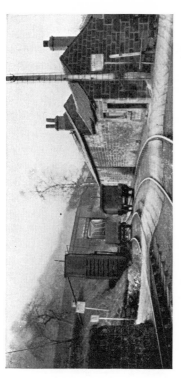

Fig. 25. Foot of Sheep Pasture incline. C. & H.P. workshops to right

Fig. 27. View towards summit, Middleton incline

Fig. 24. Catchpit near foot of Sheep Pasture incline

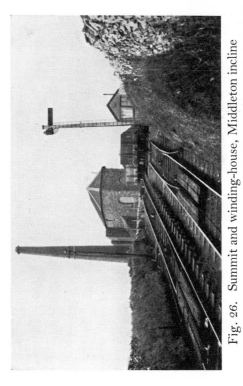

Fig. 26. Summit and winding-house, Middleton incline

The Cromford and High Peak Railway. (From *The Railway Gazette*)

worked by horses or locomotive engines, and to localize the ascents by having steep planes worked by stationary engines. According to him, the power required to move the waggons on the level is about a 200th part of the weight, but in practice should be taken as a 150th part. The rate of travelling with a locomotive may be increased to surpass that of mail coaches. The expense of locomotive haulage is less than half a farthing per ton per mile.

The ascent from Cromford by four inclined planes was to be nearly 1,000 feet, and the descent to the Peak Forest Canal, between 700 and 800 feet, by three others, the average cost of working each plane being about a halfpenny a ton.

A general meeting of the Committee and Supporters of the 'High Peak Steam Railway' was held at the Bridgewater Arms, Manchester, on December 1st, 1824, when it was resolved to go on with the undertaking. The meeting received 'with the greatest satisfaction the communication that his Grace the Duke of Devonshire consents to the Railway being made through his Grace's Estates, and most liberally without requiring any remuneration for his Land'.

The line was opened in 1830; the level portions being worked by horses. Lewin ('Early British Railways', 1925) says: 'Locomotives subsequently displaced the horses on the line, which was finally absorbed by the L. and N.W.R. in 1887, after a period of working the traffic.' Passengers were not conveyed after 1877. Certain parts of the line are still in use, including a piece of gradient of 1 in 14, worked occasionally by locomotives. One of the inclines, called the Middleton incline, is worked by a stationary engine over a hundred years old; steam pressure, 5 lb.

RAILWAYS IN SHROPSHIRE

Here the centre of interest is the Coalbrookdale Iron Works,[1] where the problem of smelting iron with coal was solved, cast-iron cylinders were first made for steam-engines, and, most probably, cast-iron rails were first laid.

The possibility of wooden railways having existed here before the middle of the seventeenth century was touched upon in Chapter I. Broseley too, where there was apparently something of the kind, is quite near.[2]

[1] Much interesting information on the subject of these works is contained in three papers published in the *Transactions of the Newcomen Society*, viz. 'Industrial History of the Coalbrookdale District', vol. iv, pp. 102–7; 'Notes on Coalbrookdale and the Darbys' and 'The Discoveries of the Darbys of Coalbrookdale', vol. v, pp. 1–14. The author is greatly indebted thereto.　　[2] See p. 6, *ante*.

At any rate, there was an early wooden line from Coalbrookdale to Horsehay, a distance of about 2½ miles, on which cast-iron rails were laid in 1767 or 1768.[1] The 'Victoria History of Shropshire' says it was made in 1750,[2] and 'extended to the new furnaces at Ketley' in 1757, so that there was a continuous railway from Ketley to the Severn, a distance of 5 miles. The account goes on:

The rails were of wood 3½ by 4½ inches, fixed on sleepers of wood laid transversely. Abraham Darby retained the accustomed size of the wagons, and adopted for them a cast iron wheel having an inside flange, and a cast iron axle-tree, on to which the wheel was wedged. These wagons, wheels and axle-trees continued to be used long after cast iron rails had been substituted for the wooden rails, and until a narrower gauge of road and a different pattern of rail was introduced.

Priestley says there was also a railway from the Horse Hay Ironworks to the Shropshire Canal (which entered the Severn at Coalport).

A manuscript history of the works is extant, which was written by W. G. Norris, the manager from 1867 to 1897. He makes it clear that Richard Reynolds, who became a partner in July 1756 and married Darby's eldest daughter, and was the manager from 1763 to 1768, was instrumental in laying down a considerable amount of iron rails between Ketley, Horsehay, and the Dale; he says that in the years 1768–71, 800 tons of cast-iron rails were laid. He also mentions that Abraham Darby II, who died in 1763, used cast-iron wheels with inside flanges, and a cast-iron axle. These wheels would of course have been used on the wooden rails, and on the first cast-iron rails, which were flat plates nailed on the wooden ones. At the present day a narrow-gauge tramway of the plate-rail type extends throughout the works, with cast-iron ties from a very ancient pattern, bearing the words 'Coalbrookdale Company'.

At some time after the death of Abraham II, probably about 1775, his widow, Abiah Darby, wrote an account of what he had done. With reference to railways, she said that the materials for the works were carried on pack-horses until 'he got roads made and laid with sleepers and rails, as they have them in the North of England'.

This evidence is rather fatal to the claims that have been made for Coalbrookdale as a pioneer of railways. Abiah's husband did not come of age until 1732.

Another interesting point in her letter is that one waggon with three horses brought as much as twenty pack-horses used to bring.

[1] See p. 142, *post*.

[2] p. 463. No authority given, but it may be correct for the wooden rails on which the iron ones were laid.

Fig. 28. Old tram-road at Coalbrookdale

Fig. 29. Old type of plate-rails used at
Coalbrookdale

Fig. 30. End of the Coalbrookdale tramway at Ironbridge. (From a photograph of 1917
by the Locomotive Publishing Co.)

Richard Reynolds, writing to Earl Gower on March 27th, 1785, stated that there were then 20 miles of iron railways in connexion with the works; which Mrs. Darby said cost over £800 per mile.

There is an interesting reference to the railways at Coalbrookdale in the book by von Oeynhausen and von Dechen (1826–7), from which part of the description of the Hetton Railway in Chapter II was taken:

> In Coalbrookdale there is a cast-iron tramroad extending from the Severn as far as the lower Ironworks of the Dale Company, which, like all the tramroads laid down in this district, is of this kind: the tram-plates are 5 and even $5\frac{1}{2}$ feet long and lie in cast-iron chairs. The tram-road at Coalbrookdale comprises really two: a small one of 20 inches gauge, which is worked with small receptacles, lies in the middle of a large one of 36 inches gauge. It is worked by horse traction and it deserves to be mentioned that here in this neighbourhood the narrowest gauge which is anywhere to be found is employed for horses; on some roads it only attains 18 inches.

John Wilkinson, who was a rival iron-manufacturer nearly opposite, on the south side of the river, evidently possessed some railways, as the following information from the 'Victoria History' shows; he made guns, not only for England, but also sent some down south to be smuggled across to France. They were taken down Tarbatch Dingle by a tramway from Willey Foundry to Willey Wharf on the Severn.

Wilkinson invented a machine for boring cannon which became a valuable ally to the steam-engine, inasmuch as by its means the cylinders could be produced far more accurately than before.

Farther to the westward, we find a line recorded in Priestley, called the Kington Railway, which went from the Hay Railway, of which presently, near Eardisley in Herefordshire, to Kington in the said county, and from thence to the Burlinjob Lime Works, in the county of Radnor, a distance of 14 miles. The Act was dated May 23rd, 1818.

From the same authority we gather that the Leominster Canal (from Kington to Stourport) had powers under an Act of 1803 (their first was obtained in 1791) to make a railway from the canal at or near Stockton in Worcestershire to the basin at or near Stourport Bridge in the same county; also one from Milton Cross to the town of Kington. But he does not say if they were made; the latter was not.

RAILWAYS IN STAFFORDSHIRE

We find the Shutt End Railway, which was made from the Earl of Dudley's colliery at Kingswinford, $3\frac{1}{2}$ miles NW. of Stourbridge, to the Staffordshire and Worcestershire Canal; opened June 2nd, 1829. The following description comes from an account of the opening in the *Birmingham Gazette* for June 9th, 1829; copied in the *Mechanics' Magazine* for June 20th.

The entire length of the railway is 3 miles and one-eighth, it commences at the colliery of the Earl of Dudley by an inclined plane of one thousand yards in length, having an inclination of 2 feet 3-10ths in a chain [1 in 29], and the carriages with coal are delivered down the plane in three minutes and a half, bringing up at the same time an equal number of empty carriages. The railroad then proceeds from the foot of the inclined plane for 1 mile and seven-eighths, at an inclination of sixteen feet in a mile [1 in 330]; and on this part of the railway the locomotive engine travels, and delivers the waggons at the head of another inclined plane of five hundred yards in length, having an inclination of two feet, thirty-five-hundredths in a chain [1 in 28] . . . At the foot of this second inclined plane there is a basin 750 yards long, communicating with the Staffordshire and Worcestershire Canal, parallel to which the rail-road is continued on both sides, affording the means of loading sixty boats at the same time; and on the middle of this basin is a handsome bridge of eleven arches, on which the road from Wordsley to New Inn passes.

Recent researches by Mr. Kenneth Brown have unearthed a railway between Stafford and Radford Wharf on the Staffordshire and Worcestershire Canal, a distance of about a mile and a half. According to 'Stafford in Olden Times', by J. L. Cherry (1890), it was opened on November 1st, 1805. The whole concern, which belonged to the Stafford Railway, Coal and Lime Company, was advertised for sale by auction in the *Staffordshire Advertiser* of July 2nd and 9th, 1814. The lots included boats and 'a quantity of Railway Carriages' (of course waggons). It was laid with 'flanch rails'.

According to the 'Victoria History of Staffordshire' there must have been many more (vol. i, pp. 291–2):

There was an early system of primitive railways in this county in connexion with the mines, e.g. there was a system of wayleaves at Newcastle-under-Lyme where colliery owners paid as much as £500 per annum for leave to draw coal over the estates of landowners, and it is probable that in 1750 every important mine had its accompanying railroad with wooden tram lines at first, followed by iron ones after 1738.

An Act was obtained in 1798 for making a navigable canal and 'Inclined Plane or Railway' from the Newcastle-under-Lyme Canal to the canal of Sir Nigel Bowyer Gresley, Bart., near the town of Newcastle-under-Lyme; but no particulars have been found of the railway part, if there was one.

STRATFORD AND MORETON RAILWAY

This line was projected by William James, and was all that materialized of a scheme for connecting the Midlands with London. Although in a map of his, dated 1820, reproduced in Fig. 82, it is shown as 'executed', its first Act was not obtained until May 28th, 1821, and modern authorities, such as Lewin, and MacDermot ('History of the G.W.R.'), give 1826 as the date of the opening.

It went from Stratford-on-Avon in Warwickshire to Moreton-in-the-Marsh, in Gloucestershire, a distance of 16 miles, with a rise from the canal at Stratford-on-Avon of 360 feet. There was a branch of $2\frac{1}{2}$ miles from Stretton-on-Fosse to Shipston-on-Stour in Worcestershire. Mac-Dermot gives the date of the opening of the branch as 1836, and goes on to describe the permanent way, thus:

> The gauge was 4 feet, and the railway consisted of light fish-bellied rails, 12 feet long and weighing 30 lb. to the yard, fixed by 6 lb. chairs to small rough stone blocks a yard apart.

But it was originally laid as a wooden railway, for in one of Rastrick's note-books there is the following note referring to this line:

> Agreed by the Committee of Works on 6th December, 1822, that the Contractors should be allowed to use elm instead of oak for rails, provided the Elm Rails be made from perfect sound wood and not less than 4 by 2 inches.

When giving evidence on the G.W.R. Bill in 1835, Rastrick mentioned this line and said he executed it.

The 'Observations' by a shareholder in the Avon and Kennet Canal (1825) say there were two viaducts, over the Avon and Stour, and several heavy embankments.

The line, which was not financially successful, fell into the hands of the Oxford, Worcester, and Wolverhampton Railway in 1844. Part of it is now the Shipston-on-Stour branch of the G.W.R.

Anderson, in his 'Recreations in Agriculture' (1801), mentions 'Railways over Blisworth hill . . . on the Grand Junction Canal—three miles and a half long', double, just finished. They were temporary ones,[1] used during the construction of the Blisworth Tunnel on the canal, 3,080 yards long. In connexion with this canal, which he calls a 'stupendous and most useful line of navigation' and which took thirteen Acts of Parliament (1793–1819) to construct, Priestley also mentions that the communication

---

[1] Priestley, p. 311.

with Northampton and the river Nene is 'by a double railway, allowing carriages, going different ways, to pass without interruption'.

RAILWAYS IN GLOUCESTERSHIRE

We now turn westwards to Gloucester, which was one of the first towns in the country to become a railway centre. The first line there was the Gloucester and Cheltenham, the Act for which was obtained April 28th, 1809. Priestley described it in the following words:

> This railway commences at the basin of the Gloucester and Berkeley Canal, within the city of Gloucester; from whence, skirting the south side of the town, it passes the village of Wotton, and thence, in a north-easterly direction, by the side of the Mail-Road between Gloucester and Cheltenham, and terminates at the Knapp Toll Gate, at the latter place. A branch is proposed to be extended to the Limestone Quarries at Leck-hampton Hill; but this is not yet executed. The length of the main line from the basin is rather more than eight miles and three quarters; but, including the length of the quay, it is nine miles.

According to the original intentions, it was to be a single line, with passing-places at every quarter of a mile. It was a plate-railway, opened June 4th, 1811. Horses were used until 1831. There is, however, evidence pointing strongly to a trial of a locomotive in 1825.

It was purchased jointly by the Cheltenham and Great Western and the Birmingham and Gloucester Railways in 1836 for £35,000; the original cost having been £40,000. A small portion was relaid and used by the purchasers; the rest continuing to be worked in the old way until 1859, when it was abandoned.

We now cross the Severn, and find ourselves in the Forest of Dean. The chief, one may almost say the only, authority on the early railways in this district is Mr. T. E. R. Morris, who wrote an admirable series of articles on the subject, published in *The Locomotive* for January to April 1931. The following account is drawn largely from those articles:

> The Forest of Dean, situated in the north-west corner of Gloucester-shire, and bounded by the rivers Severn and Wye, was noted in the middle ages as a Royal hunting ground and is still Crown property, although the boundaries have since been much curtailed. It has a coal and ironfield of an area of some thirty-five square miles, and the getting and smelting of the iron ore had been practised since the time of the Romans; in later times it became famous for the timber grown therein to supply the needs of the Navy. In the year 1800, when one of the tramroad companies was first projected, the need of better transport consequent upon the develop-ment of the mineral wealth and the felling of timber was acutely felt; the few roads that existed being described as "execrable", and impassable in

winter. There were no canals from the Forest area to the riversides, the
contour not being suitable. Some opposition to the tramroads was first
met with, one of the principal Verderers being foremost with objections—
and for seven years or so thereafter none was made.[1] We find subsequently, however, that no fewer than three separate undertakings
serving the needs of the district, and running in different directions to the
rivers Severn and Wye, were commenced within a comparatively short

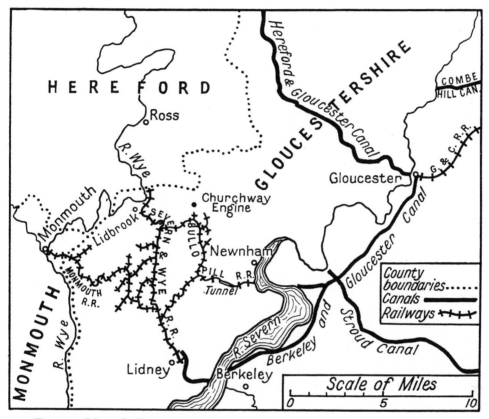

FIG. 31. Map of railways in the Forest of Dean. From Priestley's map of 1830

time of one another, namely the Bullo Pill and the Lydney and Lydbrook
(later renamed the Severn and Wye) and the Monmouth, and in their
order of construction we will deal with the first named, the Bullo Pill Co.,
afterwards—from 1826—known as the Forest of Dean Ry.

The Act of Parliament authorizing this undertaking was 49 Geo. III,
cap. 158, Royal Assent June 10th, 1809. Priestley's description is as follows:

Prior to the act of 49th George III, a railroad had been nearly
completed, without the authority of parliament,[2] from the Severn at

---

[1] A slight correction has been made here, supplied by Mr. Morris.
[2] The Act (1809) speaks of it as 'already formed and nearly completed'.

Bullo Pill, near the town of Newnham, to Cinderford Bridge, in his Majesty's Forest of Dean, by Roynon Jones, Esq., Margaret Roberts, William Fendall and James Telf, Esquires, the owners, but who, being desirous of obtaining power to extend their railway, and to make branches therefrom, applied to Parliament and obtained an act, entitled, *"An Act for making and maintaining a Railway or Tramroad, from the summit of the Hill above Churchway Engine, in the Forest of Dean, in the county of Gloucester, to a certain place in the said Forest, called Cinderford Bridge"*, by which the above parties are incorporated by the name of "The Bullo Pill Railway Company".

The line of extension which the above company are empowered to make, proceeds from the above-mentioned private railway, at Cinderford Bridge, in a northwardly direction, up a valley in the forest, to the summit of the hill above Churchway Engine, and the place where the Severn and Wye Railroad Company have subsequently formed a junction; its length is about three miles. There is also a branch from a place called the Dam, to the Upper and Lower Bilson Works; another from the same place to Kelmsley Green, and one from Nofold Engine, to the Old Engine and Nofold Green. . . .

The private railway is nearly four miles and a half long, with a tunnel upwards of five hundred yards in length,[1] situate about a mile and a half from Bullo Pill,[2] at which place are convenient wharfs for goods, intended for shipment on the Severn.

On the 5th of May 1826, the royal assent was given to another Act, entitled, *"An Act for maintaining an existing public Railway from the summit of the Hill above Churchway Engine, in the Forest of Dean, to Cinderford Bridge, and for making public a private Railway from thence to the River Severn, at or near Bullo Pill, all in the county of Gloucester; and for amending an Act of his late Majesty relating to the said Railways"*, by which a company, consisting of eighteen persons, agree to purchase the interest of the Bullo Pill Railway Company, and make the whole public, and they are by this act incorporated by the name of the "Forest of Dean Railway Company", with power to raise among themselves for these purposes, the sum of £125,000, to be divided into two thousand five hundred shares, of £50 each. Edward Protheroe, Esquire, was the principal proprietor of this concern.

Fig. 32 shows a stretch of the disused track of the Bullo Pill Railway near Cinderford. The overbridge was erected by the Cinderford Iron Company in 1827. Fig. 33 is from a photograph of an old milestone of the Forest of Dean Railway, with the date 1826 on the back.

---

[1] The first railway tunnel in the world, otherwise than those on purely mining railways. The length was 1,100 yards.

[2] Pill is a local name, on both sides of the Bristol Channel, on the lower course of the Severn, and in Cornwall, for a tidal creek on the coast, or a pool in a creek or at the confluence of a tributary stream (O.E.D.).

FIG. 32. Part of the disused track of the Forest of
Dean Tram-road

FIG. 33. Old mile-post (5½ m.) of the Forest of Dean
Tram-road

Here are some further interesting quotations from Mr. Morris's articles. There were

two distinct types of cast-iron plate rails, both in uniform lengths of 3 ft. corresponding with the distance between the sleepers [stone blocks] and set to a gauge of 48 in. The earliest type was notched at both ends, and held in position by an iron spike gripping two rails at once and thus forming the joint. Later it was found that from constant traffic passing, the spikes became worn and loose, and iron slippers or chairs were introduced. These were studded at each end, two holes being bored into the stone blocks to receive the chairs carrying the rails, which were 45 lb. each.

.   .   .   .

Mention must be made of a connexion made in 1823 with the Severn & Wye Co. at Churchway, but the gauge of the latter company being only 44 in., an adjustment of the axle washers of the tram wagons became necessary at each exchange.

.   .   .   .

No mechanical power was ever introduced, traffic being "led" by horses and mules throughout, the regular drivers in not a few cases being females and the daily hours of duty anything up to twenty-four.

The system of signalling and controlling the loaded and empty trains passing through the long tunnel near Bullo Pill must be mentioned. The last team in each direction had to carry as a token a tree branch, "Line clear" being signalled to the opposite end by a horn blown. In this manner for forty-five years, the not inconsiderable traffic on the east side of the Forest of Dean was worked. Until the close of 1929, these far-off days were recalled by a private branch, constructed by the Crump Meadon Colliery in 1829, to join the main line of the Forest of Dean Ry. at Bilson, later terminating in a wharf near the former connexion, but working in the same manner.

The Forest of Dean Railway was purchased by the South Wales Railway Company in 1850, and most of it was altered to an ordinary broad-gauge line, the tunnel being enlarged without stopping the coal traffic.

The largest and most important of the three Forest of Dean tramroads was that between Lydbrook on the Wye and Lydney on the Severn, which traversed the western part of the Forest, in a direction nearly from north to south.

The first document relating to this line which is known to the author is a little pamphlet in his collection, entitled 'Report & Estimate of the Proposed Rail-ways from the Collieries in the Forest of Dean to the Rivers Severn & Wye. By Benj. Outram, Engineer. Hereford: Printed by D. Walker High-Town. 1801'.

He gives a description of the course he proposed that the line should take, then saying:

The length of the main Line between the *Severn* at Jack's Pill, and the *Wye* near Lidbrook, will be nearly thirteen miles and three quarters. I recommend the *Rail-way* to be made substantial, on my improved plan, with stone blocks for the rails to rest upon: the rails to be of the stoutest cast iron, one yard in length, and to weigh about 37 lb. each; the waggons to carry from 30 to 40 cwt. each.

There was to be an inclined plane at Lydbrook. The cost he reckoned as £21,500.

To turn now to Priestley. Under the heading 'Severn and Wye Railway and Canal', by which it became known in 1810—a title which has nearly persisted to the present day, as it is still known as the 'Severn and Wye Joint Railway'—he says:

Commencing from the River Wye at a place called Bishop's Wood, and proceeding thirteen miles and a half through the forest, it terminates in a basin at Cross Pill, a little below Lydney, and from thence is connected with the Severn at Nass Point by a canal one mile in length. There are nine branches, amounting together in length to above twelve miles and a quarter, laid from the main line to coal and other mines in the neighbourhood; one from Ridnall's Mill; one other from Park End Bridge to the Birches; one other from Park End Bridge to Scroll's Tump; one other from Park End Bridge to Milk Wall; one other from opposite the Lodge Enclosure up Brookhall Ditches; one other from White Ley to Bixhead Quarries; one other from Cannop Hill, up, through and to the head of Howler Slade;[1] one other from Vallet's Inclosure to Wimblow Slade; and one other from Miery Stock to the summit at Churchway Engine.[2]

The first Act was dated June 10th, 1809, and incorporated the company as the 'Lydney and Lidbrook Railway'. The capital was £35,000, which was £13,500 over Outram's original estimate. On June 21st, 1810, they obtained another Act, which changed the name to 'Severn and Wye Railway and Canal Company', and authorized certain extensions, such as from Lydbrook to Bishop's Wood Furnace on the Wye, and from the Lower Forge in two branches, one on each side of a basin to a creek called Cross Pill, and a canal on to the Severn at Nass Point. A third Act of 1811 authorized them to raise another £30,000, which operation was repeated by a fourth in 1814.

The additional works are recorded as being opened for traffic in 1813, according to Mr. Morris.

[1] Slade means a valley.

[2] Whether 'Churchway Engine' was for hauling or for pumping is not known, but the references on p. 60 point to the latter.

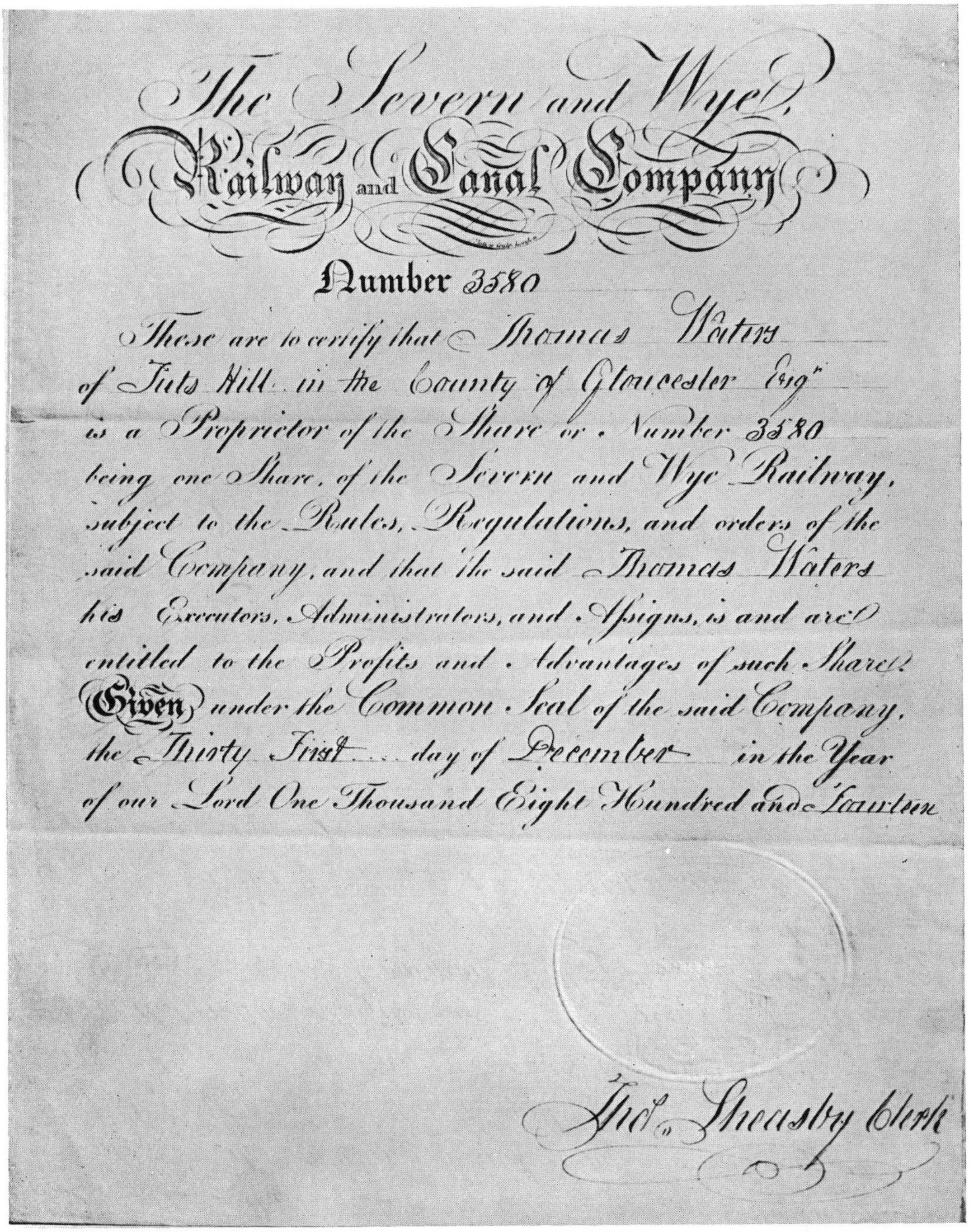
The Severn and Wye
Railway and Canal Company

Number 3580

These are to certify that Thomas Waters
of Tuts Hill in the County of Gloucester Esqr
is a Proprietor of the Share or Number 3580
being one Share, of the Severn and Wye Railway,
subject to the Rules, Regulations, and orders of the
said Company, and that the said Thomas Waters
his Executors, Administrators, and Assigns, is and are
entitled to the Profits and Advantages of such Share.
Given under the Common Seal of the said Company,
the Thirty First day of December in the Year
of our Lord One Thousand Eight Hundred and Fourteen

Thos. Sheasby Clerk

FIG. 34. A share certificate of the Severn and Wye Company, size 8 by 10 inches
(Author's collection)

FIGS. 35 & 36
Wimberry Slade, 1933

A share certificate of 1814 is illustrated. Thomas Sheasby, who signed it, was manager for thirty-five years.

Some locomotive experiments are mentioned in Chapter VI of the author's 'Two Essays in Early Locomotive History'.

The railway was purchased by the Midland and Great Western companies in 1894.

The third of the trio of ancient railways in this district was the Monmouth Railway,[1] which was in the westernmost part of the Forest of Dean. From Priestley:

> The act for this work, obtained in 1810, and entitled *'An Act for making and maintaining a Railway from Howler Slade in the Forest of Dean, in the county of Gloucester, to the town of Monmouth; and for making other Railways therein mentioned, in the county of Gloucester and Monmouth'* provides for the making of a railway or tramroad from Howler Slade in the Forest of Dean, by the villages of Newland and Redbrook and the town of Coleford to May Hill, near Monmouth, or to a place in the said town of Monmouth, extending north-eastward from Wyebridge to the Nag's Head near Dixon Gate, by passing the bridge over the Wye or by passing the river itself by a boat; and also to make branches out of the said main railway, viz. one from Winnall's Hill southwards to Winnall Colliery, with a collateral line to the mine in Clear-Well-Mead; another line from the same place northward to Wymbery Slade; one from the said line at Swan Pool to the village of Staunton; one other from the same in Lord's Grove to the Redbrook Tin Mines, there branching into two railways, one extending to Lower Redbrook Tin Mines, the other to the Wye at Cinder Bank in Newland, there crossing the river to Pool Dee in the parish of Penallt, in the county of Monmouth, and also the necessary wharfs.

The proprietors were incorporated as the 'Monmouth Railway Company'. The 'Tonnage Rates' which they were empowered to charge contain the following clause:

> For every Carriage conveying Passengers, or light Goods or Parcels, not exceeding Five Hundred Weight: 6d per Mile.

This is the first mention of passengers, so far as the author is aware, in a Railway Act[2] (Royal Assent May 24th, 1810). Probably it was not contemplated that the company would carry passengers themselves, but that others might run carriages for the purpose, on payment of the authorized toll mentioned.

The clause empowering the passage of the Wye by a boat is strange.

---

[1] Must not be confused with the Monmouthshire Railways, which were quite another affair. See Chapter V.

[2] Tomlinson ('Hist. N.E.R.', p. 32) gives this distinction to the Berwick & Kelso Act of 1811.

Mr. Morris adds the detail that the boat was to be drawn across the river by a fixed rope or chain.

The main line was formally opened on August 17th, 1812.[1] Its total length was nine miles. The subsequent history will be found in the articles in *The Locomotive* (1931, p. 128). Part of it was turned into a locomotive line under an Act of 1853. In 1876 what remained of it was bought by the Coleford Railway Company.

Fig. 37 shows a share certificate, or, as they were often called in those days, a 'ticket'; a term liable to be misunderstood. The arms are coloured; they also appear in the seal. Thinking that we might have here the first coat of arms granted to a railway company, the author inquired at the College of Arms, and received the following interesting reply:

> The Arms of which you send me a drawing "Azure three chevronels Or overall a fesse Gules", were used, without authority, by the Corporation of the Town of Monmouth.
>
> The Arms have properly no connexion with the Monmouth Railway Company unless this Company was owned by the Corporation of the Town of Monmouth, and even so they are bogus!

The Hereford Railway remains to be mentioned. Priestley gives an account of it, but it is not marked in his map. The Act, obtained in 1826, was for making a 'Tramroad or Railway from the End of the Grosmont Railway[2] at Monmouth Cap, in the parish of Llangua . . . to Wye Bridge . . . within the Liberties of the city of Hereford'.

Lewin describes it thus:

> A plate railway of $12\frac{1}{4}$ miles in length, forming a continuation of the Llanvihangel and Grosmont lines into Hereford. Opened in 1830[3], and worked by horse power, it was purchased, together with the railways just mentioned, by the Newport, Abergavenny and Hereford Railway under their Act of incorporation in 1846, the route of the Hereford company being largely adopted by the latter in the formation of their railway.

Since the above was written, details of one or two more small railways in Shropshire have been supplied by Mr. Stanley Davies, for which see the Index, under headings:

Llanymynech Rock Tramways.
Porthywaen Railway.
Rowton Mines.

---

[1] *Gloucester Journal*, August 24th, 1812.
[2] See p. 105, *post*.
[3] Actually Monday, September 21st, 1829 (*Hereford Journal*, September 23rd, 1829).

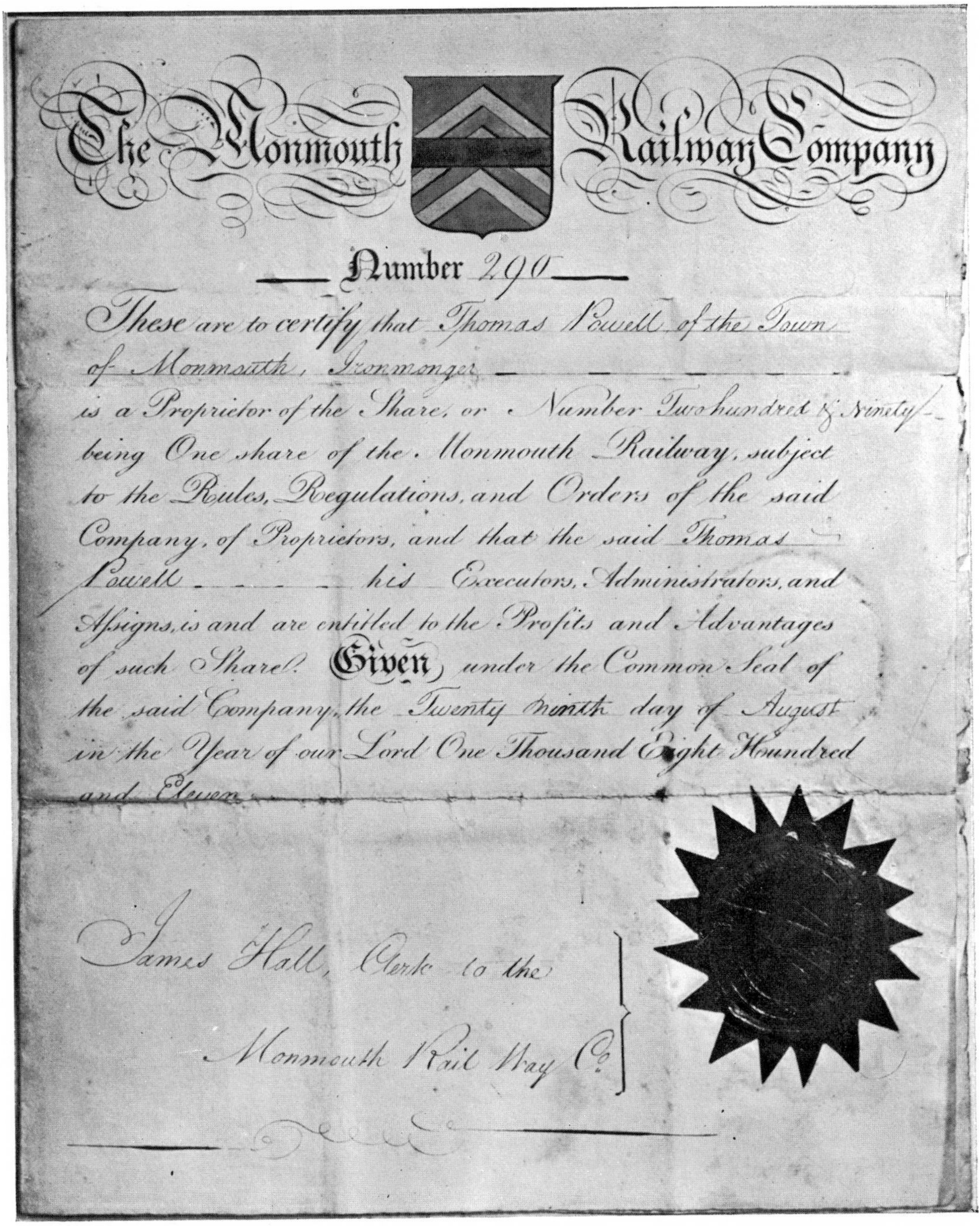

The Monmouth Railway Company

Number 290

These are to certify that Thomas Powell of the Town
of Monmouth, Ironmonger
is a Proprietor of the Share, or Number Two hundred & Ninety
being One share of the Monmouth Railway, subject
to the Rules, Regulations, and Orders of the said
Company, of Proprietors, and that the said Thomas
Powell his Executors, Administrators, and
Assigns, is and are entitled to the Profits and Advantages
of such Share. **Given** under the Common Seal of
the said Company, the Twenty ninth day of August
in the Year of our Lord One Thousand Eight Hundred
and Eleven.

James Hall, Clerk to the

Monmouth Rail Way Co.

FIG. 37.   A share certificate of the Monmouth Railway Company, size 8 by 10 inches
(Author's collection)

J. Hudson Pinx.ᵇ   J. Faber Fecit 1754

M. Allen

Fɪɢ. 38.   Ralph Allen (1694–1764)
(From the author's 'British Post Office from its beginnings down to the end of 1925')

CHAPTER IV

EARLY RAILWAYS IN THE SOUTH OF ENGLAND

THIS chapter opens with the first railway that was ever elaborately discussed in print. The description occurs in Desaguliers's 'A Course of Experimental Philosophy', vol. i, published in 1734. It was contributed by Charles Labelye, architect of the first Westminster Bridge (opened in 1750). It is headed ' *A* DESCRIPTION *of the Carriages made use of by Ralph Allen, Esq; to carry Stone from his Quarries, situated on the top of a Hill, to the Water-side of the River Avon, near the City of Bath'*.

Allen, who came of humble origin, entered the service of the Post Office at an early age and became one of its great reformers. He devised a system of 'cross-posts', thereby avoiding the necessity for letters between towns on different roads to pass through London, as had previously been the practice. These cross-posts he 'farmed' himself, amassing thereby in the course of years nearly half a million of money. He became of great importance, and was known as 'The Man of Bath'. He built a magnificent house called 'Prior Park', where he entertained many distinguished visitors, including Fielding, who drew his portrait as Squire Allworthy in 'Tom Jones', and dedicated 'Amelia' to him.

The following is an extract from 'An essay towards a description of Bath', by John Wood, Architect (1749).

The exportation of block free stone was a branch of trade which Mr. Allen engaged himself, upon the completion of the work that rendered the River Avon navigable between Bath and Bristol. He first purchased some of the Quarries on Camalodunum (Combe Down) with the land about them; and then determined to make such a Road between the summit of the Hill and the River Avon, as the gentlemen in the North of England had made between their Collieries and the River Tyne, that heavy carriages might be drawn along it with such little strength as would reduce the transportation of the stone to the Waterside to half the price of carrying it down in common waggons. Of the roads and carriages in the North the late Mr. Hedworth sent proper Models to Bath and Mr. Allen had the good fortune to meet with a person[1] whose natural genius for mechanics enabled him to improve upon the originals and to execute the intended road as well as the carriages to be worked upon it, so as to answer the purpose for which both were designed, whereby stone blocks came to be delivered at the Avon side for 7/6d a ton of 20 cubical feet, which was 2/6d a ton cheaper than it had been previously sold for.

[1] No doubt Mr. Padmore. See later.

The railway described by Desaguliers was the one made to bring down stone from Combe Down, in 1730. A view of it is given in Fig. 39, from an engraving published in 1752, after Prior Park had been built. The road is much the same today, minus the rails, except that trees interrupt the view of the house, which is now a Roman Catholic college.

There is evidence that he had made one still earlier, perhaps as soon as 1724, to serve a quarry on the other side of Bath, called Hampton Down. It is mentioned in 'Walks through Bath' by Pierce Egan (the Elder), 1819, thus:

> Proceeding some distance down the river, on the left side of which an iron rail-way from an immense steep height is to be seen. It is curious to observe the iron carriages sent up and down without horses; and by the aid of machinery the vehicles change their positions midway, the full one running down to the barge in the canal, and the empty one making its way to the top again to receive its load.
> Bathampton Church soon appears after quitting the railway.[1]

Both the above and the Combe Down lines are described at some length in R. M. Peach's 'Life and Times of Ralph Allen' (1895), but with some obvious mistakes. He says the Combe Down line was made in 1731, a statement which immediately follows a transcription of a deed of March 20th, 1730, in which it is recited that Allen 'has lately made and cut a certain Waggon-way or road for the carriage of stone'. For geographical reasons, the deed must refer to the Combe Down line, which may therefore even date from 1729.

Peach is also wrong in saying that the Combe Down line was a double track, with the loaded trucks pulling up the empty ones. This description does not agree with Desaguliers's account,[2] nor with the old prints. He must have confused it with the Hampton Down line, where, as we have seen, this system was used. The latter line is also mentioned in 'The Famous Houses of Bath', by J. T. Meehan (1901).

The Combe Down line was about a mile and a half long; more than half of which was on a gradient of 1 in 10. The full trucks descended the hill by gravity and were drawn on the level and up (empty) by horses. Their construction is shown in the accompanying illustrations, taken from Desaguliers. The wheels were of cast iron, 20 inches in diameter, with flanges stated to be no less than 6 inches deep. But they were actually 3 inches only, according to the drawings; 'six' applying to the diameter of the circle. The axles—diameter 3 inches—had one end square and the

---

[1] The reference to Bathampton, which is north-east of Bath, serves to identify the railway. Prior Park is south-east.   [2] Vol. i, pp. 181, 276.

Fig. 39. Ralph Allen's Combe Down Railway, near Bath

Fig. 40. Ralph Allen's truck

Fig. 41. Ralph Allen's truck

other round, as shown at the foot of Fig. 40, thereby permitting a differ-
ential rotation on curves. The brake gear was very elaborate.[1] It was
stated by the Rev. John Collinson in 1791 ('History and Antiquities of
the County of Somerset') that the 'carts or sledges' were the invention of
'Mr. Padmore, a very ingenious artist and mechanick'.[2]

Desaguliers's account is believed to be the first mention in print of
flanged wheels and brakes; although he does not use the latter term.

The following description occurs in a letter written by John Evelyn
to his father, Sir John Evelyn, dated November 9th, 1738.[3]

> . . . I went one morning to see Mr. Allen the Postmaster's great
> stone Quarry, and new house he is building near it, upon one of yᵉ high
> hills about a mile from yᵉ town, the Stone works easier than wood when
> first cutt out of the Quarry but hardens they say by the weather; 'tis con-
> veyed in a very cleaver manner down to yᵉ town upon carriages with low
> broad wheels, covered with iron, which run upon a wooden frame made
> yᵉ length of yᵉ hill, so that when yᵉ machine is sett agoing it runs down
> yᵉ hill without any help, only one man behind to steer[4] it, & in this
> manner above three hundred Tunn of stones are carried down at one
> load . . .

It appears probable that the above railways were the only wooden
ones that were ever made in the West Country; at all events, the author
knows of no others.

Remaining for the present in the neighbourhood of Bath, there are one
or two railways to be noticed in connexion with the Somersetshire Coal
Canal, which obtained its first Act in 1794. It ran from the Kennet and
Avon Canal at Limpley Stoke to Paulton, 3 miles NW. of Radstock and
10 miles SW. of Bath. A railway branched off from it in the parish of
South Stoke, proceeding by Wellow, Foxcote, Writhlington, and Radstock, to collieries at Welton and Clandown, in Somersetshire. Quoting
from Priestley:

> At the commencement of the undertaking, it was designed to have
> a canal branch to Radstock, running upon one level to within a few hun-
> dred yards of the main line between Coombe Hay and Mitford Bridge;
> but in consequence of their funds being exhausted in completing so much
> of the canal, the company were unable to carry their lockage down to the
> level; a short railway was in consequence made on the Radstock Branch,

---

[1] See p. 162, *post*.

[2] Desaguliers (vol. i, p. 179) speaks of 'Mr. *Padmore* of *Bristol* making a Crane for Mr.
Allen (Postmaster of *Bath*) to raise Stone out of a Quarry'.

[3] From 'History of the Evelyn Family', by Helen Evelyn (1915).

[4] Other examples occur of the words 'steer' and 'guide' used in the sense of governing,
otherwise than in direction; and brakes on railway vehicles were at first called 'tillers'.

to connect that portion of it, which was completed, with the main line of the canal, but here it may be observed, that above twenty years afterwards, a railway was substituted for the branch canal the whole distance.

To connect the Paulton line of canal with the lower level, the company, in the first instance made whimsey and jenny roads or inclined planes at Coombe Hay, in lieu of lockage, of 138 feet descent, but after a short time it was found that they did not succeed, and that the company would be obliged to substitute locks for them.

An Act of 1802 sanctioned the raising of £45,000 for this purpose, and was carried into effect.

Mr. S. Pearce Higgins has informed the author that in 1804 a canal was made from Midford to Radstock, connecting at Midford Basin with the 'Old Canal', now in parts the branch of the G.W.R. from Limpley Stoke to Camerton. At Radstock various collieries,[1] including Clandown Colliery, had tramroads of L shape leading to the basin. Owing to the canal falling into disuse—apparently difficulties arose over riparian rights—a tramroad was laid along the towpath from Radstock to Midford. It is shown in C. and I. Greenwood's map of 1820–1; a canal merely appearing in John Carey's map of 1805.

In 'Observations . . .' by a shareholder in the Kennet and Avon Canal (1825) the railroad from Radstock to the Somersetshire Canal is said to have had six miles on the level and two inclined to the canal.

It may be mentioned that the first compound engine in the world was erected at Radstock in 1782 by Jonathan Hornblower. The statement has been made that a locomotive was tried there in 1825, but the evidence is not convincing.

William Ashman, who is supposed to have built the locomotive in question, gave evidence to the following effect on the G.W.R. Bill in 1835. He had been for twenty-six years principal engineer and superintendent of the Clan Down Coal Works, and had also had the charge of four other collieries in the neighbourhood.

Our Coals are first passed along the Colliery Railway (which is about 8 miles long), when they are put upon the Somersetshire Coal Canal which joins the Kennet and Avon at Dundas about 2 miles from Midford . . . our railway has been laid down about 17 years, and is not an edge, but a plate railway, and is worked by horses.

The other two railways shown on the map (Fig. 42), namely the Avon and Gloucestershire and the Bristol and Gloucestershire, both obtained their Acts in 1828, but took some time in the making. The former, which

---

[1] Welton Hill, Wells Way, Clandown, Old, and Widlow's pits. (*Somerset County Herald*, August 28th, 1925.)

was opened in 1832, was a horse railway from the latter at Rodway Hill in the parish of Mangotsfield to the river Avon at Bitton, near Keynsham. The Bristol and Gloucestershire, which was frequently called the Coalpit Heath Railway, as it ran from Bristol to the latter place, a distance of 9 miles, was not opened until August 1835. It was worked by horses until 1844, when it was extended for another 22½ miles, and became part of the Midland Railway in the following year.

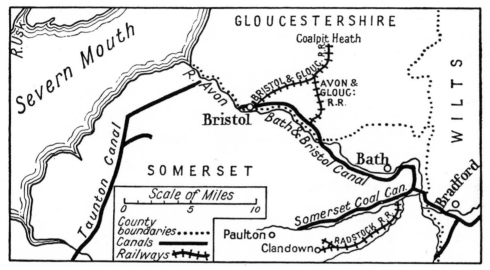

FIG. 42. Map of railways near Bath and Bristol. From Priestley's map of 1830 (Allen's not shown)

RAILWAYS IN DEVON AND CORNWALL

We will now wend our way to the Plymouth district. The first 'railway' in this district was the Hay Tor Granite Tramway, from the Hay Tor Quarries on Dartmoor, which supplied the granite for the construction of London Bridge, the National Gallery, and other public buildings, but are now disused; to the head of a short canal[1] near Teigngrace, a distance of about 7 miles. The line was made by George Templer, owner of the quarries, and was opened for traffic on September 16th, 1820. It had the striking peculiarity that the 'rails' were of granite, made of blocks about 15 inches wide, with inside curbs projecting upwards 2 or 3 inches, the gauge being about 4 feet. It was in use for about 40 years. Far up on the hill-side an almost perfect section, with a junction, remains. Another portion still more or less intact is shown in Fig. 44.[2]

[1] The canal was made in 1792–4; branching from the river Teign for the convenience of some pottery works (not the celebrated Plymouth china works, as they were transferred to Bristol in 1772).   [2] By permission of the Director of the Science Museum.

The brake used on the trolleys transporting the stone was a pole, 10 to 12 feet long, bearing on the axle, and applied by main force.

An article on this curious line, by W. B. Paley, appeared in the *Railroad Gazette* for July 21st, 1899.

There is also a quantity of information to be gathered on the subject of railways in Devonshire and Cornwall from a paper 'Early Western Railroads', by R. Hansford Worth (*Transactions of Plymouth Institution*, vol. x, 1887–90).

With regard to the Hay Tor line, he mentions that at curves the stones do not seem to have been dressed to form, but short straight stones were worked in, which by the constant friction of the wheels soon

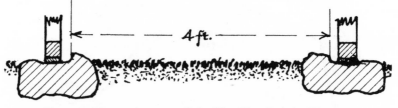

FIG. 43. Permanent way of the Hay Tor Granite Tramway

wore down to a sufficiently accurate shape. The Hay Tor granite is an exceptionally good material, and the granite-way as laid was far superior in many respects to the cast-iron rails, with their continual breakages. The wheels ran free on the axles, and the leading truck of a train usually had shafts.

TAVISTOCK CANAL

From Tavistock to the river Tamar at Morwelham, near Calstock, about 4 miles long; completed 1817. From the writer just quoted it appears that it communicated with the Tamar by an inclined plane, being 240 feet above the river. There were two lines of rails, and two winding barrels at the top. Power was derived from a waterwheel, worked by the waste waters of the canal. The descending trucks assisted the ascent of the empty ones. The incline was in places 1 in 6. The trucks had one pair of wheels 4 inches larger than the others, to keep them more or less on a level. The gauge was 4 feet 3 inches. Rails were 'rolled iron flat-headed rails'.

PLYMOUTH AND DARTMOOR RAILWAY

An excellent description of this line was given by Paley, in another article in the *Railroad Gazette*, published in the number for December 19th, 1902.

FIG. 44. Remains of the Hay Tor granite railway

FIG. 45. Passenger carriage belonging to the first plate-railway in Cornwall

The first Act for its execution was obtained in 1819, under the title of 'An Act for making and maintaining a Railway or Tramroad from Crabtree, in the parish of Egg Buckland, in the county of Devon, to communicate with the Prison of War on the Forest of Dartmoor, in the parish of Lydford, in the said county'.

This line went in a very circuitous course, and was twenty miles in length, which is about double the distance as the crow flies. It was extended a little over two miles by Acts of 1820 and 1821 to Sutton Pool, the old commercial port of Plymouth. The following particulars are derived from Paley's article.

The projector was a Sir Thomas Tyrwhitt, who believed that Dartmoor was capable of cultivation.

It was a single line, with a tunnel 620 yards long at a place called Leigham.

In the disused part, at least six different kinds of rails may be found. Two kinds are the original cast-iron parabolic or fish-bellied rails, the ends meeting in very small chairs only $4\frac{1}{2}$ inches high. Some have butt ends, others are notched so that the two rails meet with a half-lap joint. Two kinds of chairs were used, one having oval spike-holes in the foot. Wrought-iron rails consisting of two sections of flat-footed rail and two of bridge rails were laid on blocks of blue slatestone 18 inches to 2 feet square. The gauge was 4 feet 6 inches. In some of the sidings the rails are of granite. Unlike those on the Hay Tor line, the wheels ran on the inner part of the long stone blocks. The points and crossings were of cast iron.

The greater part was opened on September 26th, 1823. The last two or three miles were completed about 1825; the total length from Princetown to Sutton Pool was originally $25\frac{3}{4}$ miles. There was a steady rise from Crabtree of 1 in 100, rising over 1,200 feet in 23 miles.

The upper 11 miles from Yelverton to Princetown were purchased by the Great Western Railway in 1883, and form the present branch.

William Stuart, superintendent of the Plymouth breakwater works, was the original engineer, but the line was finished by Roger Hopkins, a West Country mining engineer. The upper terminus is about 10 miles west of the Hay Tor Quarries, but on the opposite side of Dartmoor. Financially it was a failure. A good deal of the stone for Plymouth breakwater came down the line.

There is a branch about $2\frac{1}{2}$ miles long, which was made about 1825, from Lower Crabtree, which goes eastwards, crossing the river Plym on a bridge of two cast-iron arches, then going northwards up a valley to

Cann Quarry, where slate and paving stones are produced. In 1902 the last half-mile was just as at first laid, with little notch-ended fish-belly rails, more like firebars than rails.

Not only were 'travelling vehicles' and parcels contemplated, but the transfer of convicts to Dartmoor prison was included in the original anticipation of sources of income.

The following is an account of the opening, from the *Telegraph and Chronicle*, under date 'Plymouth, September 27th, 1823':

Plymouth and Dartmoor Railway.—Our various readers, both local and distant, will learn with the sincerest pleasure that this great work, so long the object of our hopes and fears, and well designated by a worthy nobleman as the glory of the county, is now happily open for general trade. Yesterday was devoted to the celebration of the joyous event, and its festivities commenced with a public breakfast, liberally given by Sir Thomas Tyrwhitt, the original projector of the undertaking, at his wharf at Roborough Down, where three marquees were erected, and every elegant species of viand provided for the reception and gratification of the company, which comprised much of the respectability and worth of the port and its neighbourhood.

The South Devon band enlivened the scene with its choicest airs, but unhappily the weather was unfavourable, which drove many away ere the departure of the procession through the tunnel could be arranged. A long file of cars partly laden with granite and partly with stewards and other individuals, accompanied by the band, and ornamented with flags, after the breakfast set off for Plymouth, on their arrival at which place they were heartily greeted by the huzzas of a large concourse of people, anxiously awaiting their arrival, being saluted on their way by some petards at Hoo Meavy, and attended throughout the progress by a numerous cavalcade on horse and foot.

About fifty gentlemen then sat down to a handsome dinner at the Royal Hotel, who did not separate until a late hour.

PLYMOUTH BREAKWATER RAILWAY

The chief part of the three and a half million tons of stone used for Plymouth breakwater came from quarries at Oreston, on the east shore of the Cattewater, about 4 miles away, and special temporary railways were laid to bring it. They are described in great detail in 'Two Excursions to the Ports of England, Scotland, and Ireland, in 1816, 1817, and 1818; with a description of the Breakwater at Plymouth, and of the Caledonian Canal': translated from the French of Charles Dupin (1819).

Little trucks on four small wheels of cast iron, each carrying one block, and drawn by a horse, with the driver walking in front, ran 'on the grooves of an iron rail-way prepared for that purpose', and leading to the different parts of the quay. When they arrived at the latter, at which there was a sharp turn, they came to a turn-table. As the date is so early, Dupin's description is worth giving in full:

> . . . a circular plate of cast-iron, having, on two parallel curved lines, ribs or borders which form the continuation of the track of the rail-way. This plate was suspended on a pin beneath its centre (which is in the middle of the track) there being a circular ring under its circumference, which moves round freely, by means of a considerable number of small wheels or rollers, whose axles are fixed therein, upon another circular plate of iron, fixed in the ground, which prevents it from tilting on one side or the other.

> The driver having brought his truck to the plate, the two borders of which then lie in the direction of the track, he takes off his horse, and turns with his hand the plate with the truck, till the borders of the plate are in line with those of the short piece of rail-way that leads to the vessel, lying perpendicularly to the quay. A strong beam is steadfastly let into the edge of the quay. Two beams laid perpendicularly to this on the continuation of the sides of the short piece of rail-way, are fixed with solid hinges in front of the immoveable beam. The iron ribs of the road are laid along these two beams, which can be raised or lowered, by means of the hinges fastened to the fixed beam. This disengaged end of the two beams is placed on the sill of one of the stern-ports of the vessel to be loaded. According as the tide is high or low, the beams change their inclined position; but, on that account, they do not cease to rest on the port-sill.

The vessels were of special construction, with rails on the deck and in the hold.

A very similar description of turn-tables 'aided by iron friction balls running in a circular iron groove', apparently used at the London Docks, is given in Vaughan's letter to Admiral Chichagoff of 1804, mentioned in Chapter I.

Rastrick was severely critical of the arrangements for shipping the stone to the breakwater. In a letter dated November 15th, 1812, to Simon Goodrich of the Navy Office, he expressed himself thus:

> The Method in which they get the Stones and convey them to the Quays; the Construction of the vessells, the way of Loading and discharging is in my oppinion, the *verry verry worst* that could be thought of by the greatest Bungler that ever was.[1]

In 1809[2] the first tramroad in Cornwall was started, communicating between Portreath, a small seaport 4 miles north-west of Redruth, and Poldice Mine, about 2 miles east of the same place. The rails were of

---

[1] *Newcomen Society Transactions*, iv. 53.

[2] October 25th, 1809 (*Royal Cornwall Gazette*, October 28th, 1809).

cast iron, the first one being laid on October 25th, 1809, by Lord de Dunstanville, who had spent money on improving the pier at Portreath. He owned a number of mines in this district, for which Trevithick was agent. The line of which we are speaking was about 6 miles long, and was extensively used until the stoppage of the Poldice and adjacent mines about 1864, and was not dismantled until the turn of the century. Traces of the route, and stone sleepers *in situ* may still be found. The gauge was about 3 feet.

Fig. 45 shows what is probably the oldest existing railway carriage in the world. It was recently discovered in the neighbourhood of Scorrier, which was on the route, near Poldice, and is believed to have been the original carriage used by directors and officials on the line. It is built of yellow pine, with longitudinal seats for passengers to sit face to face; 6 feet long by 4 feet 6 wide. The wheels are 20 inches in diameter, of cast iron, without flanges.

We now come to a more important undertaking, the Redruth and Chasewater (or Chacewater, as it is now spelt). The latter place is $5\frac{1}{2}$ miles WSW. of Truro. The line, which obtained its Act in 1824, is thus described by Priestley:

The main line of this railway commences at the extensive tin works on the east side of the town of Redruth, whence it takes a south-easterly course round the mountain of Carn Marth; thence north-easterly by Carrarath to Twelve Heads, whence it takes a south-eastward course by Nangiles and Carnon Gate to Point Quay, situate on an estuary [Restronguet Creek] branching out of Carrick Road. Its length is nine miles, two furlongs and four chains; in the first mile and seven chains of which, to Wheel[1] Beauchamp, there is a rise of 103 feet; from thence to its termination it is one gradual inclination with a fall of 555 feet to high-water-mark. From Carnon Gate there is a branch to Narrabo of one mile one furlong; another branch from Nangiles to Wheel Fortune of three furlongs and five chains; another from Twelve Heads to Wheel Bissey, two miles, two furlongs and five chains in length and another from Wheel Beauchamp to Wheel Buller, of two furlongs four chains in length. The total length of main line and branches is thirteen miles, three furlongs and eight chains.

Lewin, 'Early British Railways', says:

It was laid with cast-iron rails in chairs fixed into stone block sleepers to the unusual gauge of 4 ft. The motive power was provided by horses up to the year 1854, when power to work with locomotives was obtained. The railway was opened in January, 1825, and has been in

---

[1] Should be Wheal; meaning, in Cornwall, a mine.

continuous use as an isolated system for ninety years. However, a
gradual decline in traffic of late years caused its working to be unprofit-
able, with the result that it was decided to close it altogether in 1915.

In the Plymouth paper previously cited, it is said that the Redruth line
was at one time laid with Barlow rails.

From the same source it may be gathered the Bude Canal had at various
points a series of inclined planes which were worked by steam power. It
does not appear, however, whether they were traversed by barges or by
waggons.

It is probable that there were other small mining railways in Cornwall,
besides those which have been mentioned, of which the author has not
come across any particulars.

We now move eastward to Portland. Priestley describes the railway
there as follows:

Portland Railway. The Act for forming this useful work was passed
in the year 1825, and is entitled *An Act for making and maintaining a
Railway or Tramroad in the Island of Portland, in the county of Dorset*, by
which certain persons are incorporated as "The Portland Railway Company", with powers to make a railway from the Priory Lands in Portland
Island, to the Stone Piers at Portland Castle. . . . The length is two miles
and four chains, and was designed by Mr. James Brown, civil engineer,
who estimated the cost at £5,689. 12s.

It was an edge-railway, worked by fixed engines, opened in October
1826.

CORFE CASTLE

In Farey's 'General View of the Agriculture of Derbyshire' (1817)
there is the following interesting note:

Collinge's patent Axle-tree has been applied to the trams on the
Rail-ways to the famous Pipe-clay pits near Corfe Castle, in Purbeck in
Dorsetshire and others in the south of England, by which there was a
great saving.

Collinge's axle, patented in 1811, was largely used for road vehicles.
Its use of course implies that the wheels revolved on a fixed axle. No
other mention of its application to railway vehicles is known.

RAILWAYS IN SURREY

Continuing to travel in an easterly direction, we come to the Surrey
Iron Railway, a line of great interest, which has been ignored by the
Surrey Archaeological Society. Though it does not appear in the index
of the 'Victoria County History of Surrey', there is a description of it in

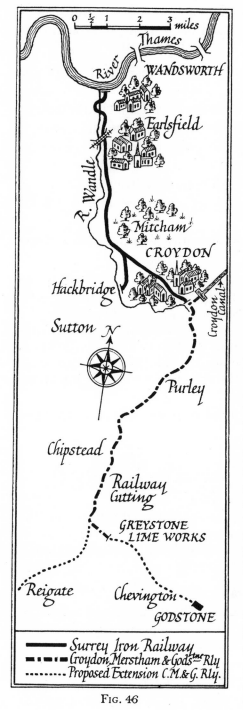

Fig. 46

vol. ii, beginning on p. 256. The Act is said (incorrectly) to have been the first for a railway. It attracted a good deal of attention at the time both among British and foreign writers and has been recently described in an excellent pamphlet entitled 'The Grand[1] Surrey Iron Railway', by F. G. Bing, printed for the Croydon Public Libraries Committee, 1931. Another recent description will be found in Chapter I of the author's 'History of the Southern Railway' (1936). Priestley's account is thus:

This railway commences at a basin which connects it with the River Thames at a place called Ram Field, in the parish of Wandsworth, and from thence proceeds in a southerly direction, running parallel with the river Wandle to Mitcham (where there is a branch from it to Hack Bridge, in the parish of Carshalton); it proceeds from thence in a south-easterly direction to a place called Pitlake Meadow, in the town of Croydon, where it unites with the Croydon, Merstham and Godstone Railway ... The length of this railway is nearly nine miles, with nowhere a greater ascent than about 1 inch in 10 feet. It was the first public railway constructed near London.

The qualification 'near London' seems to be required, although it has been stated by many writers, including the author, to have been 'the first public railway'. It was the first to be definitely empowered by an Act of Parliament to throw itself open to the

---

[1] The word 'Grand' never formed part of the title. Probably it has crept in here by confusion with the name 'Grand Surrey Canal'.

public, but, so far as the actual doing so is concerned, it seems to have been anticipated by the Loughborough and Nanpantan Railway (1789), and possibly others.

The Act was obtained on May 21st, 1801, and the line opened on July 26th, 1803. It was a plate-railway, double throughout, the gauge being about 5 feet between the centres of the stone blocks, and 4 feet

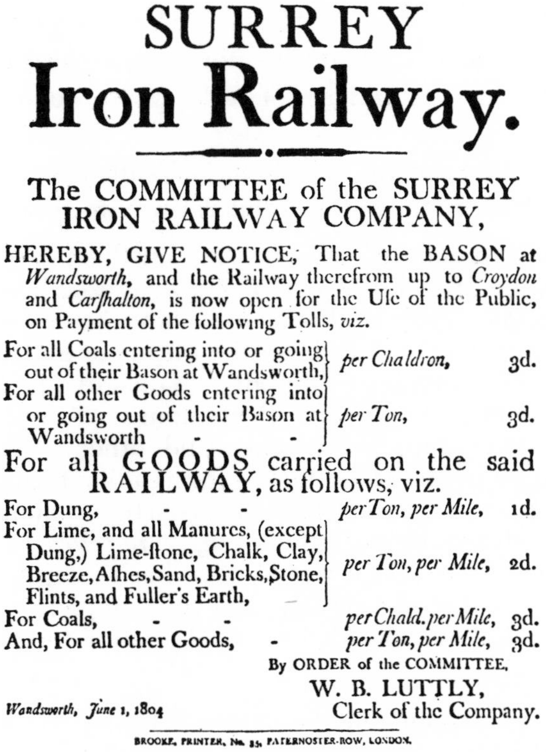

SURREY
Iron Railway.

The COMMITTEE of the SURREY IRON RAILWAY COMPANY,

HEREBY, GIVE NOTICE, That the BASON at *Wandsworth*, and the Railway therefrom up to *Croydon* and *Carshalton*, is now open for the Use of the Public, on Payment of the following Tolls, *viz.*

For all Coals entering into or going out of their Bason at Wandsworth,	*per Chaldron,*	3d.
For all other Goods entering into or going out of their Bason at Wandsworth -	*per Ton,*	3d.

For all GOODS carried on the said RAILWAY, as follows, viz.

For Dung, - -	*per Ton, per Mile,*	1d.
For Lime, and all Manures, (except Dung,) Lime-stone, Chalk, Clay, Breeze, Ashes, Sand, Bricks, Stone, Flints, and Fuller's Earth,	*per Ton, per Mile,*	2d.
For Coals, - -	*per Chald. per Mile,*	3d.
And, For all other Goods, -	*per Ton, per Mile,*	3d.

By ORDER of the COMMITTEE.

W. B. LUTTLY,
Wandsworth, June 1, 1804 Clerk of the Company.

BROOKE, PRINTER, No. 35, PATERNOSTER-ROW, LONDON.

FIG. 47. An original toll sheet of the Surrey Iron Railway

8 inches over the outer faces of the rails. The latter were of the Outram pattern, 3 feet 2 inches long, 4 inches wide on the tread, and 1 inch thick, except for 5 or 6 inches at the ends, where they were half an inch thicker. The original ones were parallel, but afterwards a rib or fish-belly was added under the outer edge, for additional strength. The flange to guide the wheels was curved, being $3\frac{3}{4}$ inches high in the middle and only $1\frac{1}{2}$ at the ends. The engineer was William Jessop.

The following account of its subsequent history is taken from the 'History of the Southern Railway':

The line, which was described by writers of the period as 'a vast and important concern', did not meet with success. It was seriously affected by the Croydon Canal from Rotherhithe, which was opened in 1809. Matters became worse, when its companion, the Croydon, Merstham and Godstone, was closed in 1838. In 1844 it was purchased by the London and South Western Railway, which company sold it to the London and Brighton company. The latter found no use for the line except where the route of the Wimbledon and Croydon intersected it, and in 1846 an Act was obtained to abandon it. The material was recovered and removed to the wharf at Wandsworth, and sold. Some of the stone sleepers were used in making banks for the dock and are still to be seen there.

It was looked upon by some of the more enthusiastic of its supporters as being the first link in a chain of railways to connect London with Portsmouth.

Sir Richard Phillips, in his 'Morning's Walk from London to Kew' (1813), was inspired by the sight of this railway to remark:

I found renewed delight on witnessing, at this place, the economy of horse labour on the Iron Railway. Yet a heavy sigh escaped me, as I thought of the inconceivable millions which have been spent about Malta, four or five of which might have been the means of extending *double lines of iron railway* from London to Edinburgh, Glasgow, Holyhead, Milford, Falmouth, Yarmouth, Dover, and Portsmouth! A reward of a single thousand would have supplied coaches and other vehicles, of various degrees of speed, with the best tackle for readily turning out; and we might, ere this, have witnessed our mail coaches running at the rate of 10 miles an hour, drawn by a single horse, or *impelled 15 miles an hour by Blenkinsop's steam-engine.* Such would have been a legitimate motive for overstepping the income of a nation; and the completion of so great and useful a work would have afforded rational ground for public triumph in general jubilees!

The Croydon, Merstham, and Godstone Railway was authorized by an Act of May 17th, 1803, to go from 'Pitlake Meadow, in the town of Croydon, to, or near to, the town of Reigate, in the county of Surrey, with a collateral Branch from the said Railway, at or near a place called Merstham . . . to, or near to, a place called Godstone Green'.

The section from Croydon to Merstham was opened to the public on July 24th, 1805. The company was unable to 'stay the course', and only penetrated as far as the Greystone Lime Works at Merstham. Priestley says: 'The railway is double throughout,[1] and is, with the carriage driver's path on each side, 24 feet in width.'

It was also engineered by William Jessop, assisted by his son Josias. Its course was more or less by the side of the Brighton main road. A piece of embankment and three overbridges still remain. The London

[1] There is some doubt about this.

FIG. 48. Embankment and bridge over the Chipstead Valley road

FIG. 49. Site of the Croydon, Merstham, and Godstone Railway at Merstham today

Fig. 50. Canal lock at north end of Surrey Iron Railway

and Brighton Railway was planned to pass over part of the route and purchased the line in 1838. An Act was passed in the following year dissolving the company.

Figs. 46, 48, and 49 are from blocks used in the 'History of the Southern Railway', lent by the Company. That of the bridge, which no longer exists, is from a water-colour drawing by G. B. Wollaston, dated 1823, in the Croydon Public Library. Fig. 50 is from a photograph taken in 1911 of the lock at Wandsworth, which has been given to the author by Mr. C. M. Cross, the Chief Engineer and General Manager of the Wandsworth and District Gas Company.

LONDON DOCKS RAILWAY

Not much can be discovered about lines at the Docks, but, so far as there were any, they were early. The letter from Vaughan to Admiral Chichagoff (1804) mentioned in Chapter I contains the following passage:

> To one of the jetties in the London Docks an inclined plane is connected, of 120 yards long, with an elevation of 20 feet, to which is connected a small steam engine of six horse power for the lifting up or letting down of loaned or empty waggons. About 730 waggon loads have been drawn up in a day by this engine, during the common working hours, with the saving of about 16 horses.

In 'The Story of Telford', by Sir Alexander Gibb (1935), it is said that Telford was employed to carry out surveys for the East and West India Docks Railway, which he did by deputy, about 1828. But this was a proposed line from the East to the West India Docks, which appears not to have been made.

Henry Palmer was engineer to the London Docks in 1832; at that time he said, in evidence on the London and Birmingham Railway Bill, that he had not executed or had the management of a railway. There were, however, or had been, two short lines on his mono-rail principle, one at the Royal Victualling Yard at Deptford, and one at Cheshunt in Herts., which will be mentioned again in Chapter VIII. Perhaps he was not very proud of them.

Fig. 51 is a reproduction of an old print (undated), apparently intended to represent the opening of an 'East London Railway', which never materialized. The only reference to this line which has been found occurs in 'A Supplement to the Short Treatise on Rail-roads', by Thomas Hill, Leeds (1829).

PURFLEET RAILWAY

The author is indebted to a friend for the following extract from a letter written by her grandmother, then Miss Deborah Coates, when driving through south Essex:

Tuesday, May 16, 1812. We reached Purfleet about $\frac{1}{2}$ past 7 in the evening; it is a small dirty garrison town. The Thames and chalkpits add greatly to the diversion of the scene. The Chalk is got into the Vessels much more easily than they used to do, by having small ridges of iron called rail roads, by which means one horse can draw 3 times as much as it could without the rail.

One more abortive scheme may be mentioned, as it was so ambitious, the Kentish Railway; the prospectus of which was published in *The Times* of December 21st, 1824, the engineer being Telford. The line was to run from London to Dover and Sandwich, by way of Woolwich, Chatham, and Canterbury, with branches to Maidstone and to Margate. The capital was £1,000,000. It was to be worked 'by locomotive machines', but the company would 'in addition thereto make use of the assistance of horses'.

S. Hemming Engineer, del.t   Printed by W. N. Wear, 24 Tabernacle Row.

Fig. 51. View of the entrance to the East India Docks with proposed East London Rail Road

CHAPTER V

EARLY RAILWAYS IN WALES

As has been mentioned in Chapter I, there is good evidence of a railway in Glamorganshire about the year 1695. It lay between Neath and Aberavon, and was constructed by Sir Humphry Mackworth.

He is described in the 'Dictionary of National Biography' as a politician and capitalist (1657–1727). He was constable of Neath Castle in 1703, sat in Parliament for Cardiganshire on and off during 1700–13, and was a fairly prolific author, dabbling in politics, finance, and religion.

The following information is contained in a 'Report of the Case of Sir Humphry Mackworth and of the Mine-Adventurers with respect to the irregular proceedings of several Justices of the Peace for Glamorgan and their Agents' (1705). The proceedings of which he complained were the forcible enlistment of workmen from his mines at Neath and the breaking-up of the waggon-way.

Richard Thomas of Neath in the county of Glamorgan, Gent., saith that he knows the way commonly called the Waggon-way between *Neath* and *Aberavon*, that the same was formerly a Pool of Dirt and Water and about eight or nine years ago made a good and firm way by Sir Humphry Mackworth for all sort of Carriages and so continued till about the eighth day of *September* last, at which time, and several times since, the said way was broke up by John Morgan and others.

Elsewhere it is stated

that the Coal Trade had been almost totally lost at *Neath*, during the space of Thirty Years and upwards, until Sir Humphry Mackworth in the year 1695 adventured great Summs of Money in finding and recovering the coal in that Neighbourhood.

Another witness deposed that Sir H. Mackworth carried on a

Level and Wind-way[1] commonly called a Foot-rid or Waggon-way, after the manner used in Shrop-shire[2] and New-Castle and at great Expenses continued the said Waggon-way on Wooden Railes from the face

---

[1] This is probably a reference to Mackworth's use of sails, of which presently. A 'wind-way' generally meant an air-way or ventilating passage in a mine.

[2] This reference is important, as it shows that there were railways in Shropshire before 1705, almost certainly before 1695. The implication to be drawn from it is that railways had been established in Shropshire and the Newcastle district before they were introduced into Wales. It also seems a fair inference that Mackworth's was the first in the latter locality.

of each Wall, of Coal twelve hundred Yards under Ground quite down to the Water-side, about three quarters of a Mile from the Mouth of the Coal-pit; the said Coal-works without the conveniency of this Foot-rid and Waggon-way, could not be carried on at any Profit.

Each waggon contained about 18 cwt. and was 'thrust forth' by two men.

And we further Certifie, that the said Sir Humphry Mackworth doth not bring his Coal in Wheel-barrows, but in Waggons, which requires great Skill as well as Labour, to keep the Waggons upon the Railes underground . . . the said waggon-way hath been quietly enjoyed for eight Years and upwards . . . and never interrupted until the eighth of *September* last, and we do verily believe, that it is the best spot of Ground for heavy Carriages in Winter time between *Neath* and *Cardiffe*.

.   .   .   .

The way commonly called the Waggon-way . . . crossing the high-way leading from Neath to Aberavon between the lands of the said Sir Humphry Mackworth was formerly a Pool of Water and Dirt and a great annoyance to all Persons travelling that Road, till about eight or nine years ago the said Sir Humphry Mackworth having occasion for frequent Carriage of Coal, and other heavy Goods that way, did at his own expense fill up the said Pool, and with Gravel, Slaggs, Cinders and Rails of Wood four inches square, did make the same a good and firm way for all Persons to pass over the same with all manner of Carriages.

The concluding words are curious, if it was an edge-railway. Possibly it requires to be amplified with the words 'provided the wheels be suitably formed'. There is perhaps a shadowy claim for the title of the 'first public railway' here.

A map showing the course of the line is reproduced in Fig. 52, from an original in the British Museum.

Another source of information is 'An Essay on the Value of the Mines Late of Sir Carbery Price. By William Waller,[1] Gent. Steward of the said Mines. Writ for the private Satisfaction of all the Partners' (1698).

The mines in question, or some of them, were in the north of Cardiganshire, near Aberdovey. Sir Humphry was concerned in the formation of a syndicate to take them over, with the imposing title of 'The Corporation of the Governor and Company of the Mine Adventurers of England', the Duke of Leeds being governor and Mackworth deputy governor. A large sum of money was raised in 1698 and 1699 for carrying on these undertakings and was spent in the construction of quays, canals, and docks.

---

[1] Mackworth's mother was a kinswoman of Edmund Waller, the poet. Doubtless William was a relation.

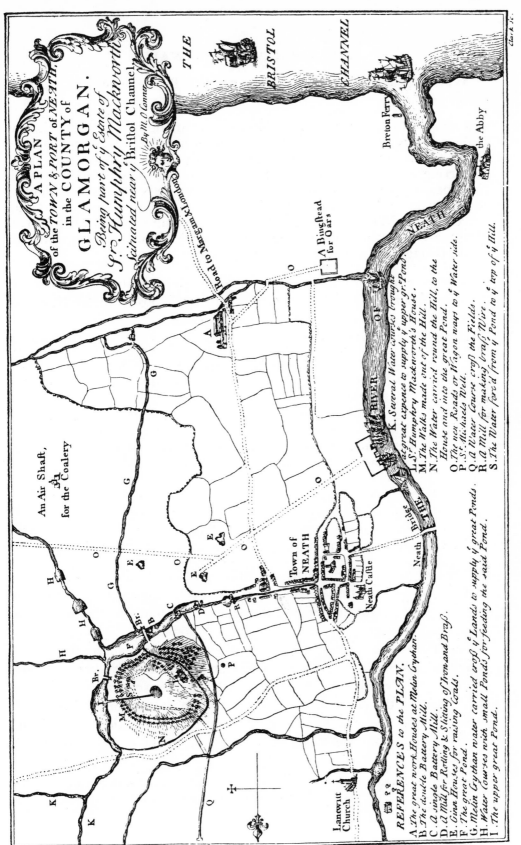

A PLAN
of the TOWN & PORT of NEATH,
in the COUNTY of
GLAMORGAN.
Being part of y Estate of
Sr Humphry Mackworth
Scituated near y Bristol Channel.
By M. O Conner.

THE BRISTOL CHANNEL

Breton Ferry

RIVER OF THE NEATH

A Bingstead for Oars

the Abby

An Air Shaft, for the Coalery

Road to Margam

Langwitt Church

Town of NEATH

Neath Castle

Neath Bridge

REFERENCES to the PLAN.

A. The great work Houses at Melon Crythan.
B. The double Battery Mill.
C. A single Battery Mill.
D. A Mill for Rolling & Slitting of Iron and Brass.
E. Ginn Houses for raising Coals.
F. The great Pond.
G. Melin Crythan river carried cross y Lands to supply y great Ponds.
H. Water courses with small Ponds for feeding the said Pond.
I. The upper great Pond.
K. Several Water courses brought at great expence to supply y upper gr. Pond
L. Sr Humphry Mackworth's House.
M. The Walks made out of the Hill.
N. The Water carried round the Hill, to the House and into the great Pond.
O. The new Roads or Wagon ways to y Water side.
P. St Michaels Well.
Q. A Water Course cross the Fields.
R. A Mill for making brass Wire.
S. The Water ford from y Pond to y top of y Hill.

FIG. 52

Waller speaks of Mackworth's enterprise in his copper-works and coal-mines at Neath,

coffering out the water from his Shafts and sinking-pits . . . and his new Sailing-Waggons, for the cheap Carriage of his Coal to the Water-side, whereby one horse does the work of ten at all times, but when any Wind is stirring (which is seldom wanting near the Sea) one man and a small Sail does the work of twenty . . . And I believe he is the first Gentleman, in this part of the World, that have set up Sailing-engines on Land, driven by the Wind, not for any Curiosity, or vain Applause, but for real Profit, whereby he could not fail of Bishop Wilkins's[1] Blessing on his Undertakings, in case he were in a Capacity to bestow it.

Mackworth's contrivances were also eulogized poetically by Thomas Yalden, about 1700. The effusion is entitled 'A Poem to Sir Humphry Mackworth, on the mines, late of Sir Carbery Price'.

Here are some verses:

> Thy fam'd inventions, Mackworth, must adorn
> The miner's art, and make the best return.
> Thy speedy sails, and useful engines, show
> A genius richer than the mines below.
>
> .   .   .   .
>
> The winds, thy slaves, their useful succour join,
> Convey thy ore, and labour at thy mine.
>
> .   .   .   .
>
> This, Mackworth, fixes thy immortal name,
> The Muses darling, and the boast of fame,
> No greater virtues on record shall stand,
> Than thus with arts to grace, with wealth enrich the land.

Mackworth sometimes made use of convict labour, and there is a story that the Government on one occasion asked if he would accept a consignment of pirates, but he declined the offer, as he felt sure the neighbourhood would object.

His third and youngest son, William Morgan, married Martha, daughter of John Praed of Trevethoe,[2] Cornwall, took the additional name of Praed, and was an ancestor of the poet. The present representative of that branch of the family is a near connexion of the author, and, curiously enough, happens to be also a 'Joliffe Trustee', being descended on his mother's side from the Joliffe who made one of the earliest railways in Durham.[3]

---

[1] Bishop of Chester; author of a book called 'Mathematical Magick', first published in 1648. He died in 1672, which explains the words with which the extract closes.

[2] Misspelt Trevathon in D.N.B.

[3] See p. 13, *ante*.

Probably there were a certain number of other wooden railways in Wales connected with the mines, but the author has only succeeded in finding one other reference: in an interesting book called 'A History of the Pioneers of the Welsh Coal-Field', by Elizabeth Phillips (1925); as follows:

As early as 1750 there were ironworks at Taibach, near Cwmavon, and coal was obtained from Cwmbychan, a little valley branching off from Cwmavon. A wooden tramway conveyed coal to the works from Mynydd Bychan, and both coal and ironstone were brought on the backs of mules from Wernlaes Level, near Merthyr.

The Rev. William Coxe, describing a 'Historical Tour in Monmouthshire' (1801), wrote thus:

In the vicinity of Blaenavon[1] we observed the process of making a rail road, so called because it is formed by a kind of frame with iron rails, or bars, laid lengthways and fastened or cramped by means of cross bars. The ground being excavated about six feet in breadth and two in depth is strewed over with broken pieces of stones, and the frame laid down; it is composed of rails, sleepers or cross bars, and under sleepers. The rail is a bar of cast iron, four feet in length, three inches thick, and one and a half broad; its extremities are respectively concave and convex, or in other words are morticed and tenanted into one another, and fastened at the ends by two wooden pegs to a cross bar called the sleeper. This sleeper was originally of iron but experience having shown that iron was liable to snap or bend, it is now made of wood, which is considerably cheaper, and requires less repair. Under each extremity of the sleeper is a square piece of wood, called the under sleeper, to which it is attached by a peg. The frame being thus laid down and filled with stones, gravel and earth, the iron rails form a ridge above the surface, over which the wheels of the carts glide by means of iron grooved rims three inches and a half broad.[2] This is the general structure of the road when carried in a strait line; at the junction of two roads, and to facilitate the passage of two cars in opposite directions, moveable iron rails, called turn rails, are occasionally used, which are fastened with screws instead of pegs, and may be pushed sideways. The level of the ground is taken with great exactness and the declivity is in general so gentle as to be almost imperceptible: the road sometimes conveyed in a straight line, sometimes winding round the sides of precipices, is a picturesque object, and the cars filled with coals or iron, and gliding along occasionally without horses, impress the traveller, who is unaccustomed to such spectacles, with pleasing astonishment. The expense of forming these roads is very considerable, varying according to the nature of the ground, or the difficulty or facility of

[1] In north-west Monmouthshire, 5½ miles NW. of Pontypool.
[2] This description suggests both internal and external flanges. The use of edge-rails in Wales was rare.

procuring proper materials; it is seldom less than a thousand pounds per mile, and sometimes exceeds that sum.

The cars from the solidity of their structure, and the quantity of iron used in the axletree and wheels, when loaded weigh not less than three tons and a half; they are drawn by a single horse, and the driver stands on a kind of footboard behind and can instantaneously stop the car by means of a lever and a drop, which falls between the wheels, and suspends their motion. In places where the declivity is more rapid than usual, the horse is taken out[1] and the car impelled forward by its own weight.

The above account, in its first few words, conveys the idea that the railway was then in process of construction. But the writer may have been merely observing the making of some extension, or siding, as a railway at Blaenavon had been in existence for some years at the time he visited it. John Fox ('General View of the Agriculture of the county of Monmouth', 1794) wrote that the Newport Canal had two branches dividing at rather less than one mile above Newport and going up to collieries and iron-works. Apparently by 'branches' he means railways, as he goes on to say that each

extends more than ten miles and the whole of the rail roads are upwards of twenty-four miles. The iron works of *Blaen-avon*, consisting of *three furnaces*, are carried on with great spirit, by Messrs. Hill and Co., and has a rail road for more than *five miles*, to bring the iron down to the head of the canal.

The following description of Welsh railways in Cumming's 'Illustrations of the origins and progress of Rail and Tram Roads' (1824) has been utilized by a number of early writers.

In Wales the tram road seems to have a preference to any other species, as such has been almost universally adopted; but we find that as late as the year 1790, there was scarcely a single rail-way in all South Wales, whilst in the year 1812, the rail-ways, in a finished state, connected with canals, collieries, iron and copper works, &c. in the counties of Monmouth, Glamorgan and Carnarvon alone, extended to upwards of one hundred and fifty miles in length, exclusive of a very considerable extent within the mines themselves, of which one company at Merthyr Tydvil possessed upwards of thirty miles, under ground, connected with the stupendous iron works at that place; and so rapid has been the increase of rail-ways in South Wales of late years, that at the present period they exceed four hundred miles, exclusive of about one hundred miles underground: and notwithstanding this vast extent, such is the

---

[1] This appears to imply the use of shafts, which are very uncommon on rail vehicles. But the writer may have expressed himself loosely. His account is of considerable interest, as it sets out the local methods, which differ in various little ways from those adopted in the north of which we have so many descriptions.

decided preference given to tram roads, that with the exception of about five miles at the head of the Pont-y-pool line of the Monmouthshire Canal, the whole are upon the tram plate principle.[1]

.   .   .   .

I have before observed, that although the rail-ways in Wales are exceedingly numerous and extensive, yet they are almost universally tram roads, and much on the same construction. Several branches were made upon the old principle, with the flaunche upon the wheel, and not upon the rail, as in tram roads in general at the present day, but were found exceedingly heavy and expensive: the rails were of cast-iron, in lengths of about three feet each, and laid four feet apart, resting on iron sleepers, with an iron rod or bar passing under the road, its extremities laid upon and made fast to each opposite sleeper for the purpose of keeping the sleepers and rails firm in their places; but it was soon found that this bar, unable to resist the weight of the waggons passing over, frequently broke in the centre of the road, and the broken end protruding, rendered it difficult as well as dangerous, for the horses to work.

These roads were principally inclined planes, with various declivities, from one-eighth to half an inch in the yard, on which one horse could, without difficulty, take down from thirty to forty tons over and above the weight of the waggons; but it would require three or four horses to bring the empty waggons up again, and even then by much the heaviest draught. There were then, and still are, a few inclined planes in the Principality, worked entirely without horses, but by the assistance of a *jenny* or *whimsey*. The loaded waggons descending, bring the empty ones up, but these machines are only made use of in cases where the declivities are very great, varying from six to eighteen inches in the yard. The lengths of these inclined planes also varies from one hundred to six hundred yards.

George Overton, who made the first survey for the Stockton and Darlington Railway, in 1818, was associated with the lines in South Wales. He wrote a book entitled 'A Description of the Faults or Dykes of the Mineral Basin of South Wales', Part I (1825). No more appears to have been published. He said he had been in the habit of making and using such roads during the greater part of the last thirty years, and had surveyed and constructed roads of some hundred miles' extent in different parts of the kingdom. He calls roads with flanges on the rails, tramways; and with flanges on the wheels, railways or railroads; expressing a strong preference for the former, considering that on them the resistance is less. The following are extracts:

About twenty-five years ago I made a tramroad (of the same description with that which is used under ground, not more than two feet and

---

[1] This statement is not strictly accurate.

a half wide,) from the Dowlais Company's limestone quarries to their blast furnaces in the parish of Merthyr, the total length being about three miles, and the fall about fifteen inches per chain [1 in 53]. Upon this road each horse hauled regularly a weight of nine or ten tons, and took the empty carriages back. This continued to be the case for many years; in fact, until that road was diverted, and a new quarry opened. I need hardly remark, that this is considerably more than could be done on a railway with so great a fall.[1]

Again, I completed a tramroad from the bottom of an inclined plane near Dowlais Works to the navigation house on the Glamorganshire Canal, a distance of upwards of nine miles, the fall on some parts of the road being upwards of one inch per yard [1 in 36], and on the remaining portion varying from two to six inches per chain [1 in 396 to 1 in 132]. Upon this road like the preceding, a single horse continued for some time to haul ten tons, and bring the empty trams back, travelling regularly a distance of nineteen miles per day. The horse here referred to, like those mentioned above, was greatly inferior to the horses generally used in the north. But I will venture to assert that no horse in the north, upon an edge-railway with a similar fall, could do the work which I have instanced upon the tramroads at Dowlais. The last-mentioned road is 4 feet 2 inches wide.

This is the celebrated Penydarren tramroad, on which a locomotive took a train for the first time in the world's history, on February 13th, 1804.

The measurement of 4 feet 2 inches was taken between the flanges, or the bottoms of the rails if they projected slightly inwards.

Penydarren is close to Dowlais, both being in the parish of Merthyr Tydfil, in the north-east corner of Glamorganshire. The 'navigation house' was at Abercynon.[2] Mr. D. V. Levien, who had charge of the Great Western Railway Company's records, wrote in the *Railway Gazette* of July 3rd, 1936:

The tramroad [Penydarren] was constructed in the year 1800 for the conveyance of limestone from the Morlais Castle collieries to the Plymouth Company's furnaces and of the manufactured iron thence to the canal at Navigation. It remained in use till 1875, but the tramplates were not removed until 1890.

It was superseded to a great extent by the Taff Vale Railway, which was opened from Cardiff to Navigation in 1840, and to Merthyr in 1841.

[1] This is an amazing remark, because it is fairly obvious that on a good 'rail road' of 1 in 53, a horse would not be able to hold up nine or ten tons going downhill, but Overton takes pride in the fact that it could be done on a tramroad (or plate-railway). Yet he maintained that the resistance was less on the latter!
[2] Called Cynon in Priestley's map. Aber is a confluence, or the mouth of a river.

FIG. 53. Penydarren Iron Works in 1811. (From 'The Principal Rivers of Wales', by J. G. Wood, 1813)

Fig. 54. The Penydarren Tram-road in 1932

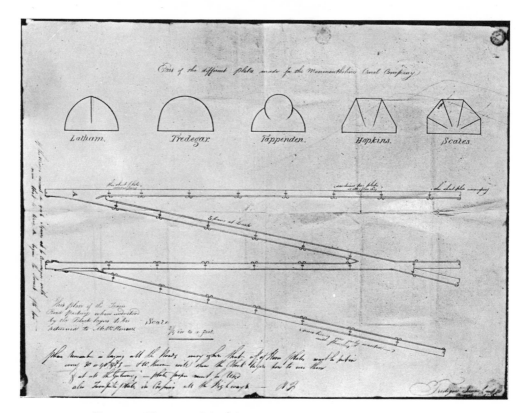

Fig. 55. Tram-road 'parting', Monmouthshire Railway, 1808

This line hugged the site of the Penydarren tramroad from Quakers' Yard up to Troedyrhiew, a distance of 3 miles, then proceeded for the rest of the way closer to the river.

A view of part of the old line in its derelict state is given in Fig. 54.

Morlais Castle is 2 miles north of Merthyr; Plymouth Furnace, a mile south of the latter.

Overton went on:

> In the principal colliery which supplied the Dowlais blast furnaces there was a railroad, over which each horse worked with one wagon. When I had completed the tramroad which I substituted in lieu of that railway, each horse regularly hauled from the farthermost part of the colliery twelve trams, carrying fifteen hundred weight each, and took the empty ones back.[1]

> It is but fair to add, that I am speaking of railroads as they existed twenty-five years ago [i.e. 1800]. Since that time their construction has been much improved; and with respect to the railroad in question, the defect arose more from the neglected state it was suffered to be kept in, than from any imperfection in principle.

> Messrs. Samuel Homfray and Company of Tredegar Works are now sending coal to Newport [Mon.], a distance of twenty-three miles over a road varying in fall from ten to four inches in a chain [1 in 79 to 1 in 198]; each horse regularly taking ten tons, and bringing the empty trams back . . . This road has been in use for more than twenty years.

> Since the introduction of the Welsh coal to the extensive lime works at Old Radnor, the beneficial effects resulting from that measure have been experienced in a great degree in the adjacent counties both of England and Wales. These lime works, although at a distance of fifty-five miles, are principally supplied from a colliery belonging to my partner and myself; the coal passing from Monmouthshire through part of Brecon and Hereford into Radnorshire, over a tramroad fifty-five miles long, if we except the intervention of seven miles of canal. This canal and tramroad are both open to the public, different parts of the tramroad belonging to different companies.

Overton preferred 'iron dove-tail sleepers' to stone blocks, and cast-iron rails to those of wrought iron.

The Glamorganshire Canal (marked 'Cardiff Canal' in Priestley's map), which is the one mentioned in connexion with the Penydarren line, ran from Merthyr down to Cardiff, a distance of about 25 miles, and was opened in February 1794. It was largely in consequence of a shortage of water in the upper parts that the line was made.

Scott's 'Highland' paper (1824), calling it the Cardiff and Merthyr Railway, says that it was $26\frac{3}{4}$ miles long, 'running near the Glamorganshire

---

[1] This seems rather a remarkable result. The colliery was no doubt Morlais Castle.

canal: at Quakers' Yard a branch of $9\frac{5}{8}$ miles goes off to Carno Mill'. With regard to the length, he evidently thought it ran all the way between the two places, whereas it went less than half the distance. Quakers' Yard is practically the terminus, being only about a mile east of Navigation.

There is a fine map in the British Museum showing the course of the 'Cardiff and Merthyr Railway' as originally projected. It is entitled:

> Plan of an intended DRAM ROAD from or near Carno Mill in the Parish of Browellty and County of Monmouth, to or near the Sea Lock below the town of Cardiff, with a branch from the same to the Limestone Rocks in the Parish of Merthyr Tydvill and County of Glamorgan. By P. Williams 1799.

The line starts just below Cardiff on the east side of the river Taff and the canal, crossing both to the west at Melin Griffith Works, passing Pentyrch Works, following the bends of the river; crossing it again at 1·5 miles up; then crossing the canal at Navigation House, close to where the river Cynon joins the Taff; 2 miles farther on it forks, close to where the river Bargoed comes in; the right fork proceeds up the east bank of the latter river for 9 miles, then turns round the head of the Carno brook to the eastward as far as the river Rumney, just opposite Carno Mill, which is half a mile south of the boundary of Breconshire and Monmouth. The position is marked by a cross in the map (Fig. 56). The left fork, which was all that was made, follows up the east bank of the Taff to Plymouth Works, then on to Penydarren Works, just north-east of Merthyr; swinging round to skirt Penydarren Place, it goes up to 'Castell Morlais'.

Priestley, under the heading 'Glamorganshire Canal', says: 'The Cardiff and Merthyr Tidvile Railway takes a parallel course with the canal from Merthyr to the aqueduct, but on the opposite side of the river.' He shows it thus in the map, but has not given it a separate article in the book.

Sir David Brewster's 'Edinburgh Encyclopaedia' (1830), in the article Navigation, Inland, speaking of the canal, says 'the upper part was sometimes short of water, hence the formation of a railway parallel to it, chiefly for the iron-works of Plymouth, Pendarren and Dowlais, but this railway has not been carried lower than Quakers-Yard, being about nine miles from its commencement'.

Rees' 'Cyclopaedia' (1819), in the article Canal, mentions an Act obtained by Homfray in 1794 for making this line. Tredgold and other writers have followed in the same line, probably only repeating from Rees.

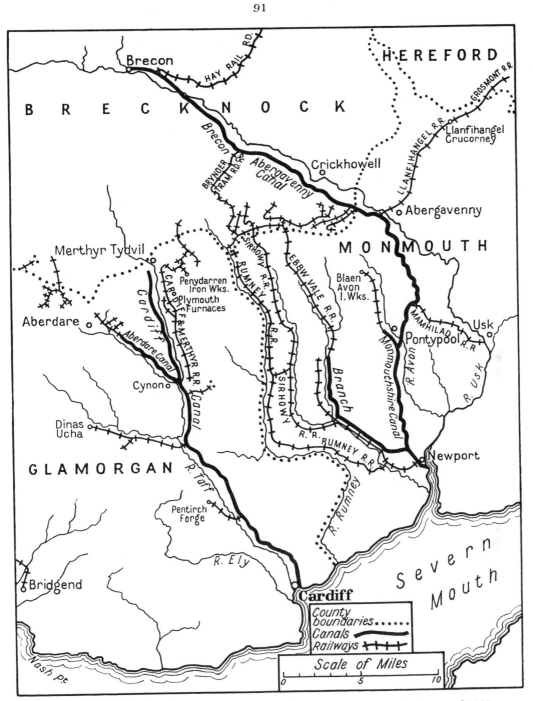

FIG. 56. Railways in the Cardiff and Newport areas. From Priestley's map of 1830

The author has found no trace of this Act, either at the British Museum or at the Inner Temple Library. The construction was not as early as 1794, and was no doubt carried out under the powers embodied in the canal company's Act.

It is, however, stated in 'Ueber Schienenwege in England, 1826 und 1827', by von Oeynhausen and von Dechen (1829), that the tramroads in the Merthyr Tydfil district were commenced in 1791, and that by 1811, 150 miles were in existence.

In connexion with the Glamorganshire Canal, Priestley adds:

There is also a railway from the mines near Glancayach,[1] to this canal . . . and there is another railway of considerable extent, which commences at the collieries at Dinas Ucha, on the west bank of the River Rhondda Vawr, along which it continues to below its junction with the River Taff, near Forest Bridge.

The Aberdare Canal communicated with the Glamorganshire Canal near an aqueduct which carried the latter over the river Taff, and proceeded nearly parallel with the river Cynon to a place called Ynys Cynon, about three-quarters of a mile from Aberdare. Priestley says that at the head of the canal there was a railroad, 2 miles long, to the Llwydcoed Furnaces, from which branches extended to Godley's and Abernant Furnaces. Scott's 'Highland' paper says:

Where the Aberdare branch of the Glamorganshire Canal terminates railways commence, passing the iron works of Abernant, Aberdare and Hirwain, and thence to the summit of a precipice, near Neath Valley, where an immense inclined plane completes the communication with the Neath Canal. Up this inclined plane the waggons are dragged by a high pressure engine of Mr. Trevithick's construction.

The above passage is copied in the 'Edinburgh Encyclopaedia'. As will be seen in Fig. 56, Priestley's map does not show the connexion with Hirwain (though there must have been one), nor the more important one with the Neath Canal, the head of which was only about 3 miles to the west of Hirwain.

Some interesting details of early railways in this neighbourhood are given in 'Pioneers of the Welsh Coal-Field' (1925). Firstly, Griffith's railway:

The year 1790 is memorable in the history of the Rhondda, for in that year Dr. Griffiths opened out the first known level at Gyfeillon.[2]

---

[1] The name cannot be traced, but it is evidently the short line shown in the map, going to the east, just below 'Cynon'.   [2] One and a half miles SW. of Pontypridd.

This turned out successfully, and he constructed three miles of tramroad —part of which is still to be seen in Pontypridd as the Broadway—and a bridge over the Taff near the old Machine House. This was known as Pont-y-doctor, and was built in 1809. He also constructed a length of canal to meet the Glamorganshire Canal, which is now filled up, but was until quite recently known as the 'Doctor's Canal'.

Then Coffin's railway:

Walter Coffin bought a farm at Dinas in 1806 and began prospecting for coal. . . . In a short time he constructed three miles of tramway, connecting Dinas with Dr. Griffiths' tramway at Gyfeillon, and thus gained access to the canal at Treforest. For many years this tramway was the only communicating link between the villages of the lower Rhondda and Pontypridd. It was a great convenience to the country folk and miners, and was the means of bringing much trade to Pontypridd. Up to that time Llantrissant had been the chief market-town within reach, but it was a weary way to tramp over the hills and return at night heavy laden, and the colliers' wives welcomed the appearance of the tramway, which provided them with many a lift homewards.

The above is, of course, the one referred to just previously in the last quotation from Priestley, as running from Dinas Ucha to the Taff.

About 20 miles west of Cardiff there was the Duffryn Llynvi and Porthcawl Railway; the Act for which was obtained in 1825. It was a horse plate-railway, $16\frac{1}{2}$ miles long, rising 490 feet, opened in 1828. At Cefn Gribbw, the Bridgend Railway communicated with it, which ran from it to Bridgend, about 4 miles. The Act was obtained in 1828, but it was not opened till 1834; rather a late date for the construction of a new plate-railway. The latter company were empowered 'to set up Fire engines or other machines; the furnace of any steam engine to consume its own smoke'. Both these lines were bought by the Llynvi Valley Railway, which afterwards became part of the G.W.R.

Proceeding some 14 miles up the coast in a north-westerly direction we find ourselves at Neath.

First, with regard to the Neath Canal: constructed under Acts of 1791 and 1798, it entered the river Neath at the town of that name, and followed the course of the river up for 14 miles to a place called Abernant, close to the border of the county. This place now appears to be called Aberpergwn. (The 'Edinburgh Encyclopaedia' gives the termination of the canal as 'Aberfergwn', evidently a misspelling of the above. There is another Abernant about 8 miles to the east, near Aberdare, which is a different place.) Priestley says there were two short railways at its head. The 'Edinburgh Encyclopaedia' mentions that a railway joined it at

'Aberfergwn' from the head of the Aberdare canal, which was evidently the one mentioned previously, under the latter heading. Priestley adds: 'A few miles above Neath the canal has a branch to the west, with which the Aberdulais Railway communicates, as do also two other railroads from copper works on the same side of the canal.' To the former line he devotes an article with the heading Dulais Railway. The Act for it was obtained in 1826. It was on one inclined plane of 8 miles 5 furlongs and 5 chains, with a rise of 426 feet. It commenced

at Aber Dulais, near the canal which crosses the River Neath at its junction with the Dulais River, runs parallel with the latter on the western bank, for nearly five miles, to Ynis-y-bout; at this place it crosses the river and keeps the eastern bank till it reaches the lime works of Cwm-Dulais.

From Priestley's account it would appear to have been a *fait accompli* at the time he wrote. The 'Penny Cyclopaedia' (1837) gives a similar description. Lewin, therefore, is probably wrong in saying it did not appear to have reached the construction stage.[1]

Another line communicating with the Neath Canal came from Penderyn, which is 5 miles NW. of Aberdare, and rather less from Aberpergwn, lying ENE. of the latter. A tramway was made from there to the canal about 1806. It contained an inclined plane at Penrhiw. Penderyn parish is 1,200 feet above sea-level.

The following details are given in 'A History of the Vale of Neath', by D. Rhys Phillips (1925):

[About 1806] a tram or rail way was constructed . . . to connect the [Neath] canal head at Glyn Neath with the limestone quarries of Penderyn and the ironworks of Hirwaen and neighbourhood.

The *Cambrian* for April 12th, 1806, mentions that "Dr. Bevan of Neath is now engaged at his own expense in making a Tram-Road from Dinas Rock in the county of Brecon, to communicate with the Neath Canal . . . being upwards of one mile and a half long. The whole line . . . will be completed by the first week in July next." The same paper for May 2nd, 1807, contained an advertisement asking for tenders for the conveyance of 30,000 Tons of Limestone (ready quarried and the drams filled at the rock); and also 500 Tons of Fire-clay (ready raised and the drams filled) from Dinas Rock . . . to the upper end of the Neath Canal . . . to be carried along the Dram-road belonging to Dr. Bevan of Neath.

The use of tram and dram as synonymous terms will be noticed. Dram is rare, being as a matter of fact the Welsh pronunciation of tram.

[1] 'Early British Railways', p. 17.

Under the heading Cefn Rhigos Tramroad, in the same book, the date of about 1780 is given for the opening of a tramroad

from Hirwaen Iron Works to Ysgubor Fawr, Penderyn, later extended through Rhigos to Glyn Neath for the conveyance of iron on trams to the boats on that canal; this extension being made early in the first decade of the XIX century by the brothers F. and R. Tappenden, the then proprietors of the Abernant Works, Aberdare, served to carry their iron from Aberdare to meet the small coasters that came up to Neath, until the Aberdare branch of the Glamorganshire Canal was opened in 1811.

Pursuing our way for a few miles to the westward, we come to Swansea.

On the Swansea Canal, which obtained an Act in 1794 empowering its construction from Swansea 'into the parish of Ystradgunlais, in the county of Brecon', Priestley says:

This canal commences in Swansea Harbour, at the mouth of the Tawe River, and running in a direction a little to the eastward of north, and parallel with the river Tawe, passes Landoor [Landore], the copperworks of J. Morris, Esq. at Morris Town; afterwards crossing the small River Twrch, it terminates at Pen Tawe, and from whence is continued a railway to the lime-works at Hen-Noyadd, in the parish of Ystradgunlais, in the county of Brecon. There are two railways branching from this canal, each about two miles in length; one near Ynis Tawe, to coal mines, and the other to coal mines and lime-works near Bryan Morgan.

. . . .

Mr. Thomas Sheasby was the engineer employed in this canal, which was completed and opened in October, 1798.[1]

We have met Mr. Sheasby before, in connexion with the Severn and Wye Railway.

The Swansea Canal Company had powers under their Act to make 'Rollers, Inclined Planes, or Railways'.

There was a steep inclined railway down from the Clydach Colliery, 5 miles NNE. of Swansea. It is mentioned by von Oeynhausen and von Dechen (1829), also in 'Pioneers of the Welsh Coal-Field' (1925), but the latter reference is obscure and appears to be inaccurate, for geographical reasons. It is probably the line shown in Fig. 57, north-east of Morriston, marked C, which is left anonymous in Priestley's map.

At Swansea we also find the Oystermouth Railway, which has a unique and very interesting history and has been called, not without some justification, the first passenger railway. It was opened for mineral traffic in

[1] It became the property of the G.W.R.

1807, under an Act of 1804 incorporating 'The Oystermouth Railway or Tramroad Company'. Priestley gives the route thus:

This railway commences at the Brewery Bank in the town of Swansea, where it communicates with the Swansea Canal; it then travels along

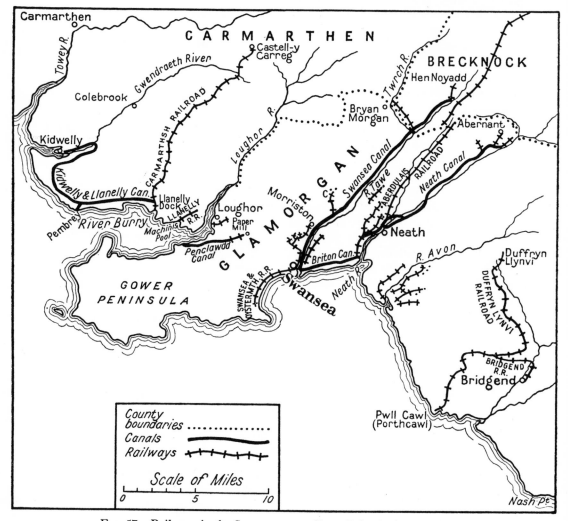

FIG. 57. Railways in the Swansea area. From Priestley's map of 1830

the banks of the Swansea Bay in a south-westerly direction past Sketty, Lelbyputt and Norton Halls, when turning to the east it terminates at Oystermouth, not far from Castle Hill Field; from Swansea northwards it is continued on the west side of the Swansea Canal as far as Morriston, communicating with several mines on the line.

Lewin says a limited passenger traffic soon sprang up, although it was not until 1877 that locomotive traction was introduced. In an article in *Modern Transport* for December 7th, 1935, it was stated that 'Passenger-carrying in vehicles resembling stage-coaches commenced almost at once, although no specific powers had been obtained'. Part of the line was converted to electrical operation in 1929.

Only one more early railway is known in Glamorganshire; it was incorporated in May 1811, by an Act, as 'The Penclawdd Canal and Railway or Tramroad Company'. According to Priestley it commenced

in the River Burry, at Penclawdd, and runs in a crooked course from west to east, to the mines not far from the Paper Mill Lands, with which it is connected by a short railroad; another railroad branches off near its opening into the river, which runs down for a short distance to the south-west. There is a short separate railroad from the river to certain mines on Loughor Common, a little to the north of the main canal.

Crossing over the border for a short distance into Carmarthenshire, we come to the railway of that name. Scott's 'Highland' paper says:

From the harbour of Lanelly on the Burry river the Caermarthenshire railway extends twentyfive miles through a productive coal-country, to the lime-works near Landebie; and on the eastern side are railways to the extensive coal-works of General Wade.[1]

The above is copied in the 'Edinburgh Encyclopaedia'. The length appears to be overstated; Llandebie is only twelve miles from Llanelly as the crow flies. Priestley, who is probably a more trustworthy guide, describes it thus:

Carmarthenshire Railway. 42 George III, Cap. 80. Royal Assent 3rd June, 1802.

This railway commences from the River Bury near a place called The Flats, in the parish of Llanelly, . . . to Castell-y Garreg Limestone Quarries, in the parish of Llanfihangel-Aberbythich. It is in length sixteen miles; and upon the line, for the purpose of carrying the same on a more gradual inclination, are many deep cuttings and embankments; among the latter is one near Munydd Maur, composed of upwards of forty thousand cubic yards of earth, &c.

Lewin says that in 1834 an Act was obtained to convert it from a plate-railway into an edge-railway capable of being worked by locomotives, but the work was never carried out and the line fell into disuse through want of repairs.

[1] The correct name is General George Warde (1760–1830). He was of a Kentish family, but lived for a time in South Wales.

The following reference to this line occurs in 'Old Llanelly', by John Innes (1902), on p. 57:

There had been in Llanelly "railroads" and waggon-ways with wooden rails and stone sleepers[1] whereon horses did the traction for a long time. Many of these were called "old" on maps dated a century ago. There was also the Great Carmarthenshire Railway to Cross Hands, made in 1804. Along its route in 1876 the Mynydd Mawr Railway was made. Another of many local mineral roads was the Box Tramway, from Messrs. Jones and Cox's pit of that name by Als, the Pottery and south side of present market to Erw and Dock.

Mynydd Mawr (Great Mount) is a hill 3 miles west of Llandebie, on which there is a lake. Cross Hands is a hamlet near by, 12 miles NE. of Llanelly. The railway, known as the Llanelly and Mynydd Mawr, was taken over by the G.W.R. in 1921. It is only used for goods and minerals.

Another line in this neighbourhood was that of the Llanelly Railway and Dock Company, the Act for which was obtained in 1828, 'for making . . . a Railway . . . from Gelly Gillie Farm, in the parish of Llanelly . . . to Machynis Pool in the same parish . . . and for making . . . a Wet Dock at the Termination . . . at Machynis Pool'. Priestley gives the length as 2 miles and 300 yards.

Lewin says the 'first portion of four miles from Llanelly was opened in 1833, locomotive traction being adopted from the start'. It was considerably extended as time went on. MacDermot gives an interesting account[2] of the subsequent developments, confirming 1833 for the opening date, but saying it was worked by horses until 1840. The original part is now Great Western.

PEMBREY RAILWAY

An Act was obtained in 1825 for 'constructing a Harbour and other Works, in the parish of Pembrey, in the county of Carmarthen, and for making a Canal and Railway from the said Harbour to the Kidwelly and Llanelly Canal', the company being called the 'New Pembrey Harbour Company'. Priestley shows a very short railway in the map, but does not speak of it in the book.

KIDWELLY CANAL

The Act for the canal was obtained in 1766. Two others, in 1812 and 1818, were for improving the harbour and 'for making . . . a navigable

---

[1] Except for the Tranent and Cockenzie Railway (described in the next chapter), this is the only reference known to the author of such a combination, and is probably a mistake, caused by confusion with memories of old iron railways.

[2] 'History of the Great Western Railway', vol. ii, pp. 76–81.

canal or Tramroads, in Kidwelly, and Llanelly', &c. Priestley says: 'There are two small detached tramroads, one at Machynis Pool, the other at the Loughor Mines.'

Retracing our steps to the eastward across Glamorganshire, we come to Monmouthshire, which by the year 1830 was as thickly covered by railways as any county in Great Britain. It may be well to remind readers that the Monmouth Railway was almost entirely outside Wales, and has been described in Chapter III. The 'Monmouthshire railways' are another story altogether. We now return to Fig. 56.

The 'Company of Proprietors of the Monmouthshire Canal Navigation' was incorporated by 32 George III, cap. 102, which obtained the Royal Assent on June 3rd, 1792. Further Acts were passed in 1797 and 1802. The 'Edinburgh Encyclopaedia' gives the following description:

> The Monmouth canal commences at Pillgwelly on the Uske, and passing Newport to Malpas, divides in two branches. Of these the one follows the channel of the Ebbw river, 11 miles to Crumlin Bridge, whence lines of railway proceed up the Ebbw 21 miles to Ebbw Vale and Beaufort Iron Works, with branches to Sirhowey etc. also up the Ebbw-vach to Nant-y-glo Iron Works. The eastern or main line [of the canal] is from the Uske to Pont Newydd[1] near Pontypool, $12\frac{1}{2}$ miles; rising 447 feet, whence a railway proceeds $5\frac{1}{2}$ miles, rising 610 feet to Blaen-Avon furnace. Various other branches of railway are connected with the navigation, but the most important is the Sirhowy line. This railway commences at the Monmouth Canal at Pillgwelly and passing through Tredegar Park up the Ebbw river, at Risca crosses that river by a bridge of sixteen arches, following afterwards the course of the Sirhowy river by Tredegar and Sirhowy Iron Works to Trevill lime works, about 28 miles. A branch proceeds to Romney Iron Works and from the same place the Brinore railway is continued over the Black Mountain to the vale of the Uske at Brecon; and from thence to Hay on the Wye . . . there are also branches from the [Sirhowy] railway to the several collieries and likewise to the Monmouthshire Canal in two places.

The above account is practically all copied from Scott's 'Highland' essay.

Mr. R. Halliday, in an excellent article which appeared in the *Great Western Railway Magazine* for February and March 1912, describes the situation thus:

> The canal was only a stage on the way to the iron works and pits, and the narrow steep valleys, along which waterways were out of the question, necessitated the use of rail or tramroads to carry traffic down to the canal.

---

[1] A mistake for Pontnewynydd. Pontnewydd is another place $5\frac{1}{4}$ miles farther south.

Railways were made from Blaenavon to Pontnewynydd and from
Beaufort to Crumlin Bridge, being finished in 1793 and 1794. They were
constructed in the first place with edge-rails and sleepers; the latter at
first iron and afterwards wood (as the Rev. Mr. Coxe bears witness).[1]

In 1800 Benjamin Outram was called in to advise the company, and of
course recommended tram-plates, most of the lines being converted and
stone blocks being introduced.

The Beaufort line mentioned above is called the Ebbw Vale Railroad
in Priestley's map. In the book he omits it.

A very interesting report was made on the Monmouthshire railways in
1849 by Captain J. L. Simmons.[2] In the previous year the canal company
had obtained an Act changing their name to 'The Monmouthshire Railway and Canal Company', and making various alterations, including the
prohibition of private users' locomotives and horses. The company
sought to impose a standard type of waggon on the traders, the wheels
having stout flanges which would enable them to run on either type of
rail. As there were 23 private locomotives and over 4,000 waggons, a
great outcry was raised, and an appeal made to the Commissioners of
Railways, hence this report.

It contains a list of all the railways which the company had made under
its Acts. It is possible some were later than 1830, but the dates of construction are not given. It mentions first the Blaenavon Railroad from
Pontnewynydd; a branch from it to the Varteg Ironworks, known as the
Cwm Frwyd Railroad, and two short branches[3] from the canal a little
below Pontypool to Trosnant Furnace and to Blaendare Furnace, adding:
'The foregoing may be distinguished as the Eastern Valleys lines.'

Later in the report it is stated that in 1849 the Eastern lines were
entirely railroads, and the Western tramroads; the former having a gauge
of 3 feet 4 inches, the latter 4 feet 4 inches. Down to that time the company provided neither power nor rolling-stock. The Act of 1848 prohibited horse haulage except on Rassa, Cwm Frwyd, and Blaendare
roads, which were too steep for locomotives.

The Western Valleys lines were:

A tramroad from Newport to Risca-bridge, thence to Crumlin, thence
to Pont Aberbyg, thence branching off to the right to Blaina and Cwm
Celyn Ironworks and to the left to Beaufort Ironworks, with another
branch tramroad from Risca-bridge to a place called the Nine Mile

[1] See description of the Blaenavon line, p. 85, *ante.*
[2] Board of Trade Reports, 1849; App. 74.
[3] No branches appear in Priestley's map, but he mentions the last two in the book.

Point. Of this line between Newport and Risca-bridge, one mile called the Park Mile (sometimes the Golden Mile) passed through Tredegar Park, the property of Sir Charles Morgan, by whom it was made under the Act of 1802, which authorized the construction of a line from Sirhowy Ironworks by Tredegar Ironworks to Newport, and incorporated another company, the Sirhowy Tramroad Company, to construct the part of the line from Sirhowy Ironworks to Nine Mile Point; the Monmouth Canal Company making the line between the last-mentioned place and Newport, except the 'Park Mile'.[1]

The line was completed in 1805, having been laid out by John Hodgkinson under the direction of Benjamin Outram. The first locomotive made its appearance in 1829.

The canal company's hand had been forced by Homfray. In the 'Early History of the Old South Wales Iron Works, 1760–1840', by John Lloyd (1906), an interesting agreement is quoted, dated December 18th, 1800, which recited

that Homfray and Company were then erecting the Tredegar Iron Works . . . and had begun to make a tramroad to convey their iron, etc. from their works to a place called Pill at Newport, and that such tramroad would take a different line to any of the roads or branches of the Canal Navigation; that in consideration of Homfray and Company abandoning their proposed line the Canal Company would undertake to make a good and sufficient tramroad from the said Works to communicate with the Monmouthshire Canal Navigation at or near Risca church: the road to be open to the public on payment of the same tolls as are taken in the Newport District of Turnpike Roads. Samuel Homfray and Partners bound themselves to send all Iron, Coal, etc. from their works to Newport by that line.

A curious old drawing is reproduced in Fig. 55,[2] showing a switch. The original was made in 1808, and was sent by Richard Fothergill, of the Tredegar Ironworks, to the Canal Company at Newport, to direct the block-layers when putting down the passing-places on parts of their tramroads then under reconstruction or repair. The description given by the authorities of the Science Museum is as follows:

The drawing shows the lay-out of a junction or "parting" on a plateway. The switch and crossing plates are indicated, there being a movable tongue on one line only; outer guard flanges were cast on the

[1] Risca, Nine Mile Point, and Crumlin are 6½, 9, and 10 miles from Newport respectively. Tredegar Park is not near the works, but at the lower end of the line, close to Newport. This branch of the canal is still in existence, now called the Crumlin Canal.

[2] By permission of the Director of the Science Museum. See plate facing p. 89.

plates opposite the crossing plate, and all the plates forming the two inner lines were similarly provided with two flanges, probably to prevent them from being obstructed by the ballast disturbed by the horses' feet. The plates were 3 ft. long and laid to a gauge of 50 in. between the flanges, that being the distance advocated by Outram. The ends of the rails were widened by ears and were secured to the stone sleepers by a spike passing through a hole formed by notches cast in the adjacent rail ends. The drawing shows also the different forms of ear used on plates made for this Company.

It appears to have been designed in church. The following amusing story was related in the *South Wales Echo* for April 7th, 1915:

> The problem of the switch was agitating the minds of engineers at this time, and Mr. Richard Fothergill, of the Tredegar Iron-Works, had been turning the matter over in his mind. He was thus occupied during the sermon at Waunypound church one Sunday; drawing plans with his stick on the sawdust-covered floor. Suddenly an idea dawned on him, and he called out "That's it, by —". The old clergyman paused, aghast at the interruption, but the culprit looked up with a smile, and said "Go on, Mr. Price, it's all right now".

Returning to the Board of Trade Report, it is stated there that at the time of the passing of the Act of 1802 the works of the company in the Western Valleys consisted of the canal to Crumlin, with a tramroad from Crumlin to Beaufort Ironworks, and a railroad called the Rassa Railroad from Beaufort Ironworks to Sirhowy Ironworks.[1] The line from Crumlin to Beaufort Ironworks had originally been laid down as a railroad, but was subsequently altered by the company into a tramroad, by taking up the edge-rails and substituting tram-plates for them (in 1848 they reversed this policy). The old road from Beaufort to Sirhowy, called the Rassa Railroad, was left in its original state as a railroad, its gradients being very unfavourable, and it being very little used, except as a lime-stone road for the neighbouring works. Quoting:

> By the Act of 42 George III this company was authorised to con-struct in addition to the lines of tramroad between the Nine Mile Point and Newport, a branch line of tramroad from Risca-bridge to Crumlin. Having done so, they afterwards laid down a branch tramroad from Pont Aberbyg to Coal Brook Vale Iron-works.[2]

In the Western Valleys an unbroken communication by tramroad

---

[1] Beaufort is about 2 miles east of Sirhowy.

[2] Is it necessary to remark that these works were not the same as Coalbrookdale? The 'company' is of course the Monmouthshire Canal Company.

extends the whole way from the different works to Newport; in the Eastern, only to the canal at and above the Pontypool.

. . . .

The various tramways have in many instances been used as high roads, and villages have been erected along them, having no other roads of communication, even from house to house; and in the town of Newport good houses have been built with no means of access to any public road except across the tramroad. On one of the lines public horse-coaches and the mails travelled daily.

An early form of ribbon development! The passenger traffic began as soon as 1822, when John Kingson of Newport ran a horse-vehicle, known as 'the Caravan', between Newport and Tredegar. Afterwards, other people carried passengers, which any one was free to do on paying 6d., later 1s., per tram at each toll-gate. When the locomotives began to get about, they were prohibited on Saturdays, for fear of accidents, as the passenger traffic to Newport market was so heavy.

The Sirhowy line, at least the portion above Nine Mile Point, fell into the hands of the L. and N.W.R., and now forms the oldest piece of the London, Midland and Scottish Railway.

One would like to know more about the connexions with Nant-y-glo, which is a little over 3 miles east of Sirhowy. The description in the 'Edinburgh Encyclopaedia', quoted on p. 99, of the line there, refers to the Ebbw Vale Railway. Priestley says (p. 455) that the Nant-y-glo branch has a rise of 518 feet. The altitude of the present railway station is 1,075 feet above sea-level. According to the *Monmouthshire Merlin* of March 27th, 1830, there was a rack locomotive there which had been in use 'for a considerable time' by the date mentioned. Unfortunately nothing can be discovered about it.

With regard to the line, Cumming, writing in 1824, says:

Another line of tramroad, recently completed, branches off from the same canal [Brecknock], at a short distance from Abergavenny, and communicates with the extensive iron works of Mr. Bailey, at Nant y glo; the distance is only about eight miles, but such were the inequalities and unfavourable state of the ground over which the road must necessarily pass, that the difficulties and obstacles appeared to many well-informed and scientific persons as near to insurmountable; yet this enterprising proprietor, fearless of expense, cut his way through tremendous rocks, and actually completed the road in a workmanlike manner in the short space of seven months, to the astonishment of all who witnessed it.

Elsewhere, Cumming writes:

Some years ago a tramroad was made by the late Benjamin Hall, Esq. M.P., branching off from the Monmouthshire canal near Abercarnan [or Abercarn], in a north-west direction, to his collieries about nine miles distant.

This line was the Ebbw Vale Railroad.

There is an interesting account of the Hall family in 'The History of the Iron, Steel, Tinplate, and other Trades of Wales', by Charles Wilkins (1903). This Benjamin Hall married the daughter of Richard Crawshay, whom Wilkins calls 'the Iron King of Cyfartha',[1] in 1801, and his father-in-law bought Rhymney Works and gave them to the young couple as a marriage dowry. Their son became Lord Llanover.

A few further details have been obtained from an interesting little book 'Glimpses of West Gwent', by Rex H. Pugh (1934). A line which was made about 1805 'for the conveyance of minerals from the colliery at Manmoel to the Monmouthshire Canal Company's tramroad at Cross Keys' was known as 'Hall's road', having been built by him. There long existed an old stone viaduct, Hall's bridge, which spanned the valley near Pontywain. Hall's road has been converted into a railway and forms part of the Great Western system. Hall's eldest son, who was afterwards ennobled, was First Commissioner of Works under Lord Palmerston's government, 1855 to 1858, and Big Ben was called after him.

The other line shown in the map parallel to the Sirhowy Railway, but on the west side of it, is the Rumney Railway, which is of later date, having been constructed under an Act of 1825. It started from the former at Bassaleg, and ran up about 22 miles to 'Rumney Iron Forges', near Bedwellty; afterwards called Rhymney Ironworks. It was bought by the Brecon and Merthyr in 1863. It must not be confused with the Rhymney Railway, which was much later and more to the westward.

All three railways were called after the rivers whose valleys they followed.

The following passage from an account of a visit by King Edward VIII, in *The Times* of November 20th, 1936, describes the condition of the neighbourhood in these days:

> The run to Blaenavon, situated on a bleak wind-swept plateau, gave a vivid impression of the desolation which grips an area where the industries which created it have vanished to more favoured sites. Here was a broad expanse of slag heaps which Nature was doing its best to cover with a hint of verdure, not very successfully, but gone were the steel-works which could supply its only justification. Down in the valley were the idle collieries, partly dismantled and scarcely likely to be worked again.

---

[1] Cyfartha Castle was close to Merthyr, as also were the celebrated ironworks.

The Monmouthshire Canal was continued from its termination about a mile south of Pontypool by the Brecknock and Abergavenny Canal, which was 33 miles long, passing Abergavenny in its course. The Act, obtained in 1793, authorized the making of a navigable canal from the town of Brecknock to the Monmouthshire Canal, near Pontypool, 'and for making and maintaining Railways and Stone Roads to several Iron Works and Mines in the counties of Brecknock and Monmouth'. The 'Edinburgh Encyclopaedia' says: 'At the iron works near Pontypool there are some lofty inclined planes.'

Proceeding up the canal, we first come to the Mamhilad Railway, otherwise known as the Usk Tramroad. It was 5 miles and 3 chains in length, and went to the town of Usk. The Act was obtained in 1814, and stipulated that the line was to be made in three years. Lewin says 'not carried out', but Priestley speaks as if it had been made, and shows it on the map. About 8 miles farther, at Govilon, the Llanfihangel Railway went off in a north-easterly direction, passing Abergavenny, to a place called Llanfihangel Crucorney, a total distance of 6 miles. The Act was obtained in 1811. In the following year another company secured an Act for an extension, which was called the Grosmont Railway, nearly 7 miles long, prolonging it to Llangua Bridge, close to the border of Herefordshire. It was eventually continued to Hereford, by the railway of that name.[1] At first they were all plate-ways.

Ten miles or so farther on, was the Brynoer Tramroad, running south 8 or 9 miles over the 'Black Mountain' to the 'Blaen Rumney', otherwise Rhymney, Ironworks.

Hay Railway. Acts 1811 and 1812. Priestley describes it thus:

This railway commences at the wharf of the Brecknock and Abergavenny Canal, not far from the town of Brecon, and pursuing a circuitous course through a mountainous district, in some parts 670 feet or more above the level of the sea, it ends at the village of Eardisley, in the county of Hereford, where a junction of the Kington Railway[2] has since been made with it.

The engineer was John Hodgkinson, who laid out a number of railways in this neighbourhood. The length was 24 miles. The author has been taken over practically the whole route by Captain F. B. Ellison, of Eardisley, who has made an exhaustive study of this line. A good deal of it ran by the sides of the present roads. The original minute-book for 1811 to

[1] See p. 64, *ante*.　　　　　　　　[2] See p. 55, *ante*.

1833 has survived, and as it is possibly a unique document a number of extracts are given.

The first of the reasons put forward for making the line was to save damage to the turnpike roads. From the list of proprietors, it is obvious that there was no hostility to the scheme; all the important landowners and inhabitants of the district appear to be included. Among the 'Commissioners', who were appointed to settle any differences that might arise between the Company and owners of land to be taken, the name of James Watt is included. (He resided not far away.)

It was enacted that where the line crossed any turnpike road or public highway, 'the ledge or Flaunch, for the purpose of guiding the wheels of the Carriages, should not exceed one inch in Height above the level of such Road'.

A share certificate was called a 'Ticket or Instrument'. What we should call 'stations' were 'Toll-Houses'; where there were sheds or sidings, 'Wharfs'; terms taken from the road and the canal.

All persons were to have 'free Liberty' to use the railway on payment of the rates. Waggons were to be properly constructed, with the owners' names painted on them in letters 3 inches high.

July 31st 1811. Resolved that an advertisement should be inserted in the Hereford Journal inviting Iron Masters and others to contract for the supply of 2,000 tons of tram plates, to be made of good strong bodied Grey Iron and of the Cheltenham Railroad Pattern, weighing not exceeding 50 pounds per plate.

The list of the Tenderers is of interest. The prices were from £6 16s. 6d. to £7 17s. 6d. per ton.

Bailey & Wayne, Nantyglo Iron Works
Frere & Co., Clydach Iron Works
Hill & Co., Blaenavon
Harford & Co., Ebbw Vale[1]
Mr. Hall, Romney Iron Works

On December 6th, 1811, the clerk was instructed to advertise for 20,000 stone blocks, to weigh 168 lb. each; the price to be $7\frac{1}{2}d$. The blocks on this line were unlike the usual ones, being utterly irregular in shape. A flat was formed to take the rails, but no attempt was made to square them up.

On January 20th, 1818, the clerk was ordered to apply to Mr. Rastrick, engineer, of Bridgnorth, for a plan of a bridge to be erected over the

---

[1] A rail preserved in the Hereford Museum has E V cast on it.

Wye at Whitney. The design, an engraving of which is in existence, was duly delivered.

March 2nd, 1818. Mr. Rastrick's Plan for an Iron Suspension Bridge was considered, and it appeared that the cost of making a Bridge would far exceed the Resources of the Company. Resolved that the Plan of a Boat or Boats for passing the Tram Wagons over the River Wye is the most advisable to be adopted, and that the Clerk make Inquiry respecting the Boat at Chepstow recommended by Mr. Rastrick, and correspond with Mr. Rastrick respecting the necessary machinery.

The eventual solution consisted in laying the rails over the road bridge at Whitney, which of course involved the payment of tolls, eventually compounded for at £100 a year. This bridge, which was originally made under an Act of 20 George III, still exists, after two destructions and reconstructions, and tolls are levied and paid to the representatives of the original owners; a state of affairs which the Herefordshire County Council are endeavouring to bring to an end. Over the bridge, the rails were trough-shaped, for greater safety.

On December 11th, 1818, the clerk was reimbursed the sum of 'ffive Pounds the Price of ffour Tons of Coal given to the Poor on the opening of the Road to Eardisley' and a similar sum for gratuities to the workmen.

On August 8th, 1820, it was ordered that 'the Company supply the contractor with iron sleepers . . .'; unfortunately the rest of the minute is so badly written as to be illegible.

In September 1828 it was laid down that no waggon was to be allowed 'unless the Axle Trees of the Wheels be at least three ffeet & one Inch apart'. A year later it was determined that 'all the Hauliers be compelled to use Shafts to their foremost Waggon and that not more than eight Waggons be allowed to follow each other'.

The amounts paid for land seem to be very moderate; those for repairs—mostly to Hodgkinson—very heavy.

Lewin says this line was sold in 1860 to the Hereford, Hay and Brecon Railway, by whom portions of the old route were utilized in forming their line, which was absorbed by the Midland Railway in 1886.

The only remaining railways in Wales were in the north. From Tredgold we gather one in Denbighshire, which is just mentioned in passing by Priestley, viz. the Ruabon Brook Railway. This line, Tredgold tells us,

commences from an extensive basin at Pontcysylte, on the north bank of the river Dee; it is a double rail-way, and proceeds with a gentle ascent past Mr. Hazeldine's iron-works, and through numerous collieries to Ruabon Brook, a distance of 3 miles.

At Pontcysylte there was Telford's famous cast-iron aqueduct which carried the Ellesmere and Chester Canal over the Dee. Hazeldine was Rastrick's partner in the works at Stourbridge.

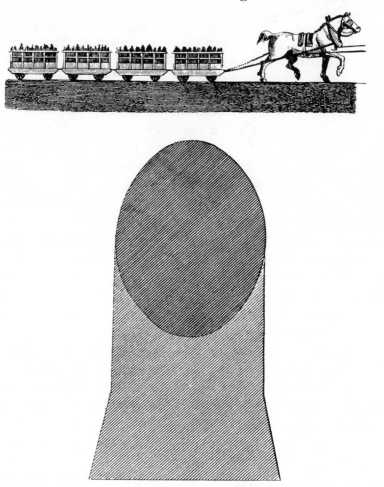

FIG. 58.   Penrhyn Railway, with section of rail

Moving north-westward, we come to a railway at the Penrhyn slate-quarries, which is of rather unique interest. There is a very interesting 'Account of the Penrhyn Iron Railway' in 'Repertory of Arts and Manufactures', vol. iii, 2nd series (1803). It was 'communicated by the Inventor, Mr. Benjamin Wyatt, of Lime Grove near Bangor', and illustrated by the plate reproduced in Fig. 58. He said:

The rail hitherto made use of in most railways is a flat one, three feet in length, with a rib on one edge, to give it strength, and to prevent the wheels (which have a flat rim) from running off. Observing that these rails were frequently obstructed by stones and dirt lodging upon them; that they were obliged to be fastened to single stones or blocks on account of their not rising sufficiently high above the sills to admit of gravelling the horse-path, that the sharp rib standing up was dangerous for the horses, that the strength of the rail was applied the wrong way; and that less surface would create less friction; led me to consider if some better form of rail could not be applied; the oval presented itself as the best adapted to correct all the faults of the flat rail, and I have the satisfaction to say that it has completely answered the purpose in a railway lately executed for Lord Penrhyn, from his Lordship's slate-quarries in Carnarvonshire, to Port Penrhyn (the place of shipping). The wheel made use of on this rail has a concave rim, so contrived in its form, and the wheels so fixed on their axes, as to move with the greatest facility in the sharpest curves that can be required.

The Penrhyn Railway (which was close to Bangor) was $6\frac{1}{4}$ miles in length, divided into four stages. It had $\frac{3}{8}$ inch fall in a yard (1 in 96), with three inclines. Port Penrhyn is at the upper end of the Menai Straits.

It was begun in October 1800 and finished in July 1801. Two horses drew 24 waggons one stage six times a day, carrying 24 tons each journey. The rails were 4 feet 6 inches long, weight 36 lb. 'The part below the oval was cast to each end of the rail 3 inches long, to let into the sills, which have a dovetail notch to receive them.' By sills, Wyatt meant sleepers, which were cast iron, curved downwards in the middle.

Hebert ('Practical Treatise on Railroads', 1837) says Wyatt found that the oval form of rail quickly wore the concave rims of the wheels into hollows, and rendered it necessary to change them very often. He therefore made the tops of the rails flat, the central part of the rims of the wheels being also flattened, with flanges on both sides. Tredgold gives a drawing of the improved form, which shows the curved 'sills'. This railway is ignored by Priestley, on account of its private character.

At the southern end of the Menai Straits there was the Nantlle Railway, made under Acts of 1825, 1827, and 1828, being opened in the latter year. It commenced

at the Gloddfarlon Slate Quarries, near Nantlle Pool, and proceeding in a westerly direction for some distance, it turns at right angles to the north, in which direction it proceeds to its termination at the shipping quay at Carnarvon. (Priestley.)

The length was $9\frac{1}{4}$ miles. It was eventually absorbed by the Carnarvonshire Railway Company, and today forms a branch of the L.M. & S.R.

There is an interesting letter relating to this line in the Phillimore collection, addressed to 'Geo. Stephenson Esqr., Railway Office, Liverpool'; dated from Carnarvon, August 8th, 1827.

Dear Brother,

According to your instructions I went up the line to the slate quarries to examine the quality of the slate. I found by enquiry the blue ones will stand the weather well. Mr. Smedley was with me at the time when we agreed with a person to find the stone and bore any quantity wanted. I here send you a copy of his proposal for your approval.

Gentlemen, I hereby undertake to supply your company with thirty-three thousand stone blocks not less in size and equal in every respect quality &c. to four blocks now in penrhyn quarry yard under the care of Wm. Jones at three shillings pr. dozen to be delivered as I may hereafter be directed on any part of the rail-way on this side of peny y groes within three months from this date each block to have two holes four inches deep $\frac{3}{4}$ in. diameter. Mr. R. Stephenson or Mr. Gillespie to have the power on the part of Company to reject any blocks they may not approve. Cilgwyn Augt 2d. 1827. Signed John Edwards.

The same person also agrees to supply the company with sixty thousand oak pins for the blocks and put them in at 6d. pr. dozen. I intent to try to bore the white slate, it can be had of any size they will make an excellent block for the joints. With respect to the state of rail-way you may expect a report in a short time we have not had time to take the proper levels, there is four miles ready to lay we only wait for iron and carriages I beg you'll forward the chairs from Mr. Kennedy's foundry. I will have a wheel pattern finished soon which I'll send to Liverpool. I think the way will be better a little wider than three feet six, for that will only allow a carriage to come between the wheels three feet two. The road is so uncommonly curved that I think short carriages will suit the quick curves best, as long ones the sole ends are liable to pass each other. The cut at Carnarvon large cut & tunnel at Dinas are carried on as bad as possible in every respect. The Gentlemen here at a meeting desired us not interfere with Mr. Williams he to have the whole management of the works, we only to lay the way. I fear we can render the company little service until the present agents are removed. The company are losing a fine season they have some large cuts and embankments to make yet and those they have made are only half finished. I remain Dear Brother,

Yours respectfully,
Robt. Stephenson.

Only two more railways remain to be described in Wales, so far as the author's researches have carried him. There was the Anglesey Railway, called by Priestley the Penrhynmaur Railway. Authorized under an

Act of 1812, it was to run from Penrhynmawr in a north-easterly direction to Red Wharf Bay, on the north coast of Anglesey, the length being 7 miles and 4 chains. Clapham, in the second edition of his 'Economic History of Modern Britain', vol. i, (1930) described it thus:

a curious little line, seven miles long, ran from the tiny scrap of coal measures, which a geological accident has preserved in the heart of Anglesey, across the Holyhead high road to the sea at Red Wharf Bay.

In fact this line was never constructed, although it appears as an accomplished work in Joseph Priestley's 'Historical Account of the Navigable Rivers, Canals, and Railways throughout Great Britain' (1831) and later in at least four other authorities.[1]

It may be noted that Scott's 'Highland' paper gives a detail not mentioned by other writers, saying: 'The slate-quarries above Bangor and Carnarvon situate on the Menai Straits have iron rail-roads, with several inclined planes.'

Another 'slate railway' was from slate-quarries in the north of Merionethshire to Port Madoc just over the border of Carnarvonshire, attaining the latter point over an embankment across the mouth of the Traeth Mawr, made in 1807. Part of the route was used later for the Festiniog Railway.[2]

Since writing the above chapter, some information of great interest has been received from Mr. Stanley Davies, which will be found in the Index, under headings:

Bersham
Chirk
Ewloe
Saltney
Stondart Quarry Railway.

[1] Kenneth Brown, 'Anglesey's Ghost Railway', *Railway Magazine*, July 1940, pp. 1–3; and *Railway Magazine*, January 1941, p. 36, where the evidence is summarized. Two other authors who spotted the error are H. G. Lewin, 'Early British Railways' (1925), p. 7, and A. H. Dodd, 'The Industrial Revolution in North Wales' (1933), p. 111.

[2] See J. I. C. Boyd, 'The Festiniog Railway', vol. i, 1800–89 (1st edn. 1956, 3rd edn. 1966), pp. 1–15; M. J. T. Lewis, 'How Ffestiniog got its Railway' (1968); E. Beazley, 'Madocks and the Wonders of Wales' (1967), ch. XII.

CHAPTER VI

EARLY RAILWAYS IN SCOTLAND AND IRELAND

Rᴏʙᴇʀᴛ Sᴛᴇᴠᴇɴsᴏɴ's report of 1818 on Edinburgh railways is valuable in connexion with Scottish lines. Although those forming its subject were not made—immediately, at all events—there is much useful information about the lines already in existence at the time. The following are some extracts:

> In the recollection of some persons still living . . . owing to the miserable and circumscribed state of the roads, or rather the want of formed roads altogether, pit-coal continued to be conveyed in sacks and on horse back, for supplying the city of Edinburgh.

> We might mention the name of the late Mr. Jᴇssᴏᴘ as the first engineer of eminence who seems to have introduced Railways in the South. He was also the engineer for the magnificent works of his Grace the Duke of Pᴏʀᴛʟᴀɴᴅ in Scotland, connected with which there is a double Railway from Kilmarnock to Troon, which is ten miles in length. The other railways in Scotland of any extent are those at the works of the Carron Company, Lord Eʟɢɪɴ's, Mr. Eʀsᴋɪɴᴇ of Mar's, Sir Jᴏʜɴ Hᴏᴘᴇ's, and other coal-works. A Public Railway has also been projected from Berwick-upon-Tweed to Glasgow; an extent of country of about 125 miles; and an act of Parliament has already been obtained, for completing part of this track, viz. from Berwick to Kelso.

> Since this Report was put to press Mr. Rᴜᴛʜᴠᴇɴ, who some time since obtained a patent for an improved Printing Press, has made several experiments upon the Railway at the works of Mr. Cᴀᴅᴇʟʟ of Cockenzie, with a view to apply the principle of the crank so successfully used in his Printing Press, to propel waggons up an inclined plane.

The earliest tramway north of the Border was that between Tranent and Cockenzie; the latter place being on the coast 1 mile east of Prestonpans, and adjoining Port Seton.

In 1719 the York Buildings Company acquired the estate of Tranent, part of the lands of the Earl of Winton, who was attainted after the rebellion of 1715. A short note on the subject of this interesting company will perhaps not be out of place—gathered from 'The York Buildings Society', by David Murray (1883).

On May 7th, 1675, Charles II granted Letters Patent under the Great

Seal to Ralph Bucknall and Richard Wayne, empowering them for a period of 99 years to erect a 'water work' and water house near the river Thames, upon part of the grounds of York House, in York House garden, and to dig and lay ponds, pipes, and cisterns for the purpose of supplying the inhabitants of St. James's Fields and Piccadilly with water at reasonable rents.

The water was at first pumped up by a machine worked by two horses; then by a Savery engine, erected about 1712, followed by one of Newcomen's, put up in 1725. The company (which had been incorporated by an Act of Parliament in 1691 as 'The Governor and Company of Undertakers for raising Thames Water in York Buildings') was dissolved in 1829. They made large purchases by way of investment in the forfeited estates of the Highlanders, which, of course, no Scotsman would touch.

In connexion with the development of their estate, they renovated and enlarged the harbour of Cockenzie, and in 1722 constructed a railway from the coal-pits in the neighbourhood of Tranent, to the harbour, which was about two miles away.

The following information has been supplied to the author by Mr. Lewis I. Cadell, of Edinburgh.

The line ran on a gradual slope downwards to the sea, crossing a marsh on an embankment which played its part in history, as will be seen. At first, wooden rails were used, laid on stone blocks. The collieries were operated by various tenants during the ownership of the York Buildings Company, who sold the estate by auction in the year 1779; when it was purchased by John Cadell, who, along with his elder brother, William, had for some time been tenants of the colliery, and carried on salt-making and other industries in the neighbourhood. The ships which brought rock salt from Sweden usually took back a cargo of coal, and there was a good coastal trade as well.

In 1815 iron rails were substituted for the old wooden rails and the railway was continued with waggons each weighing 2 tons gross. On the downward journey for the greater part of the way the waggons descended by their own weight, and the horse walked behind, a man walking on one side with a sprag with which to brake the wheels if the waggons went too fast. The principal work for the horse was to bring up the empty waggons.

The railway was a single line with two crossing-places, and continued in operation till between 1880 and 1890. By this time the small vessels which suited Cockenzie Harbour were being superseded by larger steamers and most of the coal for shipment was sent by railway line to Leith, and the use of the old line was discontinued. The southern portion was adapted and used for a railway siding connecting the collieries to the south with the North British Railway, while the section between the railway line and Cockenzie Harbour was abandoned for transport purposes.

An interesting historical episode occurred in the rebellion of 1745, when Sir John Cope stationed six or seven pieces of cannon on the embankment at the battle of Prestonpans.

The experiments made by Ruthven on this line to which Stevenson referred are described in the Highland Society's *Transactions* as an arrangement worked by a winch handle turned by a man; the description is difficult to follow. The editor cautiously says: 'Experience is still wanting to show that Mr. Ruthven's machine would be useful upon a railway to the extent alleged, although this may be worthy of a further trial.'

Scott's essay, speaking of this line, says: 'The breadth of the horse-track is 3 feet 3 inches.' Whether by that he is referring to the actual gauge does not appear.

Moving a little westwards, we come to Sir John Hope's line, of Pinkie. It is mentioned by Cumming and in Stevenson's Report, also in Scott's essay. Cumming gives it the credit for the first introduction of malleable iron rails, but this is unlikely to be correct.[1] Maclaren ('Railways compared with Canals & Common Roads', 1825) says:

On the dead-level Railway constructed by Mr. John Grieve for Sir John Hope near Musselburgh, which is one of the most perfect in Britain, a single horse draws five loaded waggons, each containing 30 cwt. of coals, at the rate of four miles an hour—in all $7\frac{1}{2}$ tons, exclusive of the waggons, which weigh 3 tons more.

It was not a 'dead-level' railway. Telford's memorandum book, quoted in his 'Life', on p. 689, gives these details:

Distance, 2 Miles.

Pinkie single railroad
- 1st —$\frac{1}{3}$—descends at 1 in 72.
- 2d —$\frac{1}{3}$—nearly level.
- 3d —$\frac{1}{3}$—rises 1 in 700.

One horse draws 4 waggons, with $1\frac{1}{2}$ tons each: waggon weighs about 12 cwt. Horse makes 5 trips a day.

The exact location would be unknown, were it not for the fact that it has been painted in by a contemporary hand, together with the Tranent and Cockenzie, in the map in the author's copy of Stevenson's Report; as

[1] See p. 151, *post*.

sketched in Fig. 59. The map as printed only showed the railways proposed by Stevenson, but some former owner has added neatly in green 'Existing Railways', and the probabilities are that they are fairly correct.

The railway shown in Fig. 59 to the westward, which has also been added to the author's map, appears to be the only one of Stevenson's railway schemes which was carried out at the time. Tomlinson mentions it in his 'History of the North Eastern Railway', saying that Stevenson (in 1818) 'had just completed the Newton or Edmonston Railway (from Newton Colliery to the Edinburgh and Dalkeith road, near Little France).' Scott just mentions it, as a line belonging to Mr. Wauchope of Edmonston.[1]

Besides the numerous lines proposed in his Report of 1818, which were all within a comparatively small radius of Edinburgh, Stevenson also formulated schemes which were more ambitious. There is a map of 1819 in the Phillimore collection showing lines projected by him from Aberdeen to Perth, Crieff to Dunfermline, Stirling, &c. He was just a few years before his time.

Among the railways near Edinburgh, Robertson's 'Highland' essay (1824) mentions 'Mr. Laing's railway near Edinburgh'; edge-rails, $3\frac{3}{4}$ miles long. This line has not been identified.

The Edinburgh and Dalkeith Railway was authorized by an Act of 1826 entitled 'An Act for making . . . a Railway from Edinburgh to the South Side of the River North Esk, near Dalkeith and Newbattle, with Branches therefrom'. It was a horse railway, intended for the purpose of conveying coals to Edinburgh. Although Priestley describes it, and the branches, as if it had been completed at the time he was writing, it was not opened until 1831. He says that at Redrow it communicated with the Edmonston Railway. It was purchased by the N.B.R. in 1845.

The West Lothian Railway Company was incorporated under an Act of 1825. Priestley says:

This railway commences at the Edinburgh and Glasgow Union Canal, near Ryhall, in the parish of Uphall, and proceeds south-westerly to Houston, where a branch goes off to the Silver Mines; it is then continued to Housden, where another branch runs off to Balbardie; the main line, passing Whiteburn, proceeds to Shotts, where it terminates. . . .

The length of this railway is about fifteen miles, with a rise of 322 feet; the Silver Mines branch is four miles and seven chains in length, with a rise of 410 feet; and the Balbardie branch is four miles and four chains, with a rise of 69 feet.

[1] Andrew Wauchope of 'Edmonstone in Midlothian' is known to have been the purchaser of a Newcomen engine early in the eighteenth century. See 'The Collected Papers of Rhys Jenkins' (1936), p. 84.

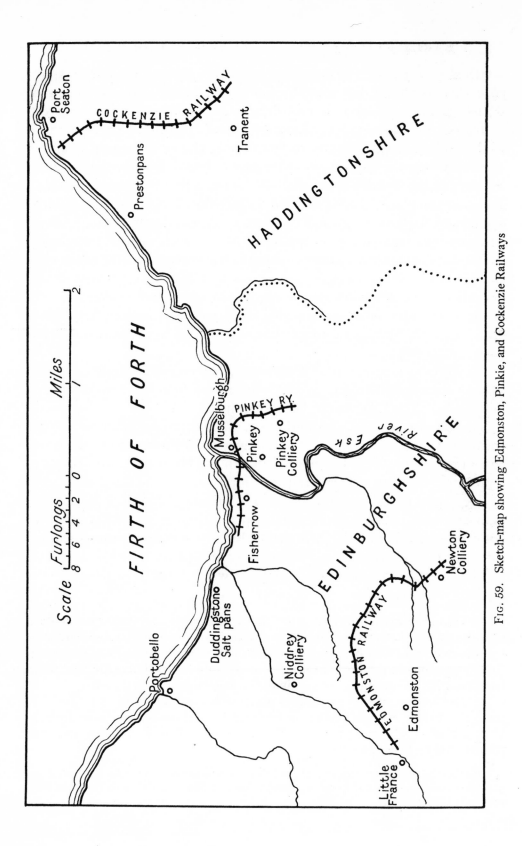

FIG. 59. Sketch-map showing Edmonston, Pinkie, and Cockenzie Railways

The author has a copy of a report on this line dated December 18th, 1824, by Hugh Baird, who surveyed it. Cast-iron rails were to be used, and, of course, horses for traction. The 'Silver Mines' were then limeworks.

Priestley's description, coupled with the fact that he shows it in the map, leads one to think it was made, but Lewin says it was never carried out.

At the Shotts Ironworks, where it terminated, or was intended to, there had been an earlier-railway, as it is recorded in a 'General Report of the Agricultural State and Political Circumstances of Scotland' (vol. iii, 1814) that 'a horse in 1813 drew three tons of iron in a common cart up an ascent of 1 in 15 at the Shotts Iron Works'. The term 'common cart' suggests that it was a plate-railway, which was a rarity in Scotland. Scott also just mentions it. Shotts is about 20 miles south-east of Glasgow.

Before proceeding to the latter locality, we will cross to the north side of the Forth, and deal with an interesting line about which very little has appeared in railway literature. To begin with Scott's description in his 'Highland' essay:

> The railway on Lord Elgin's works between Dunfermline and Lime-kilns in Fife, for design and execution, is inferior to none. On this line of railway there are two inclined planes; executed with all the requisite machinery, for the loaded waggons drawing up the empty ones; the longest of these is about 511 yards, with a declivity of about one in twenty. Between the two inclined planes the ground had been originally level to some extent: an ingenious advantage is taken of this level, by commencing, at a short distance from the foot of the upper inclined plane, and cutting out a track for a railway, with an easy slope in the line of the main descending railway for the loaded waggons, by banking up the earth, and facing it with a stone wall; another railway is formed with a similar slope, but in a contrary direction, towards the foot of the upper inclined plane. In this manner the two railways are carried forward until they reach the top or bank-head of the under inclined plane, where the difference of perpendicular height between the two appears to be about ten feet; the one-half of this height gives a declivity to the loaded waggons to proceed downwards; and the other half a declivity to the empty waggons to proceed to the foot of the upper inclined plane: the brake or drag of the loaded waggons has only to be attended to, for regulating their motion to the place where they start on the inclined plane.

The construction of the embankment, with the two lines on different levels, is shown in Fig. 60, which is reproduced from an old water-colour sketch.

Through the kindness of Lord Elgin, it is possible to supply a considerable amount of information about the railway made by his ancestor. The following details have been obtained from 'Limekilns and Passagium

Reginae', compiled under the instructions of the Rt. Hon. the Lord Wavertree of Delamere, 1929 (for private circulation; 215 copies only).

In the early nineteenth century a railway line came down from the coal-mines on the east[1] side of the Broomhall estate and terminated at Lime-kilns, a small seaport village on the north side of the Forth, a little to the west of Rosyth. The Broomhall estate is on high ground immediately above Limekilns, and belongs to Lord Elgin.

The lime of Limekilns and Charlestown (a village close by on the west, also possessing a small harbour) was famous and was used for building many harbours.[2] The lime from Charlestown was formerly shipped from the piers of Limekilns and Brucehaven (which is close by). A railway was run from Charlestown kilns to these piers, first of all narrow rails for 'hutches',[3] and then wider ones for waggons which brought it to the near approaches of the harbours, drawn, of course, by horses in the early times. There are still to be seen the old stables at Charlestown (now a shop and post office) where Lord Elgin's horses were kept for this purpose. Horse-haulage, and not rope-haulage, was used for the quarries to the docks in 1760.

Coming to comparatively recent times, we read:

In the sixties of last century the Charlestown and Dunfermline Railway took over most of the transportation of lime, and by 1870 we might say that shipping from Limekilns and Brucehaven received its death-blow, though it lingered on at Charlestown for a time.

In the 'Statistical Account of Scotland', published in 1794, there is the following passage, speaking of Charles, fifth Earl of Elgin:

In the years 1777 and 1778 his lordship began to build nine large draw-kilns,[4] a harbour, waggon-ways for drawing the stone from the quarries to kilnheads, and a village for accommodating his work people which, after himself, was called Charlestown.

The dates are too late, as the fifth Earl died in 1771, and statistics of the works dated in that year are still in existence. It is suggested that 1767 and 1768 would be nearer the mark.

The present Lord Elgin has a scroll about 3 feet 6 inches long, dated 1784, which describes the 'hutches', or coal-waggons. At the top there is a drawing of one hauled by a horse, which has a strong resemblance to the Buddle truck shown in Fig. 6, although not so 'flared'. Like the

[1] Originally so. But when Charlestown Harbour was built, a new line was made on the west side, as shown in the map (Fig. 63).
[2] e.g. Leith and Dundee.   [3] Small waggons.
[4] Kilns so constructed that the burnt lime is drawn out at the bottom.

Fig. 60. An embankment on the Elgin Railway

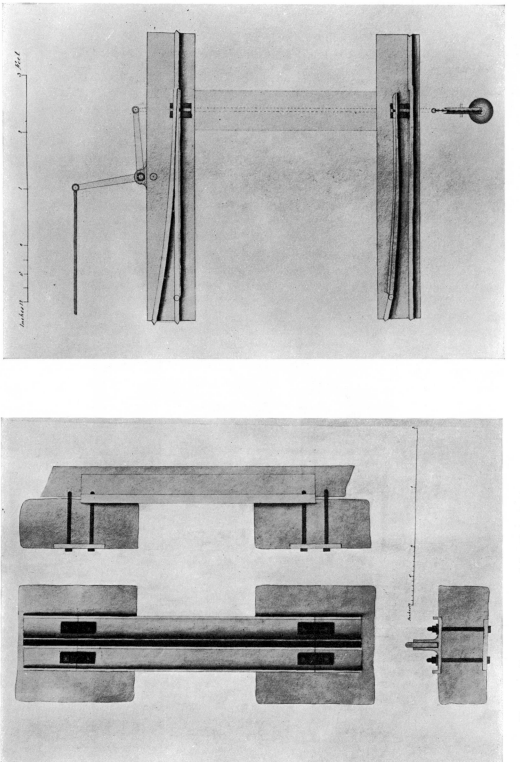

Fig. 62. Switch, Elgin Railway

Fig. 61. Permanent way of the Elgin Railway

latter, the front wheels were of cast iron, with spokes; and the rear wheels, solid wooden disks. They held '$2\frac{1}{2}$ tons of Great Coal' (enlarged to 3 tons by 1796), and cost £13.[1] The iron wheels were 41 inches diameter, with 10 spokes, and cost £3 3s. 0d. the pair; the wooden ones were 42 inches, 'rough from the wood', and were priced at 18s. There were 378 nails of various sizes (4s. 7d.).

Lord Elgin has a number of very interesting large drawings, undated, but on paper watermarked from 1821 to 1823, showing inclined planes, cuttings, tunnels, &c. From these Figs. 60–2 have been reproduced. The construction in longitudinal iron troughs must have been very costly.

The drawings also show an early example of tapered points (Fig. 62). As late as 1839, Bourne's 'London and Birmingham Railway' shows the movable rail parallel, with a square end. The drawings of the inclined planes depict loaded trucks pulling up empty ones by a rope passing over a wheel. These evidently apply to an alteration in the line which was effected in 1821, and is mentioned presently, but that of the embankment is presented in a manner which is almost certainly meant to indicate that it was copied from an older drawing. Others also show this peculiarity.

The rails are no doubt those which were adopted when the line was remodelled in 1821. The original line must have been a wooden one.

Further information can be gathered from a 'Historical and Statistical Account of Dunfermline', by the Rev. Peter Chalmers, vol. i, 1844, vol. ii, 1859.

Some remarks he makes about the beginning of the coal industry in Scotland are of great interest. Coal was wrought near Dunfermline in very early times, as a charter of 1291 is in existence, whereby William de Oberwill, proprietor of Pittencrieff estate, adjoining the town, granted to the Abbot and Convent of Dunfermline the privilege of working a coal-pit on his property for their own use, but not for purposes of sale. Mr. Chalmers also gives a quotation from an account of Scotland written by Boethius, at the beginning of the sixteenth century, as follows:

There are black stones also digged out of the ground, which are very good for firing, and such is their intolerable heat, that they resolve and melt iron, and therefore, are very profitable for smiths and such artificers as deal with other metals; neither are they found anywhere else (that I know of) but between the Tay and Tyne,[2] within the whole Island.

[1] Ralph Allen's trucks, it may be remarked, cost upwards of £30 each.
[2] He may have been referring not to the Tyne in Northumberland, but to one of the same name flowing in a north-easterly direction through Haddingtonshire roughly parallel with the south shore of the Firth of Forth and entering the sea near Dunbar.

With reference to Lord Elgin's railway, it says that his coal

is conveyed to his limeworks and shipping at Charleston by a railroad, the two inclined planes of which, near the town of Dunfermline, are much admired, and were executed on a change of the line of the rail-road in 1821, at a very great expense, under the direction of the late ingenious Mr. Landale of Dundee. The Wellwood coal for exportation is now also conveyed along this railway, which is connected with that Colliery by a branch line.

The railway is about six miles in length, but longer when the branches to the different pits, etc., are taken into account. There are from 100 to 500 tons of coal generally conveyed along it in a day, according to the demand, or the number of vessels lying in the Charleston harbour waiting for them. . . . There have been at times 2,000 tons sent down by the Elgin Railway in one fortnight.

It was exported to the Baltic and Mediterranean ports; also France, where the steamboats plying between Paris and Rouen used it almost entirely.

The Wellwood branch does not appear in the map, from which Fig. 63 has been adapted. No details are given of the Halbeath Railway shown on the map, except that there were 15 horses employed on it (20 to 24 on the Elgin line).

Passengers were conveyed at an early period. In 1834 a branch was made

to the Elgin railroad from the bottom of the town of Dunfermline, along which goods of various kinds are transported to and from the packets at Charleston; and an Omnibus runs at various hours every day, to and from the same harbour, for the conveyance of passengers by the steamboats on the Forth.

Figures are given, for the years 1838 to 1843, of 'passengers shipped and landed at Charleston, most of whom travelled by this railway', averaging just over 23,000 per year. It had, therefore, become a public railway.

In Mr. Chalmers' second volume, which appeared in 1859, we find some information on the subject of later developments, for instance:

Steam was for the first time introduced on the Railway to Charleston in February 1852, whereby that seaport is brought within 10 or 15 minutes of Dunfermline. There is one large railway carriage, able to accommodate about 50 passengers.

A junction is mentioned (Colton), which had been made with the

Stirling and Dunfermline Railway, then belonging to the Edinburgh and Glasgow Company.

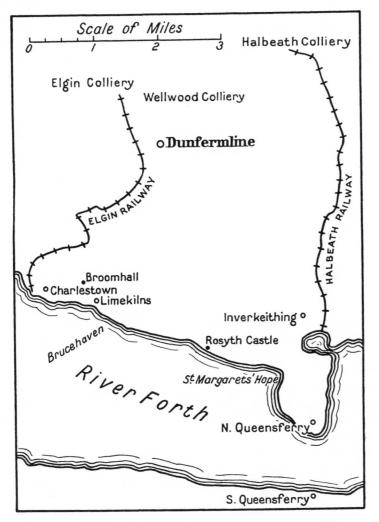

FIG. 63. Sketch-map showing the Elgin and Halbeath Railways

The working of the Elgin line after the introduction of locomotives is thus described:

There are two inclines on the railroad near to the town of Dunfermline and a third at the shore. The coals are conveyed by a locomotive engine from the pits to the top of the first incline at the Colton station, east end of Golf Drum Street, and from the bottom of it they are drawn a short distance by horses, to the top of the second incline, which commences a little south of Pittencrieff toll-bar, and are afterwards conveyed by another locomotive, which takes also goods and passengers from the Nethertown station in the town of Dunfermline to the steamboats that ply between Stirling and Granton pier.

The upper and lower portions of the Elgin Railway now form mineral branches of the L. & N.E.R.; the middle portion through the Burgh of Dunfermline, including the inclines, having been discontinued.

ALLOA RAILWAY

Some information concerning lines about 12 miles to the west of the Elgin Railway has been obtained from a description of Alloa in Clackmannanshire, given in 'The Statistical Account of Scotland' by Sir John Sinclair, vol. viii (1793), as follows:

To the west of the ferry stands a glass house, for making bottles, which is thought to be the most conveniently situated of any in Britain. It can have whatever quantity of coals it requires, at a very easy rate, as they are conveyed from the pits, to the very doors of the glass house, by a waggon way.

In 1768 a waggon way was made to the Alloa pits, which proved to be so great an advantage, that it induced the proprietor to extend it to the Collyland, in 1771. . . . In 1785 the Alloa waggon way was worn out, and required to be renewed. This was done on a new plan; and it is now acknowledged to be the most complete in Britain. . . . The sleepers are very broad, and only 18 inches from centre to centre. A rail of foreign fir, 4 inches square, is pinned down to them, and another rail, of the same dimensions, is laid over it, and the whole well beat up in good clay; on the top of the upper rail is laid a bar of malleable iron, of $1\frac{3}{4}$ inches breadth and nearly six-8ths thick. The waggons have cast iron wheels, $27\frac{1}{2}$ inches diameter, and are supposed to weigh altogether about a ton. A waggon carries 30 cwt. of coals and 3 waggons are linked together by chains; so that 1 horse draws $4\frac{1}{2}$ tons of coal at once; and the declivity of the way is so gentle that the same horse draws with ease the 3 empty waggons back to the coal-hill. . . .

The first expense of making this kind of waggon way is undoubtedly great, being at least 10s. per running yard.

Tredgold says the Alloa Railway was $2\frac{1}{2}$ miles long.

In 'A General View of the Coal Trade of Scotland . . .' by Robert Bald, civil engineer, Alloa (1808), it is stated that John Francis Erskine of Mar was proprietor of the Alloa collieries. In the year 1709 John, Earl of Mar, sent the manager of his works to Newcastle to inspect the machinery of that district. 'At that time, waggon-ways were in use at Newcastle, but they were not introduced into Scotland till a considerable time afterwards.'

FIG. 64. Iron bridge, Carron Railway (1810–1905)

Returning across the Forth, a letter written by William Brown in 1754 (quoted in T. V. Simpson's paper on Old Mining Records which has been previously mentioned) refers to an underground railway at Bo'ness, thus:

At Burroughstones I was assisting to contrive a Waggon Way underground on which will have to bring the Coales 600 yards at first starting tho at present they are Convey'd from the face of the workings to the pitts Bottoms and in some places up the Shafts upon womans Backs which poor Creatures Carries some of them 13 Stones weight of Coales at a time in there Creals.

THE CARRON COMPANY

A little to the westward we come to the Carron Railways. With reference to them, Mr. George Pate, the manager of the Carron Company, has kindly supplied the following information.

Their first line, from Kinnaird Colliery into the interior of Carron Works, a distance of about 2 miles, was constructed in about 1766. The rails in that instance were of wood, covered with a sort of hoop iron.[1]

What was known as the 'Old Wagon Road' was laid down in 1810, and connected the works with Bainsford Basin on the Forth and Clyde Canal. It was rather narrower than the standard gauge and ran alongside the public road for a distance of nearly 2 miles. It continued in use until about 1860, but, owing to its situation and construction, locomotives were never employed upon it, the waggons being drawn by horses. Its main purpose was to convey pig-iron, sugar pans, &c., to Burnhouse Basin, at which point the company's own sailing-ships were loaded for Liverpool.

An iron bridge, shown in the accompanying illustration, was suspended from the side of a stone bridge which had been erected in 1775; prior to which all materials, &c., to and from the Carron Works had to be ferried across the river in carts. The iron girders extended right through the stone arches to the other side. Both stone and iron bridges were demolished in 1905, a new bridge being substituted to take a line of electric tramcars which were introduced at that time, to serve Falkirk and the district.

According to the article Railway[2] in the 'Edinburgh Encyclopaedia' (1830), the introduction of railways reduced the average monthly expenditure of the company from £1,200 to £300.

[1] See p. 141, *post*.
[2] This article is ascribed by Tredgold to Robert Stevenson ('Treatise on Railroads', p. 26).

The Carron Company has a most interesting history. In addition to being early railway builders they were pioneers in canal construction, having, in the latter part of the eighteenth century, constructed a private canal connecting the harbour at the works with the river Carron at Carronshore; thus enabling vessels from the works to reach the outlet of the river at Grangemouth. This canal remained in use until the end of the nineteenth century. One of the original founders of the company (in 1756) was Dr. Roebuck, the friend and first financial assistant of James Watt. The following account of the beginnings of the company is given in 'James Watt and the Steam Engine', by H. W. Dickinson and Rhys Jenkins (1927).

> Dr. Roebuck . . . had recently turned his attention to the manufacture of iron in Scotland, and had formed a company—in which he was the chief figure—composed of himself, his brothers, Garbett,[1] and the firm of Cadell and Sons.[2] Roebuck chose for the site of the new works a spot on the river Carron, some nine miles south-east of Stirling, not far from where the Carron flows into the Firth of Forth. For water-power there was the Carron, for water-way the Forth, while all about them were ironstone, limestone and coal. Much of the machinery was contrived by Smeaton, and the first furnace was blown in at Carron on Jan. 1. 1760.

There are some very interesting descriptions and drawings of machinery designed for the company, 1769–79, by Smeaton, in the first volume of his Reports (pp. 359 to end). They include a blowing engine and boring machines for cylinders and guns, all driven by water-wheels.

John Adam, one of the celebrated architect brothers, was one of the earliest partners in the Carron firm—an association which has left many beautiful marks on their products down to the present day.

An interesting account of this company, which Faujas de St. Fond described after a visit in 1784 as 'the greatest iron-foundry in Europe', is given in chapters ix and x of 'The Story of the Forth' by Dr. H. M. Cadell (1913).

GLASGOW RAILWAYS

Still pursuing a westerly course we come upon an interesting group of railways in the Glasgow area. The demand for these first arose in the district of Old and New Monkland, in the Middle Ward of Lanarkshire, which are rich in coal and iron, the workings being of great antiquity. The author has on his house a bell, which has been there for many years, with 'BELL FOUNDED MUNKLAND 1636 REFOUNDED 1719' cast on it in raised letters.

---

[1] Samuel Garbett, a merchant of Birmingham.   [2] Of Cockenzie, Haddingtonshire.

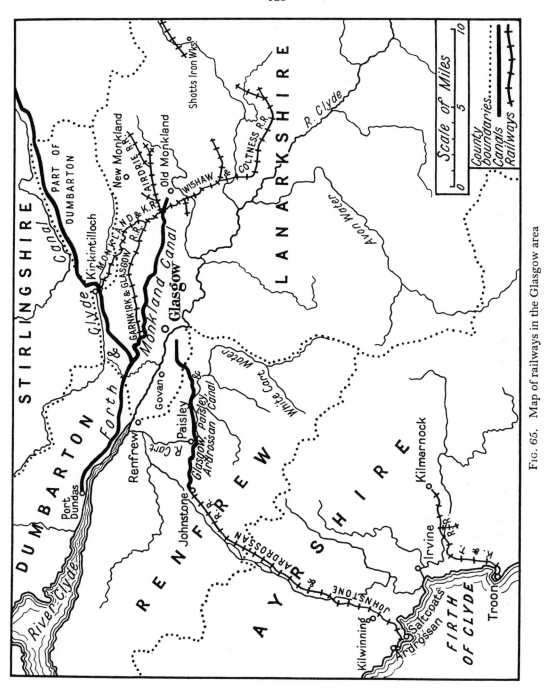

FIG. 65.   Map of railways in the Glasgow area

The first known suggestion of railway construction is contained in an Act, 10 Geo. III, cap. 105 (1770), 'for making and maintaining a new cut or Canal, and Waggon way from the Collieries in the parishes of Old and New Monkland to the City of Glasgow'. The canal went 'to or near the City', and a road or waggon-way was to go 'from the west end of the said cut or Canal at or near Jermeston to the River Clyde at or near Glasgow, with a side Road or Waggon way into the City of Glasgow'. The company was called the Monkland Navigation.[1] Priestley describes the canal, but does not say anything about the waggon-way.

Over fifty years seem to have passed before any further developments took place. Then they came quickly.

The best description of them is an 'Account of the Lanarkshire Railways', written by George Buchanan and appended to D. O. Hill's 'Views of the opening of the Garnkirk and Glasgow Railway' (1832). He states that in the spring of 1824 an Act (5 Geo. IV, cap. 49) was obtained for making a railway from the Monkland coal-field to the Forth and Clyde Canal near Kirkintilloch in Dumbartonshire, and called the Monkland and Kirkintilloch Railway. There is an engraving of a horse drawing 14 loaded trucks, entitled 'Horse "Dragon" with Train on Monkland and Kirkintilloch Railway, 27th February 1828. Load 50 tons. $6\frac{3}{4}$ miles in 1 hour 43 minutes'. He describes the line thus:

This railway commences at Palace Craig and Cairnhill Collieries about a mile south-west of Airdrie, and nine or ten miles east of Glasgow in a straight line. From this point it runs about a mile westwards, passing close to the north of the Calder Iron Works; it then turns to the north-west, and about half a mile farther on, crosses the Edinburgh and Glasgow road by Airdrie, at the same point this road crosses the Monkland Canal by the Coat Bridge. This is nine miles from the Cross at Glasgow, and two miles west of Airdrie. From this point the line continues nearly due north for a quarter of a mile, and here a small branch goes off eastwards about three fourths of a mile, to the Colliery of Kipps. The line then advances northwards for about a mile, passing to the east of Gartsherrie Coal and Iron Works, and on to Gargill Colliery, where it turns nearly north for two miles; and turning again to the north-westwards with several turns till it reaches the canal opposite Kirkintilloch.

The whole length from Carnhill Bridge to the Forth and Clyde Canal is ten miles and the fall about 127 feet. In some parts it is quite level, and in others runs with a gentle but variable declination. The works were commenced in June 1824 and the railway was opened to the public in October 1826. It was originally laid with a single line of rails and passing places. Ground was taken, however, to lay a double line all

---

[1] Became the property of the Caledonian Ry. Co.

the way and this has since been gradually carrying into effect. The expense of the original line was about L. 3700 a mile.

The work on this railway is now chiefly performed by two locomotive engines,[1] the same plying between the collieries and the tunnel at Bedlay, where its progress is interrupted, the other between the tunnel and the canal. By an operation now going on, the tunnel will soon be converted into an open cut, to admit the locomotive engines, and the one engine will be capable of performing nearly the work of both.

Nearly a twelvemonth before the Monkland and Kirkintilloch Railway was completed, its utility and importance to the mineral proprietors in the line appeared so manifest, that those interested in the adjacent extensive and valuable mineral district of New Monkland, on the east of the railway, and lying in the high grounds immediately to the north and north-east of Airdrie became anxious to obtain access to so convenient an outlet for their produce; and a company was immediately formed for making a railway to connect this district with the Monkland and Kirkintilloch Railway. This was termed the Ballochney Railway,[2] from the name of the extreme colliery to which it extended. It was commenced in the summer of 1826 and opened to the public 8th August 1828. Leaving the Monkland and Kirkintilloch Railway at the extremity of the branch to Kipps Colliery already described, the Ballochney Railway advances in an easterly direction, about $1\frac{3}{4}$ miles to a point near the farm of Raw Yards, on the Stirling and Carlisle road, rising at the same time very rapidly into the high grounds, and passing about a quarter of a mile north of Airdrie. At this point a branch about $1\frac{1}{4}$ mile in length, goes off to the south-east embracing Raw Yards, South Colliery and the lands of Colliertree, and terminating at West Moffat Colliery, belonging to Dr. Clerk, where it crosses the Edinburgh and Glasgow road about $1\frac{3}{4}$ mile east of Airdrie. From the point at Raw Yards the main line advances to the north-west about 2 miles, embracing Raw Yards North Colliery and other properties containing valuable minerals. It then turns eastwards about half a mile further, where a branch about half a mile in length goes off to the north-west to embrace the extensive colliery of Whiterig, and the coal and ironstone mines of Stanrig, and which has been recently extended to the ironstone mines of Gavil and others. From this point the railway continues in an easterly direction about $1\frac{1}{4}$ mile, and terminates at the extensive colliery of Ballochney. The whole length of the railway is four miles and a furlong and of the branches $1\frac{1}{2}$ mile.

From near the eastern extremity at Ballochney Colliery the line has a gentle descent all the way to the separation of the branch to Clerkston, and the branches have a similar declination to the main line; all of

---

[1] These were built by Murdock and Aitken of Glasgow (the first constructed in that city). They were designed by Isaac Dodds, and delivered in May and September 1831. They were of the Killingworth type, but with tubular boilers, and gave great satisfaction. Previously to their arrival horses were used.

[2] Thus also Priestley in his book. But on the map he calls it Airdrie Railway. The Act was obtained in May 1826.

which is extremely favourable for the transit of the minerals, which in many places advance by their own gravity, leaving the horses only to bring back the empty waggons (a useful contrivance . . . has been adopted for the ease of the animal in descending; instead of causing it to run behind the waggon, a carriage is made, in which the horse stands at his ease all the time the waggons are descending, and starts perfectly fresh to his task of drawing them back. This plan was first practised in North America on the Mauchunk Railway).

The branch to Clerkston is quite level as far as Collierstree, thence it descends 14 feet to Moffat Colliery. From the point of separation of the Clerkston branch to Kipps Colliery the ground descends too rapidly to admit of the waggons descending of themselves. The only resource here was in inclined planes; and two of them have been formed, down which 3, 4 or 5 waggons descending by a rope, bring up an equal number of empty ones attached to the other extremity, the rope passing over a wheel or pulley at the top. The length of the upper end of the inclined plane is 2000 feet and the perpendicular descent from top to bottom is 94 feet; the inclination of the plane varies from 1 in 25 at the top to 1 in 38 at the bottom; the length of the lower is 3000 feet, the perpendicular descent 118 feet and the inclination varies from 1 in 22 at the top to 1 in 36 at the bottom. The whole railway is laid with a single line of rails and passing places at convenient distances. On the inclined planes there are three single rails throughout, excepting the middle, where there are four single rails, or a double line for the waggons passing each other.

The act for the Garnkirk and Glasgow line was obtained in the spring of 1826. It commences at the Monkland and Kirkintilloch Railway at Gargill Colliery and runs about half a mile in a north-westerly direction, and turning then more to the west, advances about two and a half miles on in a straight line passing Gartcloss on the west, Whitehill and Gartcosh on the south. It then turns west, inclining to south, and again advances in a straight line for nearly two miles passing by Blackfauld and crossing the Glasgow and Cumbernauld road, near Step's Inn. Turning again to the south-west, the line advances quite straight for three quarters of a mile, crossing Robroyston Moss. Here it turns again, a little to the west, and then advances in a line perfectly straight for two miles, to the entrance of the depot at St. Rollox. The whole length of the line, to the west end of the depot, is very nearly eight and one fourth mile, and the fall 95 feet. For the first five and a half miles, the line runs on a level, from thence to the depot, it declines regularly at the rate of 1 in 144. . . .

There appeared in the first mile an embankment in Gartcloss Valley nearly three quarters of a mile long, in some parts 27 feet high and this on a very soft and mossy formation. Another west of Gartcosh, nearly half a mile long, and fifteen feet high and the bottom a perfect moss, a third considerable one at Proven Mill, and a fourth and the most formidable of all, across the valley of Germiston, nearly three quarters of a mile in length and a considerable part of it upwards of 45 feet high. The cuttings appeared also very considerable, one at Gartcosh, a quarter of a mile long, and in some parts 24 feet deep, one near Blackfauld, nearly half a mile long; another a mile and a quarter in length through Robroyston Moss and by Proven Mill farm in some parts upwards of 40 feet deep.

All these lines were laid with the 'malleable iron patent rails' from Bedlington Ironworks.

The Garnkirk and Glasgow was not opened until September 27th, 1831, with two locomotives built by Stephenson & Co.

Priestley does not add anything material to the above account, except that all these three lines were laid out by Thomas Grainger. Most of them are in use at the present day, part of the Monkland and Kirkintilloch forming a section of the west-coast route to Scotland. By an Act of June 1829, powers were obtained to construct the Wishaw and Coltness Railway, which extended the M. & K. for 11 miles to the south-east, but it was not opened until 1833.

The gauge of these lines was 4 feet 6 inches.[1] Longitudinal sleepers were used, partly, at all events, on the Garnkirk and Glasgow Railway.[2]

The Ballochney Company, on July 8th, 1828, commenced running a springless coach, with accommodation for thirty passengers, between Airdrie and Kirkintilloch, and were much perturbed at being called upon to pay Government duty at the rate of 3d. per mile.[3]

Another short railway in the neighbourhood was from the Govan Colliery to Tradeston, which is part of Glasgow. Priestley mentions it in connexion with the Polloc (sic) and Govan Railway, the Act for which was not obtained until May 1830, and which, according to Lewin, was only opened for horse-traffic in 1840 and was absorbed in the Caledonian system six years later, being now partly embodied in the main L.M. & S. route to the north. Part of it, however, appears to have been opened earlier, as Lewin says it was about three miles long, but Priestley wrote thus in 1830:

This railway commences from the River Clyde, at the south quay of the Broomielaw in the city of Glasgow, from whence it crosses the road leading from Paisley to the last-mentioned place, then crosses and runs parallel with the private railway leading from the Govan Colliery to Tradestown; and shortly afterwards it crosses, at right angles, the Glasgow, Paisley and Ardrossan Canal, near its termination at Port Eglinton; thence to Port Eglinton Street, where it terminates after forming a junction with the Govan Railway.

[1] Warren, 'A Century of Locomotive Building', p. 331.   [2] Ibid., p. 334.
[3] Tomlinson, 'Hist. N.E.R.', p. 159.

It is in length only one thousand four hundred and eighty-eight yards.

In a pamphlet of 1829, which deals with a 'proposed Railway and Tunnel from the North quarter of Glasgow to the Broomielaw', the 'Rail-road from Govan Colliery' is spoken of as having been in existence for nearly fifty years.

GLASGOW, PAISLEY, AND ARDROSSAN CANAL AND RAILWAY

In 1804 Telford was employed by the Earl of Eglinton and others to survey a canal from Glasgow to Ardrossan, where the Earl owned the property, and had formed the intention of making a great port, hoping thus to by-pass the Clyde, on which navigation was exceedingly difficult owing to its numerous bends and shallows. Sir Alexander Gibb, in 'The Story of Telford' (1935), says:

The projected canal, besides leaving the rich city of Glasgow in its hinterland, would also pass through an area full of coal, iron and lime-stone, and the prospects are thought to be exceptionally encouraging. But the promoters—naturally—got little help from Glasgow, whose citizens were intent on improving their river.

An Act was obtained in June 1806, and work was begun immediately, but the canal never got beyond Johnstone. Quoting Sir Alexander Gibb again:

Houston for some time popularised the canal by running fast passenger boats on it between Glasgow and Paisley which were much patronised, and quite met the feeble threats of the first railways. The example was followed by other canals. But another "unexpected discovery came into competition" in the form of locomotive steam carriages upon the Turnpike Road between Glasgow and Paisley, which carried passengers more quickly and cheaply even than the canal boats. Long after, in 1827, the Company obtained powers to make a railway from Johnstone to Ardrossan, and later the course of the canal itself from Johnstone to Glasgow was used for a railway line.

Priestley's map shows the railway for the full length, but Lewin says:

The authorised line was about $22\frac{1}{2}$ miles long, but again, owing to financial difficulties, its construction was limited to a distance of $5\frac{1}{2}$ miles between Ardrossan and Kilwinning. The railway was opened in 1831 for horse traction.

The Earl of Eglinton had possessed an earlier railway, as Robertson, in the second of the 'Highland' essays (1824), mentions his line at Ardrossan, 'a concave iron-track about half a mile long' (presumably meaning a plate-railway).

The Act for the canal authorized a 'collateral Cut from the said Canal to the Coal Works at Hurlet, in the county of Renfrew', which was probably never made; it is not shown in the map of the canal in the 'Atlas to the Life of Telford'. But there was a railway at Hurlet, which is about three miles south of Paisley. It is referred to thus in the article Railways in the 'Encyclopaedia Britannica' of 1824:

We have been favoured with the following account . . . by an engineer (Mr. Neilson of Glasgow) who has formed several of the kind.

"One of these is on the property of the Earl of Glasgow, commencing at the Hurlet extensive coal and limeworks, and extending to the Paisley canal, a distance of about two miles. It is formed of flat bar iron two and one-forth inches deep, by nearly three-quarters of an inch thick, and the rails in lengths of nine feet, each rail supported at every three feet by a sleeper and cast-iron chair. The joinings are formed by a cast-iron dovetailed socket suitable to receive the jointed ends of the bar, and a dovetailed glut or key, by which means the several rails are joined as if into one continuous bar."

Cumming gives an almost identical description of the Hurlet line.

KILMARNOCK AND TROON RAILWAY

Farther south we come upon a railway which was the first in Scotland to obtain an Act of its own; the Royal Assent being given on May 27th, 1808.

The Phillimore collection contains a letter belonging to the inception of this line. It is dated 'Welbeck, April 22, 1806', and is from the Marquis of Titchfield[1] to the Earl of Eglinton, and is as follows:

My Lord,
  I take the liberty of troubling your Lordship with this letter for the purpose of submitting to your consideration a plan, which if it should be so fortunate as to meet with the approbation of those Landed Proprietors whose property it may touch, it is my intention to bring before Parliament. The plan to which I allude is for the purpose of making an iron rail road or railway from the Troon Point to Kilmarnock, which (unless those who may be professionally consulted should propose a more eligible line) I should at present propose to bring through the estates of Mr. McKerrol, Lord Montgomerie and Sir Wm. Cunningham of Robertland on the South Side of the Water of Irvine. I should propose to take it across that river at or near the Cockhill Burn, and to continue it on your Lordship's property on the North Bank of that River, untill it came into

[1] Afterwards fourth Duke of Portland.

mine. It is my intention to propose that the several proprietors of Lands above stated should (if they think proper) be joint proprietors of the undertaking, and hold shares in it, in proportion to the extent of their property over which the railway may pass. But as the advantages to be derived to the Public from all undertakings of this nature, must almost wholly depend upon the terms on which they are made, It becomes necessary for me to add, that it is my intention to propose that the tonnage on this Railway should be limited not to exceed the rate of 3d per ton per mile, and that a clause should be introduced into the bill providing, that whenever the clear profits of the Company should be found to have exceeded from the commencement of their works, the rate of £20 per cent, on the capital invested. The tonnage should be reduced at the rate of one halfpenny per ton per mile, and that in succeeding years, under the same circumstances, it should in the same manner continue to be reduced, untill it is brought down as low as one penny per ton per mile—below which sum it should never be—I flatter myself it will appear to your Lordship that while these terms afford to the owners of coal a fair prospect of exporting it to considerable advantage, they also hold out to those Proprietors of Land, who may now have that inducement to become subscribers, a reasonable return for any money they may choose to embark. It remains for me to explain to your Lordship the reasons which have induced me to prefer the proposition, which I have now the honor of submitting to your Lordship, to that of a canal which was originally proposed by Colonel Fullarton. This preference has arisen from the consideration that the adoption of it will be attended with much less prejudice to the land through which it may pass, and that, as it can be completed at a much less expence than a canal, it will eventually allow the business of the country to be done on much cheaper terms. It now only remains for me to express my hope that this plan may meet with your Lordship's concurrence and approbation and if it should be so fortunate, to request that you would have the goodness to inform me whether and to what extent you would choose to take any share in the concern. I have the honor to be My Lord,

Your Lordship's most obedient Servant,

Scott Titchfield

I will beg your Lordship to direct your answer to me at Burlington House.

The author's collection contains a map 27½ by 8¾ inches, entitled 'Plan of a Proposed line of RAILWAY or TRAM ROAD, from KILMARNOCK TO TROON on the West Coast of AYRSHIRE, 1807'. 'Copied by Peter Potter from a plan of twice the present scale signed John Wilson. Neele sculp.'

The plan, reproduced on a reduced scale in Fig. 66, shows that the railway was made exactly as proposed in Lord Titchfield's letter. The length of the main line was 9 miles 6 furlongs. A branch is shown, to 'coal works belonging to Sir William Cunninghame of Robertland, Bart.; in length 4 furlongs 107 yards nearly'.

The line was opened in 1812. The tonnage rates, as proposed in the letter, were fixed at 3d. per ton per mile 'for all Goods, Wares, Merchandise and other Things whatsoever'. The engineer was William Jessop, whose estimate was £38,167 10s. 0d. The original subscribers were the Marquis of Titchfield, 74 shares (of £500 each); Lord Montgomerie, 1 share; Lord Montgomerie Eglinton, 1 share, and John Boyle, Esq., 1 share; making in all £38,500.

The best contemporary description is given by Strickland in his 'Reports on Canals, &c.', of 1826, as follows:

Among the plate railways which I have visited, that of the Duke of Portland, constructed from the Troon harbour near Irvine, to Kilmarnock in Ayrshire, Scotland, is of the most importance.

The work was commenced many years ago, and is upon the old construction, formed with flat tram rails four inches in width, having a flange on the inside, rising three inches above the path of the wagon wheel, and supported by foundation stone three feet apart. The rails are joined together with a square joint, and are nailed to the stone through a small square hole formed half way in each end of the rails.[1]

The road is a double line, formed with cast iron rails, rising eighty four feet in nine miles, or about one-sixteenth of an inch to the yard [1 in 576]. The attendant and horse paths are four feet in width, and are raised or made up to a level with the top of the flange.

From this mode of construction, the flat part of the rail is frequently filled with dirt and gravel; so much so, as to be little better than a common hard road. Horses only are used as the propelling power, and they convey thirteen wagons in convoy, each containing about one ton, at the rate of two and a half miles per hour. This reduced speed is occasioned principally by the great friction caused by the broad construction of the rails, and the wheels of the wagons come in contact with the soil, which is constantly thrown off from the horse path.

Besides the rail wagons, common carts are introduced upon the rails; which has a very injurious effect, arising from the roughness of the tire of their wheels, and from the soil which adheres to them being deposited on the flat part of the rails.

More than three miles of this road is formed through a bog or moor, without any other precaution than a low embankment, made of sand and gravel, mixed with loam. The top surface is coated over with fine coal, brought from the collieries in the neighbourhood, and a good drain is formed on each side of the embankment, which is raised about two or three feet above the level of the moor. The foundation props are laid level or flush with the surface of the attendant path: these in many

[1] For illustration, see Fig. 68, facing p. 146.

places have given way and left the rails in great disorder; besides which, they are laid too near the surface to withstand the action of the frost.

The whole line is straight, passing through a level country, with few difficulties, and little embanking or deep cutting. The traffic chiefly consists of coal, brought from a few collieries in the neighbourhood of Kilmarnock, to the harbour of the Troon; from whence it is shipped to Belfast, and the northern parts of Ireland.

The railway was carried across the river Irvine by a fine stone bridge of four arches, of 40 feet span and rising 25 feet above the river. It is still standing, but in a very bad state of repair.

A branch line, believed to have been made about 1818, connected the Fairlie Collieries with Drybridge, about 2½ miles south-west. Curiously enough, the gauge, &c., did not correspond with the main line, the branch being laid with edge-rails 3 feet 4 inches apart.

There was an unsuccessful attempt to introduce a locomotive in 1817.

Although there were no powers to convey passengers in the Act they were nevertheless taken. Stevenson makes the following remark (p. 38):

In so far as the Reporter knows, a regular system of Travelling on Railways, or the conveyance of passengers, has not been attempted, excepting, perhaps, from Kilmarnock to Troon in Ayrshire. But we see no objection to this, by a properly constructed Railway and carriage.

Dupin, in his 'Excursions to the Ports of England etc. in the years 1816, 1817 and 1818', also mentions passengers:

I saw some diligences established on the iron railway from Kilmarnock to Troon Bay; they convey the idea of an enormous wandering vehicle,[1] and nevertheless are drawn without difficulty by a single horse.

In an article in the *Locomotive Magazine* of April 14th, 1906, it is stated that passengers were conveyed shortly after the opening of the line (fare 1s., single) in two vehicles, one, Willie Wight's 'Caledonia', and the other, an open carriage called 'The Boat'.

In 1837 an Act was obtained for the conversion of the line for use by locomotives, which were reintroduced in 1841. In 1845 it was leased to the Glasgow, Paisley, and Kilmarnock Railway for 999 years, but on account of frequent questions arising as to what was to be paid to it for 'wayleave' in the case of coals passing over the line, the lease was cancelled later and the Glasgow and South-Western, as it had then become, purchased the line, which now belongs to the L.M. & S.R.

---

[1] 'Wandering vehicle' is represented in the original French by *voiture nomade*, by which he doubtless meant a gipsy caravan.

A few miles farther south there was a railway at Messrs. Taylor's works at Ayr, as Stevenson's Report of 1818 mentions them as having been the scene of experiments with malleable iron rails. Robertson's 'Highland' essay (1824) speaks of it as an 'edge rail-track' about one mile long.

Two schemes call for brief mention, although they proved abortive, as they attracted much attention at the time, and some interesting literature has survived concerning them. One was for a railway from Glasgow to Berwick, which would have been 125 miles long. Mr. Kenneth Brown possesses a map of it, entitled 'PLAN AND SECTIONS of the Track of a proposed CAST IRON RAILWAY from the City of Glasgow to Berwick-upon-Tweed passing through the Counties of Lanark, Peebles, Selkirk, Roxburgh, Berwick and Northumberland. London March 1810, Thos. Telford.' The author has a copy of Telford's Report on the line. It was to be a cast-iron railway, the cost being estimated at £365,700 0s. 9d. In Glasgow:

> Access with all the principal streets is preserved, which having declivities from the railway, renders it easy to transport coals by merely removing the waggon-chest from the rail-road wheels, and placing it upon others suitable for passing along the streets of the city.

From the above it may be concluded that edge-rails were intended, although the Report does not specify the form.

A contemporary scheme was for a line between Berwick and Kelso. Mr. Phillimore has a copy of a 'Report by Mr. John Rennie, Engineer, respecting the proposed Rail-way from Kelso to Berwick', printed at Kelso in 1810, and including a map. This line succeeded in obtaining an Act (51 Geo. III, cap. 133, Royal Assent May 31st, 1811). It appears to have been the second one—not, as frequently stated, the first—to contain a clause empowering the conveyance of passengers.[1] The line was never made, and the company was dissolved in 1838.

For a note on temporary railways used during the construction of the Caledonian Canal, see Index.

EARLY RAILWAYS IN IRELAND

There were no public railways during the period covered by this book. Whishaw in 'The Railways of Great Britain and Ireland' (1840) wrote:

> Although several Acts of Parliament have been passed for the construction of railways in Ireland by joint-stock companies, two only at

---

[1] The first railway to have this distinction was the Monmouth Railway, a year and a week earlier. See p. 63, *ante*.

present are in active operation—the Dublin and Kingstown, and part of the Ulster Railway.

The Acts for these lines were obtained in 1831 and 1836 respectively. In the 'Edinburgh Encyclopaedia' (1830) we read, in the article Railways:

In Ireland there are yet few railways, excepting those at the Harbour-works at Dublin, and at quarries and other works of that description, which, from their temporary nature, are not generally calculated to afford good specimens of the art; but in the progress of the improvement of that fine country, we may look forward to the period, when such works will be more generally established, and conducted with all the improvement and systematic precision of the sister kingdom.

In the same work, under the heading Navigation, Inland, the following passage occurs:

The Tyrone Canal extends from Coalisland, county Tyrone, three miles to the Blackwater river and from thence by a short cut across the isthmus of Maghery into Lough Neagh. There are eight locks to the Colliery basin, from whence a wooden railway extends to the mines. This canal is chiefly remarkable, as being the first in this country, on which inclined planes and railways were employed to unite canal ponds of very different levels.[1]

Matthias Dunn, in his 'View of the Coal Trade' (1844), says that he was employed in 1827 to inspect the Castle Comer mines, which about 1829 were 'fitted up with tram-ways'.

There is an ambitious prospectus in the British Museum of the Hibernian General Railway Company, published in 1825. It contemplated railways all through Ireland, intending to start with one from Waterford to Limerick. The Presidents and Vice-Presidents included about twenty Peers.

The University of London possesses a 'Report of Alexander Nimmo on the proposed Railway between Limerick and Waterford', addressed to the Secretary of the Hibernian Railway Company, dated November 15th, 1825. The line adopted is spoken of as being an improvement on 'that formerly projected', so there had evidently been a previous scheme. The length of the main line was about 73 miles, and there were to be branches to Thurles and the Killenaule Collieries. Quoting:

We will be enabled not only to make use of horses, but also of locomotive engines in drawing the carriages, and to proceed with any degree of speed that may be deemed advisable.

[1] See p. 155, *post*.

I propose to make the railway of malleable iron, similar in principle to those I have introduced at the public works in Limerick, Courtown, &c., being at once simple, durable and effectual, and in facility of application or removal, greatly superior to cast iron, and less liable to injury.

These railways are made of the ordinary flat bar of merchantable iron placed on edge, the materials being intended for sale after the temporary purposes for which they are laid down is served. But for a permanent railway I would have them rolled thicker at top, as well for strength as to lessen the wear of wheels, and to enable them, if any pilferage be attempted, to be more readily identified. I do not, however, from the experience I have had in the country, anticipate much risk of this kind. Of course persons must be stationed along the road for the purpose of taking care of it.

.   .   .   .

The waggon wheels used in the works above alluded to, have an inch groove cast in the middle of a flat tier of three inches broad, so that the waggon will travel on the common roads occasionally.

.   .   .   .

There seems no limit to the velocity that may be obtained, excepting the safety of the goods or passengers . . . however, it does not seem advisable to carry this mode of transport to a greater velocity than . . . six or seven miles an hour.

He mentions the possibility of using turf fuel in the locomotives, and was sure it could be used for the stationary engines (of which there were to be six).

The Waterford and Limerick Railway obtained an Act in 1826, but did not materialize until 1854.

Strickland, in his Report of 1826, dealing with Dublin Breakwater and Harbour, mentions a line which was doubtless only a temporary one:

In the commencement of the work, a tram road was laid from the strand to the granite quarries at the hill of Corrick, a distance of about two miles south-east from Kingstown. This road is formed into several branches at the quarries, which are elevated between two and three hundred feet above the level of the sea; and the branches meet in a double line of way, forming a succession of inclined planes, with brakes that regulate the descent and ascent of the laden and empty truck-wagons, to the foot and top of the hill. After the laden wagons have been let down, they are carried forward by horses, upon a slightly inclined road, which leads to, and along the top of the breakwater.

Richard Lovell Edgeworth speaks of having used trucks with cast-iron wheels and roller bearings on a temporary wooden railway about 1788, no doubt on his estate near Edgeworthstown. See p. 180, *post*.

CHAPTER VII

THE VARIOUS FORMS OF RAILS AND THE INTRODUCTION OF IRON

The article in Desaguliers (1734) on Ralph Allen's 'carriages', from which some illustrations were given at the beginning of Chapter IV, does not go into any detail with regard to the rails. In the drawings they are shown as rectangular in section, and formed of one thickness of wood.

The earliest description of one of these wooden railways which the author has succeeded in discovering is in Jars' 'Voyages Métallurgiques' in 1765;[1] a translation of which is given by Wood.[2] It is generally similar to the first paragraph of the following one, which is taken from John Brand's 'History and Antiquities of Newcastle-on-Tyne' (1789):

> After the road is formed, pieces of timber, about six feet long and six inches diameter, called sleepers, are laid across it, being eighteen or twenty-four inches distant from each other. Upon these sleepers other pieces of timber, called rails, of four or five inches square, are laid in a lateral direction four feet distant from one another, for the waggon wheels to run upon; the wheels being either of solid wood or cast iron. . . . The waggons carry 50 cwt. of coals. . . . The fellies or rims of the waggon wheels are hollow.
>
> Many of the superannuated workmen earn a little livelihood by what they call "creesing", that is, crevicing or cleaning out the crevices of the rails on these waggonways, upon which in steep places they are employed in laying cinders, to prevent their becoming too slippery, and the waggons from running amain. When the axle of a loaded waggon breaks, it causes a great stop to the other waggons, and is called by the waggon-men a caud (i.e. cold) pie.

The expression 'hollow' applied to the rims of the wheels suggests flanges on both sides. An indication of a similar kind in another part of the country occurs in the second of the Highland essays, by George Robertson. He describes railway-making in Scotland as firstly with wooden rails, 'raised convexly above the surface of the ground, the rims of the wheels being concave, to fit them'.

Hutchinson, in 'A View of Northumberland' (1778), speaks of wheels with hollow rims.[3] Farey (1817), of 'pulley wheels' and 'pulley-formed' wheels.[4] Coxe[5] (1801) and Scott[6] (1824) both speak of grooved rims.

---

[1] Vol. i, p. 200, published in 1774.
[3] See p. 12, *ante.*
[5] See p. 85, *ante.*

[2] First edn. p. 36; 2nd, p. 13; 3rd, p. 8.
[4] See pp. 43, 44, *ante.*
[6] See p. 142, *post.*

One can only infer, from so many witnesses, that flanges on both sides of the wheel were in common use. When there was one only, it seems to have been always on the inside.

With reference to the allusion to 'creesing', which term Brand appears to derive from the word 'crevice', the following passage from Baillie's 'Impartial History of Newcastle-upon-Tyne' (1801) is of interest:

> The flange was known to the old waggon-men as the "crease" and the men employed to keep the rails clear for the free passage of the flange were called "creasers".
>
> In fact it is recorded that to 500 waggon-men employed in the Coal Trade on the River Wear in 1792 there were 80 "creasers" for the ways.

The next improvement consisted in laying another wooden rail on the tops of the existing ones, which could be more easily renewed. This arrangement was known as a 'double road', and the lower rails were sometimes called 'sleepers'.

The following description was written by John Buddle in 1807, and is taken from vol. 15, p. 202, of his papers, belonging to the North of England Institute of Mining and Mechanical Engineers:

> The best wood for construction is oak for sleepers and bottom rails and beech for the top rails. Norway fir is most commonly used for the bottom rails. The strength of the way must be proportional to the weight it has to bear. For a Newcastle chaldron waggon, coals 53 cwt., waggon 17 cwt., sleepers of small oak trees unsquared 5 to 7 inches diameter. Bottom rails $4\frac{1}{2}$ by 5 inches. Top rails 4 by 5 laid the flat way.
>
> The bottom rail is fastened to the sleepers by oak trunails [sic] as is also the top rail to the bottom rail. It is advisable to have the bottom rails in long lengths and the top rails placed so as to cross the joinings of the bottom rails. The principal point in which wooden ways are inferior to iron, is that a horse on the average will do more work by 3 chaldrons, frequently 50 to 100 per cent. If the way is wanted for a number of years the expense of upkeep is less with iron. The difference in expense in way for a Newcastle chaldron waggon: iron 16 shillings, wood 8 shillings per yard. Iron railways for trains or small waggons 5s. 6d. or 6s. per yard.

It is not possible to find the date when, or the place where, the additional rail was first laid on the top to take the wear. Buddle's account of 1807, which has just been given, is the earliest mention of it, so far as the author knows. It is not referred to in Fisher's description of the Whitehaven Railways in 1793,[1] nor in Bailey and Culley's account of Northumberland in 1797.[2]

---

[1] See p. 28, *ante*.   [2] See p. 14, *ante*.

The first introduction of iron appears to have been a kind of armouring with wrought-iron plates. The evidence available does not go into particulars satisfactorily. Dr. Anderson ('Recreations in Agriculture', 1801, from which extensive quotations are given in Chapter IX) says: 'At the first, rods of bar iron were nailed on the original wooden rails.'

Wood's first mention of the use of iron is as follows:[1]

> In some parts of the road, where occasional acclivities occurred which could not be levelled, or where sudden windings of the road were obliged to be made, thin plates of wrought iron were laid on the surface of the Rails, and fastened down with common nails.

Unfortunately, he gives no place nor date. There is one, and only one, instance of a contemporary account of this practice which the author has succeeded in discovering, and that is the description of the re-laying of the Alloa Railway in 1785, given in 'The Statistical Account of Scotland' (1793), and quoted on p. 122, *ante*. Here a bar of malleable iron $\frac{3}{4}$ inch thick and $1\frac{3}{4}$ inches broad was laid on a double thickness of wooden rail. This is excellent history, of course, but it is rather late.

Cumming (1824) says:

> On the introduction of iron, the first attempt to form a rail-way of that material was, by fixing flat bars of iron on the top of wooden rails; but after a great variety of unsuccessful attempts, the wood was wholly laid aside, and the rails themselves wholly composed of cast iron bars, in short lengths.

In Mackenzie's 'History of Northumberland' (1825), speaking of wooden railways, it is stated that the tops of the rails were planed smooth and round and sometimes covered with plates of wrought iron.

One more example may be given, from Hebert's 'Engineers' and Mechanics' Encyclopaedia' (1836):

> The origin of edge-rails cannot easily be traced. The wooden rails partook of this character, for they were generally rounded a little on their upper surfaces, and flanges were put on the peripheries of the wheels . . . and in some cases square wrought iron bars were fastened over the wooden rails, partly with a view to strengthen them, as well as to form guides to the wheels.

The earliest instance of both a date and locality is that given recently by Mr. George Pate, and quoted on p. 123, *ante*, namely 'about 1766', by the Carron Co.

In reply to an inquiry as to the authority for his statement, he referred

[1] First edn., p. 42.

to a book, first published in 1868, 'Round About Falkirk', by Robert
Gillespie, where, on p. 154, the following passage occurs (speaking of
the Carron Company):

The first line, stretching from Kinnaird Colliery into the interior of
the works, was constructed in 1766. The rails in that instance were of wood,
covered with a sort of hoop-iron. In the course of the following year,
however, rails wholly of iron were cast at Colebrook Dale Iron-Works.

The above is an improvement on a statement of 1935, but does not go
back as far as one would wish.

There is an interesting passage in 'The Penny Cyclopaedia' (1841)
which gives an earlier date—alas, without authority—but no place:

As it was desirable that, as far as possible, the power of the horses
should be equally applied in every part of the road, it became usual at an
early period, at least as early as 1716, to nail thin plates of malleable iron
upon the surface of the wooden rails, wherever a steep ascent or a sharp
curve rendered the draught harder than usual, so that the horse might
travel with a full load upon the ordinary portions of the line, and yet, by
the help of the greater smoothness of an iron surface, be able to pass the
difficult points without inconvenience.

The above seems rather a cheap authority to put forward, but the
author has great faith in Charles Knight.

Turning again to the invaluable 'Highland' papers of 1824, Scott gives
an unsatisfactory reference to the subject of the introduction of cast iron,
thus:

A late anonymous author (1821) says, without advancing his
authority, "that in 1738 cast-iron rails were first substituted for wooden
ones, but owing to the old waggons continuing to be employed, which
were of too much weight for the cast-iron, they did not completely succeed
at the first attempt. However, about 1768, a simple contrivance was
attempted,[1] which was, to make a number of smaller waggons, and link
them together; and by thus diffusing the weight of one large waggon into
many, the principal cause of the failure in the first instance was removed,
because the weight was more divided upon the line".

The method of bringing coals from the wall-face to the pit-bottom,
was greatly improved by the introduction of cast-iron railroads below
ground, in place of wooden ones. For this improvement, the mining interest is indebted to Mr. John Carr [Curr], who introduced them, about the
year 1776, into his Grace the Duke of Norfolk's works, near Sheffield.

The wooden railways of the present day are generally formed in
this manner. Rails of timber (called sleepers), about six feet long, and
six inches square, are laid across the road, at the distance of 18 to 24

[1] By R. L. Edgeworth. See p. 180, *post*.

inches from each other; and, upon these sleepers, other pieces of timber, called rails, of four or five inches square, are laid in two parallel lines, 4 feet distant from each other. The waggon-wheels are constructed with a groove to correspond with the rails, and thus run with little friction. The friction is also, in some instances, materially lessened by covering the wooden rails with malleable iron. The cast-iron tracks of the earlier railways were made flat, of about four inches in breadth on the tread, with a projecting ridge (to keep the wheels within the track) and of a thickness suitable to the weight they had to carry.

The introduction of cast iron in 1738, vouched for by the 'anonymous author', has been sometimes placed at Whitehaven. The following passage occurs in Longstaffe's 'History and Antiquities of Darlington' (1854):

About 1767 iron plates were first laid down upon wooden rails in Shropshire. This is no evidence of their use in the north; but we can scarcely doubt that in this district they were introduced long before. Rails wholly of iron are said to have been unsuccessfully tried at Whitehaven in 1738.

Smiles, in the first chapter of his 'Lives of G. and R. Stephenson', says, 'the first iron rails are supposed to have been laid down at Whitehaven as early as 1738'. He was probably relying on Longstaffe, whose book he is certain to have read.

On the other hand, several writers, quoted in Chapter II, give 1738 as the date of the introduction of wooden railways at Whitehaven, which seems more likely. That year seems to have been an *annus mirabilis* of some sort there, but exactly what happened is not perfectly clear.

Altogether, the evidence favours Coalbrookdale as the scene of the introduction of cast iron, at all events at the end of 1767. The older writers who take this view usually rely on a statement by Jabez Hornblower of 1809. It is given, nearly in full, in the 'Repertory of Arts and Manufactures' for 1811; the reference being merely 'from the Reports of the House of Commons'. The author eventually succeeded in tracing it to its source, viz.:

'Committee on the Acts now in force, regarding the use of Broad Wheels and on the Preservation of the Turnpike Roads and Highways of the Kingdom. 3rd Report, 19th June 1809; p. 154 (Additional Appendix).'

Observations by Mr. Hornblower on the subject of Roads and Carriages, addressed to Sir John Sinclair, Bart., M.P.

Railways, I observe, are a part of the desiderata of this important business, and next to the inordinate expence attending the execution there is one circumstance that strongly militates against the design, and that is, a complete revolution in the habits and customs of travelling from one place to another. Waggoners must undergo fresh discipline, coachmen must be content to form a cavalcade, and our saddle-horses must be trained to the gig (if such ways are to be formed according to the present practice).

Railways have been in use in this kingdom time out of mind, and they were usually formed of scantlings of good sound oak, laid on sills or sleepers of the same timber, and pinned together with the same stuff. But it was not until the Proprietors of Colebrook-Dale Ironworks, a very respectable and opulent Company, determined to cover these oak rails with cast-iron, not altogether as a necessary expedient of improvement, but in part as a well-digested measure of economy in support of their trade.

From some adventitious circumstances (which I need not take time to relate) the price of pigs became very low, and their works being of great extent, in order to keep the furnaces on, they thought it would be the best means of stocking their pigs to lay it on the wooden railways, as it would help to pay the interest by reducing the repairs of the rails, and if iron should take any sudden rise, there was nothing to do but to take them up, and send them away as pigs.

But these scantlings of iron (as I may call them) were not as those which are now laid in some places, they were about five feet long, four inches broad, and one inch and a quarter thick, with three holes (as in the figure),[1] by which they were fastened to the rails, and very complete it was both in design and execution. Hence it was not difficult if two persons on horseback should meet on this road, for either to turn his horse out of the road, which on the railways now introduced would be attended with some serious doubt as to the consequences.

J. C. Hornblower.

At first sight 'persons on horseback' looks like ordinary equestrians, but Hornblower evidently meant men riding on horses drawing a truck behind them. It is fairly obvious that the rails were merely flat plates, without any ledge. But there must have been flanges on the wheels, so the suggested turning aside would have been accompanied by a more or less violent jerk.

The Hornblowers were a family of Cornish engineers; Jonathan was the father (1717–80) of six sons and seven daughters, all of whom received biblical names beginning with J. They were rather a hornet's nest for Watt.[2] Jabez Carter (1744–1814), the eldest of the family, was the author of the extract given above.

---

[1] Here is a little sketch showing a flat rectangular bar, with small projections at the middle and ends, where the holes came. They were laid flat, not on edge.

[2] Jonathan, one of the younger sons, invented the compound engine in 1776. Josiah, an uncle, took the first steam-engine to America in 1753, and founded a family over there.

Unfortunately, he does not give a date for the episode, which, it is clear, consisted in laying cast-iron bars on the tops of the old wooden rails.

Robert Stevenson's Report of 1818 says:

> The plan of cast-iron Railways seems to have been originally introduced by the great Iron Company of Colebroke Dale in Shropshire, only about the year 1786, as an improvement on the tram or wooden Railway.

The figure 1786 must be a misprint for 1768, as in his remarks at the end of the Highland Society essays (1824) he wrote thus:

> There seems to be no doubt of the wooden-railway or tram-road having been first known, in practice, in the neighbourhood of Newcastle. The wooden rails came afterwards to be clad or covered with plates of iron; and this metal has ultimately become the only material used for the purpose. We have reason to believe that the first introduction of rails wholly of iron took place about 56 years ago, or between 1766 and 1768.

> I some years ago visited the great Iron-works of Coalbrookdale in Shropshire, where cast-iron was indisputably first applied to the construction of bridges; and according to the information which I have been able to obtain, it was here also that railways of that material were first constructed. It appears from the books of this extensive and long-established Company that between 5 and 6 tons of rails were cast on the 13th November 1767 as an experiment on the suggestion of Mr. Reynolds, one of the partners.

Were the 'rails' cast on November 13th, 1767, the bars described by Hornblower, or were they complete rails adopted as a logical development from the bars? However that may be, there is good evidence that 800 tons of cast-iron rails were laid at Coalbrookdale in the years 1768 to 1771.[1]

Farey gave an instance of a railway in Derbyshire laid in 1777 with 'Cast iron Bars, spiked down on wooden sleepers',[2] which is also described thus by Rees ('Cyclopaedia', article Canal):

cast iron rails on the extension of the Caldon branch of the Trent and Mersey Canal, to Mr. Gilbert's lime-works, four miles in length (which was in use long before 1794), were fastened down on longitudinal rails of wood, which lay across wooden sleepers embedded in the gravel.

There is more interesting history in Stevenson's 'Remarks', which proceed thus:

> The first Public Railway Company seems to have been established at Loughborough in the year 1789, under the direction of the late Mr. William Jessop. Here this eminent engineer introduced the edge-rail,

---

[1] See p. 54, *ante.*   [2] See p. 46, *ante.*

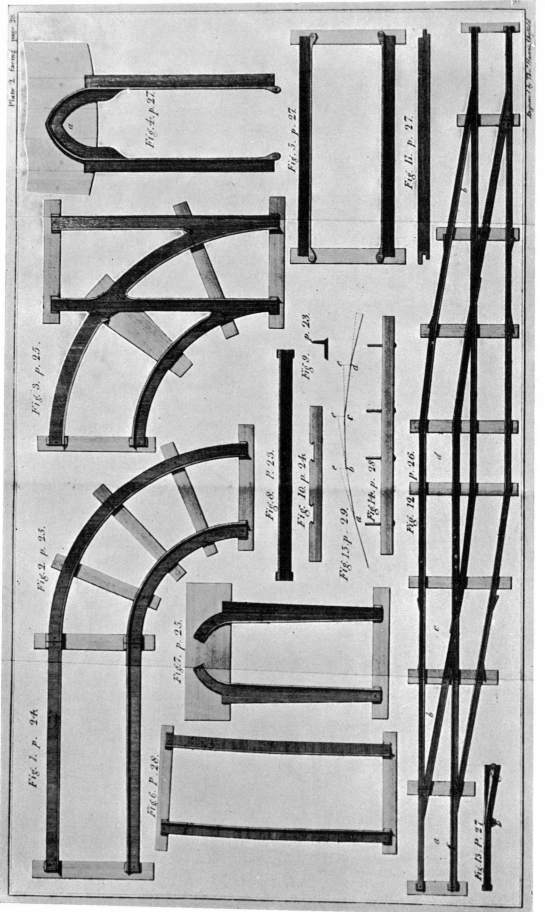

Plate 2 facing page 2

Fig. 4. p. 27.

Fig. 5. p. 27.

Fig. 11. p. 27.

Fig. 3. p. 25.

Fig. 9. p. 23.

Fig. 8. P. 23.

Fig. 2. p. 25.

Fig. 10. p. 24.

Fig. 13. p. 29.

Fig. 14. p. 28.

Fig. 7. p. 25.

Fig. 12. p. 26.

Fig. 1. p. 24.

Fig. 6. P. 28.

Fig. 13. P. 27.

Fig. 67. John Curr's cast iron tram-plates. (From his 'Coal Viewer', 1796)

FIG. 68. Rails, Kilmarnock and Troon Railway. (After Strickland, 1825)

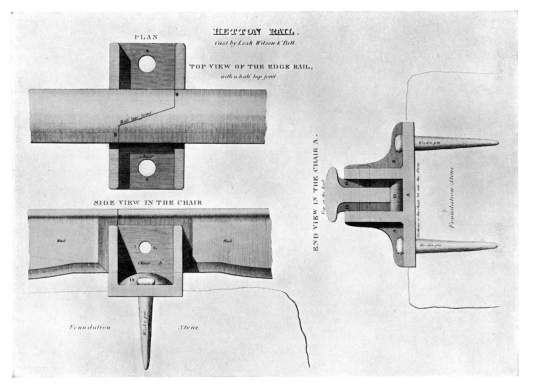

FIG. 69. Hetton rails. (After Strickland)

the upper surface of which was an elliptical figure, with flanges upon the wheels to guide them upon the tracks of the road, for hitherto the Plate or broad rail, under various forms, is understood to have been solely in use. About ten years afterwards Mr. Benjamin Outram, an engineer of acknowledged ingenuity and merit, constructed the public railway of Little Eton in Derbyshire. Here the plate-rail was adopted, with the flanges cast upon the rails, instead of having them upon the wheels, as is the case in the edge-railway. Here also, the improvement of stone props was introduced, instead of timber, for supporting the ends and joinings of the rails.

From this point the plate rail with stone-props seems to have become general, both in England and Wales, but experience, it is believed, has shown that the edge-rail possesses many advantages over the plate or flat track. Malleable iron is every day coming more and more into use for edge railways. It appears to have been first introduced about the year 1815 at Lord Carlisle's coal-works on Tindall Fell in Cumberland.

We will return to Tindale Fell anon; for the present we will keep to cast iron.

The 'plate-rail', i.e. that on which the wheels were guided by a vertical flange (cast on the rail), seems to have been introduced by John Curr, at Sheffield, at first underground. He was 'Superintendent of the Coal Works' to the Duke of Norfolk from 1780 to 1801. He wrote an excellent book on the subject, 'The Coal Viewer, and Engine Builder's Practical Companion', 1797. The author's copy is, however, dated 1796, and was probably a proof.[1] The 1797 copies, of which there are not many, have a more elaborate title-page.

In the preface Curr stated that 'the making and use of [iron] rail-roads and corves were the first of my inventions, and were introduced at the Sheffield Colliery about twenty-one years ago', i.e. he was working in Sheffield about 1776. The Duke of Norfolk's Sheffield Colliery was leased out until 1780. During this lease a wooden waggon-way or 'Newcastle road' was laid between the colliery and Sheffield, probably in 1774. There is no evidence that Curr was associated with its construction, or indeed that he was in Sheffield as early as 1774. In 1780 the Duke began to mine his coal directly, with Curr as manager. His rails were at first used only underground, and tribute to their efficiency was paid in a report by John Buddle, made in March 1787, which in dealing with the costs of 'the new scheme for hurrying the coals' includes 'Expenses of Cast Iron Plates, and Barrow-way'.[2] This antedates the line at Wingerworth, of 1788, said by Farey to be the first plate-line.[3]

The design of Curr's rails is shown in Fig. 67. The plates were '6 feet long, 3 inches broad on the trod, and $\frac{1}{2}$ an inch thick'. He went on: 'The

---

[1] C. E. Lee, introduction to 1970 reprint of 'The Coal Viewer . . .' (1797).

[2] Ashton and Sykes, 'The Coal Industry of the Eighteenth Century' (1929).

[3] See p. 43, *ante*.

margin stands 2 inches high above the plate, and is $\frac{1}{2}$ an inch thick where it joins upon it, but is tapered to the top, (which is rounded) to $\frac{3}{8}$ of an inch thick, for the convenience of moulding.' More minute instructions follow, and the weight is given as from 47 to 50 lb.

The rest of the book is taken up with the most elaborate description of a Newcomen pumping engine, at the highest stage of its development, that ever appeared.

The iron rails as described in his book are recommended for use underground. But he says he had used the gravity method of conveyance (loaded waggons pulling up the empty ones) above the ground, for 300 yards; probably on iron rails.

The wooden railway he made out of doors about 1774, and the riot it occasioned, has been mentioned at the beginning of Chapter III. It was replaced by plate-rails from Butterley, said to have been cast from Curr's drawings.

Curr's own book shows that the flanges were on the inside of the rails, but it may be remarked that they are shown incorrectly, on the outside, by Hebert in his 'Engineers' and Mechanics' Cyclopaedia' (1836) and his 'Practical Treatise on Rail-roads' (1837); also in all three editions of Wood.

The plate-rail, laid on stone blocks, became the standard almost all over the country, except in the north, the lines being usually called Outram ways, from their principal constructor, whence the false derivation of 'tramways' has arisen. A typical example is shown in Fig. 68, which is from Strickland's illustration of the Kilmarnock and Troon track of 1810.

Channel-shaped rails were used occasionally, perhaps only in exceptional places, such as over bridges, &c., e.g. Silkstone[1] and Hay[2] Railways.

An approach to the modern form of rail was introduced by Outram's partner, William Jessop; being a reversion to the form of the original wooden railway, but constructed entirely of cast iron, while the flange went back to the wheels once more. This innovation was made on the Loughborough and Nanpantan Railway in 1789, as has been mentioned in Chapter III. Hebert's 'Encyclopaedia' (1836) says the upper surface of the rails was flat, and the under of an elliptical shape. Jessop did not patent them.

The 'edge-rails' made their way but slowly in the Midlands and south of England. Even the Surrey Iron was laid with plate-rails, as in fact were the majority of the early nineteenth-century lines. That the ques-

[1] See p. 40, *ante*. [2] See p. 107, *ante*.

tion was by no means considered settled at the time of the Stockton and Darlington Railway is shown by the following report made by George Stephenson on the subject, the original of which is in the Railway Museum, York.

OBSERVATIONS ON EDGE AND TRAM RAILWAYS

Observation 1st. From the end view of an Edge Rail as represented in Losh & Stephenson specification;—it is evident that nearly the whole of the substance is applied in the depth of the Rail. And according to Gregory's Mechanics "In rectangular beams the lateral strengths are conjointly as the breadths and squares of the depths". Hence the substance in edge Rails is disposed of in the most advantagous manner viz by increasing the depth.

Obsn. 2d. In the Tram plate Rail nearly half of the substance is contained in the Base, which evidently constitutes a beam with its broader face upwards; which from the above extract is the most disadvantagous position in which a Beam or substance of the Rail can be disposed of:—It is evident therefore that the Tram Rail must be considerably increased in weight to be equal in strength to the Edge Rail, which is generally done by introducing a ledge on the under side of the Base.

Obsn. 3d. The elevated surface or trod of the Edge Rail prevents dust or other inconveniences lodging thereon but the plate Rail on the contrary is an actual harbour for such obstacles (especially in windy weather) which will consequently increase the friction of the wheels moving on such a Railway.

Obsn. 4th. I have found from experience that all Railways when not lying due North & South: the wheels (of the carriages) & Rails on the South side wear more than those on the North and the difference of wear is considerably more on a Tram than an Edge Railway; since it is known that all metallic surfaces wear much more when they are dry than wet. Hence suppose a Tram Railway lying E & W and the face of the Rails to be in a humid state the South Rail will evidently be dryed sooner than the North; the trod of the former being immediately exposed to the Rays of the sun whilst the trod of the latter is defended therefrom by the upright ledge of the Rail. Then since the South wheels must wear faster it is evident that the North wheels will outrun them and by so doing will rub excessively against the ledge of the North Rail which will very much retard the velocity of the Carriages.

Obsn. 5th. It must be understood the form of Edge Railway wheels are conical that is the outer is rather less than the inner diameter about 3/16 of an inch. Then from a small irregularity of the Railway the wheels may be thrown a little to the Right or a little to the left, when the former happens the right wheel will expose a larger and the left one a smaller diameter to the bearing surface of the Rail which will cause the latter to loose ground of the former but at the same time in moving forward it gradually exposes a greater diameter to the Rail while the right one on the contrary is gradually exposing a lesser which will cause it to loose ground of the left one but will regain it on its progress as has been described alternately gaining and loosing ground of each other which will cause the wheels to proceed in an occillatory but easy motion on the Rails.

I beg to observe that the above observations are the results of actual experiments & should a doubt be entertained by any gentleman, abundant proofs can be given in testimony of what has been stated from authorities which cannot be doubted or if Col. Chaters or any number of gentlemen will take the trouble of inspecting the various apparatus which have led to the above conclusions I shall be happy to receive them at any time they may please to appoint.

George Stephenson.

Killingworth Colliery, May 19th 1821.

A more able and interesting exposition of the subject can hardly be imagined. The patent in Losh's and his name (No. 4067 of 1816) covered a larger area than would be permitted nowadays. It not only embraced a locomotive with 'steam springs', but also a new form of rail, the ends of which were tapered in a vertical plane, fitting together in a chair. According to Wood, they were very satisfactory, and were 'almost universally adopted on all new lines of road', but in the third edition he admitted that on almost all the modern railways square joints were used.

Rails according to the patent mentioned above, which were used at Hetton, are shown in Fig. 69.

It is interesting to see that the practice of coning the wheels was in use as early as 1821.

The forms of rails varied very much, all kinds of sections being tried. We have seen that the rails at Blaenavon, which were probably laid before 1794,[1] were bars 3 inches thick and 1½ broad, 'morticed and tenanted' at the ends.

In Chapter II authorities were given for the date and place of the first iron railway in the north, namely Lawson Main, or Walker Colliery, in 1797.[2]

It very fortunately happens that drawings have survived, in the Boulton and Watt collection of papers at the Birmingham Library. They are reproduced in Figs. 70 and 71. They are not dated, but there can be no doubt that they represent the rails of 1797, especially as they

---

[1] See p. 85, *ante*.   [2] See p. 16, *ante*.

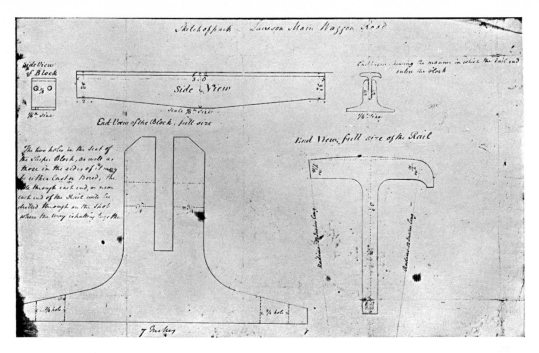

FIG. 70

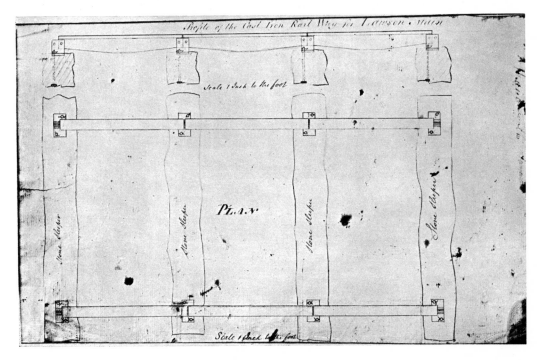

FIG. 71
Drawings of rails, Lawson Main Waggon Road

show stone sleepers, which Wood describes (stating it was the first use of stone supports). What is even more interesting, they show the first known chairs.

The first use of isolated square stone blocks, which became almost universal for both kinds of rails for a time, was, as we have seen,[1] stated by Stevenson to have been by Outram at Little Eaton (1800). But we know they were used on the Belvoir Castle line (1793), a feature probably taken from Outram; and there is a fairly strong possibility that they were adopted at Sheffield, where Outram was *persona grata*, when Curr's line was relaid, in order to have something more difficult for enemies to uproot, or burn, than wooden sleepers.

If Cadell's source of information is reliable,[2] they were used, as we saw in the last chapter, on the Tranent and Cockenzie Railway, as early as 1722, in conjunction with wooden rails.

Evidence has been given of the use of iron sleepers about this time in Wales.[3]

The first iron railways in the Midlands seem to have been laid down by Joseph Wilkes, by 1799; at Measham, Derbyshire, and Brinsley, Notts. He gave a description of them, which is quoted in Chapter III,[4] but says nothing about the section, so it was probably a simple one.

In the fifth chapter, Wyatt's rails on the Penrhyn Iron Railway are described from his own account in 1803.[5]

There were, of course, ideas put forward and patented of which no application can be discovered.

Woodhouse designed a hollow rail with a curved channel for the wheel (1803).

Charles Le Caan, whose name is also known in connexion with a brake which he proposed,[6] received twenty guineas from the Society of Arts in 1807 'for improved Tram-Plates for Carriages on Rail Roads'. He formed the rails with a tenon and mortise at the ends, and plugs cast on, to enter the blocks, and abolish nailing.[7]

Hawks proposed a cast-iron face on a wrought-iron bar in 1817.

The Elgin Railway, described in the last chapter, was of course *sui generis*.

A very late application of cast iron is shown in Fig. 72, from the High Peak Railway, opened in 1830; and in Fig. 73, a curious section cut from

---

[1] See p. 145, *ante*.
[2] Further inquiries have elicited the fact that he was depending upon family tradition. This is probably correct; he points out that stone could be obtained for nothing, whereas timber would have had to be purchased. [3] See pp. 85, 87, 89, *ante*.
[4] See p. 41, *ante*. [5] See p. 109, and Fig. 58, *ante*.
[6] See p. 166, *post*. [7] *Journal Soc. Arts*, vol. xxv, p. 87.

an actual rail, in the author's collection, which came from Dowlais, and marks the transition from plate-rail to edge-rail, being adapted to carry trucks intended for either.

It is interesting to note that a scheme for a plate-railway between Liverpool and Manchester was put forward as recently as 1898, by Alfred Holt, and was solemnly discussed by the Liverpool Chamber of Commerce. Particulars are given in a 'Report of a Select Committee on Light Railways', published at Liverpool in the year mentioned. The scheme was *not* recommended.

Benjamin Thompson claimed that he used the first 'edge rolly rails' at

FIG. 72. Cast-iron rail, Cromford and High Peak Railway (1830)

Ouston Colliery in 1816. By that he means on lines underground. But whether they were the first edge-rails used in a mine or not, we shall never know. He could not possibly be aware of what everybody was doing underground!

The *Mining Journal* for April 5th, 1862, contains an interesting letter written by Robert Stephenson in his nineteenth year, dated September 26th, 1821. He says cast iron was first introduced at Coalbrookdale; malleable at Lord Carlisle's coal-works at Brampton 'about five years since'. The line had been originally laid with cast-iron rails,

about twenty years ago. Malleable iron railways are now getting into pretty general use in Scotland; but perhaps the best example of this kind of railroad is to be found at Bedlington Iron Works in Northumberland, where Mr. Longridge has laid about three miles of it.

Turning to 'malleable' iron, Wood says that it was first introduced about the year 1805,

at Walbottle Colliery near Newcastle-upon-Tyne by Mr. C. Nixon; the rails were square bars, two feet in length, they were joined together by a half-lap joint, with one pin, one end of the rail projecting beyond the end of the adjoining one, two or three inches. Their use at that time was not extended, the narrowness of their surface would cut and indent the periphery of the wheels of the carriages; and they were on that account superseded, by the cast-iron rails with a broader surface.

As Walbottle was in Wood's own territory, it may be assumed that the above account is correct.

Robert Stevenson did not know of the above-described experiment. In his 1818 Report the following paragraph occurs, which bore rich fruit, as it led to the modern method of rail manufacture.

One point, however, deserves particular notice here, as likely to be attended with the most important advantages to the Railway system, which is the application of Malleable Iron instead of Cast Iron Rails. Three miles and a half of this description of Railway have been in use for about eight years on Lord Carlile's works at Tindal Fell in Cumberland, where there are also two miles of cast-iron rail; but the malleable iron road is found to answer the purpose in every respect better. Experiments with Malleable Iron Rails have also been made at Mr. Taylor's works at Ayr, and Sir John Hope's at Pinkie; and, upon the whole, this method, in the case of the Tindall Fell Railway, is not only considerably cheaper in the first cost than the Cast-iron Railway, but is also much less liable to accident. In the use of Malleable Iron bars, the joints of the Railway are conveniently obtained, about 12 feet apart, and three pedestals are generally placed between each pair of joints.

From the above, one would take 1810 as the approximate date of the experiment at Tindale Fell, but in Stevenson's 'Remarks' at the conclusion of the 'Highland' essays, written six years later, he gives 1815. Many of the early writers mention the episode, all giving slightly varying dates. The correct date is 1808, as appears in a letter from James Thompson, to be given presently.

The 'Edinburgh Encyclopaedia' (1824), in the article Railways, puts forward its own theory (still keeping the credit in Scotland), thus (it is followed by Cumming):

Malleable Iron was first introduced in Rail-Ways, we believe, by Mr. George Grieve, at Sir John Hope's Collieries, near Edinburgh [otherwise Pinkie], where it was first tried in the lighter work, which is done under ground. The Rails consist of square bars, one inch and one and a quarter inch square, nine feet long, resting on one or two sleepers in the middle, and resting and made fast to sleepers at the extremities; a simple knee being formed on each end of the bar, and the two knees of each two adjacent Rails jammed into one socket on the sleeper. The use of these Rails was found so beneficial, that they have since entirely superseded the Flat Cast Iron Rail in general use at the time of their invention.

Here follows the passage describing the Hurlet Railway, which was quoted on p. 131. The account goes on:

An improvement has lately been made in the construction of the Malleable Iron Rails, which promises to be of essential utility. It consists in the use of Bars, not rectangular, but of a wedge form, or swelled out on the upper edge.

. . . .

This has been accomplished by Mr. Birkinshaw of the Bedlington Iron Works, who has obtained a patent for these broad topped Rails. The peculiar shape is given them in the rolling of the Metal, by means of grooves cut in the rollers, corresponding with the requisite breadth and depth, and curvature of the proposed Rail. Mr. B. recommends his Rails to be eighteen feet in length. We have seen one of these Patent Rails at Sir John Hope's Colliery.

The rail they saw at Pinkie could not have been one of the first batch which was laid down there.

Another (unsuccessful) experiment was made at Wylam.[1]

John Birkinshaw's patent, dated December 2nd, 1820, was for the construction of malleable iron rails by passing them between rollers of appropriate profile, while hot.

The specification was published, with explanatory matter, and various supplementary information, in six editions, the bibliographical details of which are given in Chapter XII. Fig. 74 shows the illustration in the first two editions, reduced, and Fig. 75 part of the folding plate which appeared in that of 1824. The engine in the latter is evidently a representation of one of those built for Hetton, as it is practically identical with the illustration given by Strickland. The artist has omitted the exhaust pipe to the chimney; the horizontal pipe running between the cylinders should go straight on. He has added the interesting embellishments of the royal arms and a plate inscribed 'Stephenson's Patent Locomotive Steam Engine'. Whether these were imaginary, or ever appeared on an engine, one does not know: probably not.

In the 1827 edition, the plate illustrating the opening of the Stockton and Darlington Railway appeared, and this engine was copied very closely, with the intention of portraying Locomotion. The coupling chains were omitted, but no substitute supplied. The same simple crosshead guides were shown, instead of Locomotion's parallel motion; and steam springs; the plates with the coat of arms and description being retained.

There is an interesting proposal at the end of the specification, which is a very short one; as follows:

And, in order still further to remedy the evil arising from the joint of the Rail-Road, I propose to weld the ends of the Bars together as they are laid down, so as to form a considerable length of Iron Rail in one piece.

[1] See p. 154, *post.*

FIG. 73. Section of a compound rail from Dowlais, to act either as plate- or edge-rail. Early
nineteenth century. (Exact size)

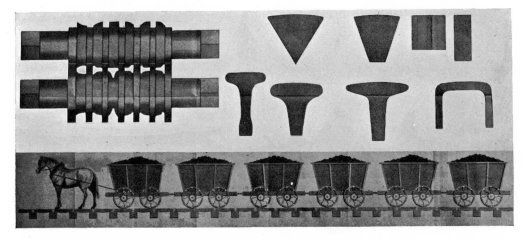

FIG. 74. First rolled rails, Birkinshaw's patent, 1820

In the 'Remarks', it is said:

The attention of the Patentee was first drawn to the subject of substituting *Malleable* for *Cast* Iron Rails, by reading the Report of Mr. Stevenson, on the Edinburgh Railway.

With regard to this point, the following letter from George Stephenson to Robert Stevenson, dated June 28th, 1821, is interesting:[1]

With this you will receive . . . a specification of a patent malleable rail invented by John Birkinshaw of Bedlington near Morpeth. The hints were got from your Report on Railways . . . Your reference to Tindall Fell Railway led the inventor to make some experiments on malleable iron bars, the result of which convinced him of the superiority of the malleable over the cast iron—so much so, that he took out a patent.

There are some interesting points in letters which are reproduced in the pamphlet.

It appears that William Chapman, in a 'Report on the Cost and separate Advantages of a Ship Canal and of a Rail-way from Newcastle to Carlisle' —which were rival schemes on foot at the time—had disparaged rolled rails, saying they were liable to 'separate in thin Laminae'. Birkinshaw asked, in a letter dated November 23rd, 1824, on what railway that effect was produced, going on to say that there were only two on which his rails had been travelled over by locomotives; namely Killingworth, where they were laid in 1820, and Heaton in 1821 (thereby confirming the existence of an engine there).

The letter to which reference has been made as settling the date of the malleable rails at Tindale Fell, from James Thompson, is dated 'Tindle Fell Colliery, December 7th, 1824', and begins thus:

Sir,—Having read in the Newcastle Courant, the Discussion between you and William Chapman, Esq. respecting the Lamination of Malleable Iron Rails used for Rail-Roads, and having under my care a Rail-way, whereon several Miles both of Cast and Wrought Iron Rails are used, I have sent you herewith a Piece of the latter, *which has been laid sixteen Years, and certainly has no Appearance of Lamination.*

That fixes the year as 1808.[2] James Thompson was the Earl of Carlisle's Colliery Agent, and was instrumental in purchasing the Rocket in 1837. George Stephenson gave him a milk-jug decorated with a picture of a train, which is now in the author's collection.

In the edition of 1832, a copy of a letter from Longridge to George Buchanan, the Scottish railway engineer, is given in which he describes how the idea was suggested by Stevenson's Report, and says the matter

---

[1] 'Life of Robert Stevenson', p. 128.   [2] See also 'Life of Telford', p. 684.

arose in consequence of an offer from a colliery company in 1818 to supply the Bedlington Iron Company with coals at a reduced price, if the latter would lay a railway to the colliery. Tomlinson, in the 'History of the North Eastern Railway', gives some interesting details of this line. The colliery was the 'Willowbridge or Bedlington Glebe'. The account is as follows:

Shortly afterwards George Stephenson, by the advice of Mr. Long-ridge, joined Thomas Mason, the lessee, as a partner, and the Bedlington Iron Company laid the proposed road for him. This waggonway, which George Stephenson probably set out himself, is now used as a footpath by the side of the Morpeth branch (Blyth and Tyne section) of the North Eastern Railway from the neighbourhood of Choppington Station to Bedlington Colliery, from which, to the old staith at the east side of the Bedlington Viaduct, it exists as a strip of waste ground fenced off from the present road to the disused Iron-works.

Tomlinson goes on to say that 'the importance of this waggonway in the evolution of the iron road can scarcely be over-estimated'.

It was visited by William James and Robert Stevenson, who both called it the best they had seen;[1] and by the deputation from the Liverpool and Manchester Company in 1824.

Returning to Longridge's letter to Buchanan, he says that malleable iron rails had been tried at Wylam, as well as at Tindale Fell. The former were bars about 2 inches broad, and $\frac{3}{4}$ of an inch thick, which were placed *edge-ways*. They were found so injurious to the waggon wheels, as to oblige the proprietors of the colliery to remove them. The railway bars at Tindal Fell were bars one and a half inches square; the objections against them were chiefly; 1st, that the surface upon which the wheels ran was too narrow, and 2ndly, that the depth of the rail could not be increased without adding so much to its weight, and consequently to its cost, as to prevent malleable rails being generally used. . . .

Mr. John Birkinshaw, the principal Agent at these Works, suggested the idea of making these Railway bars "*wedge-form*" . . . By the recommendation of John Buddle, Esq., we afterwards made the rails with a swell or curvature in the middle. . . .

The Stockton and Darlington Railway Company were the first public company who adopted the use of malleable iron Railway bars. . . . with the advice of Mr. Stephenson . . . who, although *interested* in favour of cast iron (being a joint-patentee of the best cast iron Railway bars then in use); yet had the candour to recommend the others as superior.

The 'wedge-form' was changed to that of a T.

---

[1] Compare Robert Stephenson also, p. 150, *ante*.

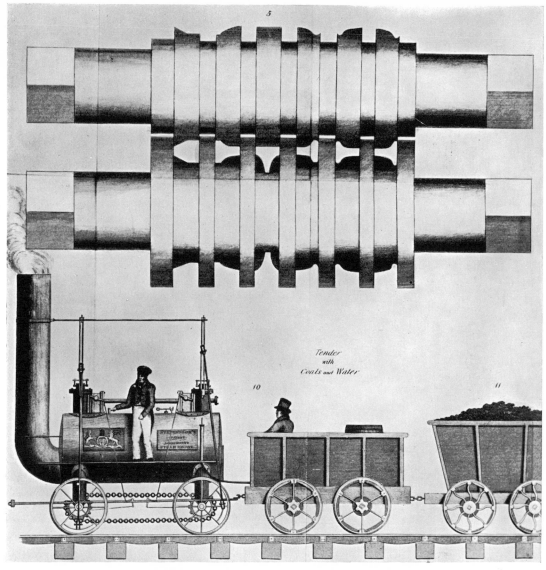

FIG. 75. Birkinshaw's rolls for rails and a Stephenson locomotive

FIG. 76. Bedlington Iron Works near Morpeth. (From a lithograph of 1827)

CHAPTER VIII

INCLINED-PLANE WORKING: BRAKES: SOME 'FREAK' SYSTEMS

THE first appearance of the idea of causing full waggons in their descent to draw empty ones back is in Michael Meinzies' patent No. 653 of 1750. His invention was described as

a Machine for the carrying Coals from the Coal Walls where they are Dug to the Bottom of the Pit or Shaft and from the Mouth of the Pitt or Shaft to the Heaps at some Distance therefrom and in some Cases of carrying them to the Staiths, or Places where they are Put on Board Keels or Ships, without the Assistance either of Horses in drawing Empty or Loaded Waggons, and of a New Method of . . . drawing the coals from the Bottom of the Pit . . . to the . . . top. . . .

He proposed a double waggon-way, inclined; loaded 'boxes' bringing up empty ones by an endless rope passing round pulleys at the ends. They could also be drawn by a vessel full of water. To draw coals from the heaps to the staiths, the arrangement was similar, or the waggon-way might be single, with a passing-place. There could be waggons of water to increase the weight. (The method proposed for 'winding' the coals was to draw them up the shaft by a counterbalance of water in a cistern.)

The beauty of the idea does not seem to have appealed to any one at the time; various people are given the credit in the old books, Meinzies being apparently quite forgotten by the time his method of working inclined planes was put into practice.

The system was first employed in connexion with canals, as a sub-stitute for locks; the earliest successful application being at Ketley in Shropshire, by William Reynolds,[1] in 1789.

William Chapman, in 'Observations on the various systems of Canal Navigation' (1797), says:

The merit of this invention, or, at least, the first introducing it into practice (which was I believe totally unknown to Mr. Reynolds) is due to the late Mr. Davis Dukart, an Engineer in the Sardinian service, who settled in Ireland, and became engaged in the Tyrone collieries. . . .

This work was executed a little prior to the year 1777, but except-ing in passing a few boats by way of trial, nothing more was done, as Mr. Dukart could not obtain money to complete some of the intervening

[1] Eldest son of Richard Reynolds. See p. 54, ante.

levels, and died soon after the time mentioned. The works were then entirely laid aside; and, a few years since, a common railroad, cutting off a considerable portion of the distance, has with propriety been adopted in their stead.[1]

It may be mentioned that Smeaton made a report on the Tyrone Canal, dated April 30th, 1774,[2] in which he gave a rather half-hearted recommendation that Dukart's scheme should be tried.

Returning to Ketley, Chapman gives the following account:

The system lately introduced into this kingdom by Mr. William Reynolds of Ketley, viz. that of connecting . . . different levels of Canals, of great intervening height, by means of an inclined plane, with two parallel rail-ways; up and down which, by the aid of a rope passing over a wheel at the head of the plane, boats of 8 tons burthen alternately pass upon carriages, over which they are floated at each extremity of the fall. The loaded boat (the trade being descending) draws up a light boat, or occasionally a half laden one. The first of these works was at Ketley in Shropshire. The carriage downwards was principally coals, and about four hundred tons daily. . . .

The chief difficulty in going from a higher to a lower level, without waste of water, lay in passing the ridge, or dam, which retains the water at the end of the upper level. This he overcame two ways.

In the first method, which he carried with effect about seven years since, he avoided the ascent from the upper level to the ridge holding up the water, by the means of two parallel Locks at the head of the inclined plane; into one of which the laden boat floated on its carriage; and the light boat, when ascended into the other was by the admission of water floated off. The water consumed in these Locks was let into a side reservoir, and in dry seasons pumped back by a steam engine to the other level. Mr. Reynolds has great merit in the invention of this method.

The second method, as practised, at the inclined plane below the iron bridge at Broseley, in Shropshire, differs from the former in having no Locks, and the boats being drawn upon the ridge by a steam engine; which also occasionally draws up the light boats, without waiting for the laden ones. The boats, as in the other, are floated upon four-wheeled carriages, which ascend and descend alternately.

Figs. 77 and 78 show a contemporary token depicting on one side the inclined plane at Ketley, and giving its date as 1789, which must therefore be taken as authentic, though it is usually said to be 1788. This plane is one of the few still remaining, and was in use within the present century.

[1] See p. 136, *ante.*   [2] Smeaton's Reports, vol. ii, p. 278.

Drawings of the other one are given in 'Mémoires sur les Travaux Publics de l'Angleterre', by J. Dutens, 1819 (which also contains an illustrated description of the Surrey Iron Railway); described as 'at Hay, on the Shropshire Canal at two miles from the iron bridge'. There is a 'Hay House' near by, close to Coalport.

One other arrangement of the kind may be mentioned as it attracted a great deal of attention at the time, and has the additional interest of

FIGS. 77 & 78. Coalbrookdale token, 1792. (Author's collection)

being underground; which is described thus in the 'Edinburgh Encyclopaedia' (article Railway):

> A highly interesting work also occurs at the Duke of Bridgewater's underground works at Worsley, about seven miles from Manchester. Here the works are so accommodated that boats containing about ten tons of coal are let down upon an inclined plane fitted with cast-iron plate-rails measuring eight inches broad, and an inch and a half in thickness, laid with a uniform bearing upon solid rock from one canal to another, the empty boats being at the same time passed upwards. This inclined plane is 150 yards in length, having a declivity of one perpendicular to four horizontal.

Chapman says, in a footnote to p. 52 of his 'Observations', that he was informed the inclined plane was 'now completed', i.e. in 1797. In 1800, the Duke presented a description of it to the Society of Arts, for which he received a gold medal.

The best guide to the subject of inclined-plane working on land railways appears to be Wood.

In the *Newcastle Magazine* for 1822 (vol. i, p. 205), he wrote: 'The utilisation of loaded waggons to pull up empties was first adopted on Mr. Brandling's rail-road.' Unfortunately he did not say when. The upper part of Brandling's plane has been shown in Fig. 19, as it appeared to Strickland in 1825.

In Wood's 'Treatise on Railroads', another device is described, thus:[1]

The first self-acting plane,[2] erected near Newcastle-upon-Tyne,[2] was by the late ingenious Mr. Barnes, on which the descending train of waggons drew up, out of a pit or well sunk at the summit, a plummet of considerable weight; which plummet, in its descent, drew the empty carriages up the plane.

The locality and date are supplied by Matthias Dunn, 'View of the Coal Trade of the North of England', 1844 (p. 52):

The first self-acting plane was effected by Mr. Barnes at Benwell Colliery, in 1797; the full waggons descending by their own gravity, and the empty ones being drawn back by means of a balance weight. The first attempt under engine power was made under the direction of Mr. Curr,[3] about the year 1805, who applied an engine to raise the coals from the valley at Birtley to the high grounds of Black Fell, and which was immediately followed by the magnificent project of Harrison, Cook and Co., in 1808, of conveying the coals from Urpeth Colliery to the river Tyne, over the heights of Ayton Banks, by a succession of inclined planes, partly wrought by engines.[4] The practicability was thereby fully established; but the cost so far exceeded all calculation, that the company was utterly ruined, and the concern shortly afterwards changed hands.

The usual system was the simple one in which the rope was passed round a large wheel revolving in a horizontal plane, to which brakes were applied. There were, however, more complicated arrangements. Wood illustrates one, in which the ropes are alternately wound and unwound on two drums with their axes horizontal, geared together, and capable of being driven round by a steam-engine. He mentions the erection of an engine on Birtley[5] Fell by Mr. S. Cooke in 1808, 'to draw the loaded carriages of the Urpeth[5] colliery across the Durham and Newcastle turnpike road, up a steep ascent'.

There is a curious and interesting method of keeping a waggon horizontal when on an incline, described in Hebert's 'Treatise on Railroads' (1837). It was proposed by Scott, who wrote the brilliant 'Highland' essay which has been of so much assistance in writing the present work. It is hardly likely to have been put into practice, because it involved four lines of rail. The front wheels of the waggon were on a narrow gauge,

[1] First edn., p. 104.
[2] Were these commas intentional? Because they have an important bearing on the meaning. He retained them in all three editions.
[3] Who is Mr. Curr? Our friend from Sheffield?
[4] The pit was Bewicke Main.
[5] These names are misspelt in the 1st edn., but corrected in the 2nd. For an account of the opening, on May 17th, 1809, see p. 19, ante.

and the rear wheels broad.   The wide rails ran on walls outside the inner track, and began to ascend at a distance equal to the wheel-base behind the point where the narrow ones started to go up.   Another of Scott's proposals was to pull up the waggons by buckets on a rope, filled with water. Hebert states that some of Mr. Scott's propositions had been carried into effect in a modified form.

A curious device, by which the horse was enabled to ride downhill, was the 'dandy cart'.   Where it was at first used, is not known.   An illustration in Tomlinson's 'History of the N.E.R.' shows three different applications, on the Stockton and Darlington, Ballochney, and Throckley Railways.

The following description, from the *Liverpool Mercury* of July 18th, 1828, relates to the first mentioned:

Improvement on the Darlington Rail Road.

There is something very ingenious, and, at the same time, whimsical in the plan we are about to describe.   As one good turn deserves another, we vastly like the notion of treating the horse to a ride in his own carriage.

A gentleman of this town has lately made a contrivance, which is equally curious and useful.   On the Darlington Rail-way the descents are so great that the loaded waggons will run down of themselves twelve miles out of twenty.   It is usual to take off the horse, and hang him by a halter to trot after the waggons, by which he is very much shaken, and more injured and fatigued, than by going the same distance at a lower rate with a load.   It has been found necessary, in conveyance, to make use of light horses, of little power, ill suited to the rest of the work.   The invention is intended to remedy this inconvenience, and consists of a light truck upon two wheels,[1] which is fastened behind a common waggon, and has a small manger in front.   The horse being placed in this, down what are called the runs, quietly eats his provender, and is quite refreshed when his services are again required.   He seems greatly pleased with his conveyance, and to be aware of how much labour he is spared; he gallops up and jumps into it at full speed and can be got out and attached again without stopping.   The driver can give greater velocity to the waggons, and is thereby enabled not only to save time, but also to run over a great extent of level ground, where power is otherwise required.   Should the dreadful accidents, which have recently occurred from explosions, lead to the abandonment of the locomotive engine, the saving to the Darlington Railway from this contrivance, cannot be estimated at less than a thousand a year.   The committee have determined upon its adoption, and have ordered a considerable number to be made.   It will also have a great effect in diminishing the expense of constructing future railways, as it renders a certain "undulation" in the line less objectionable.

[1] If 'two' is correct, it must apply to a first proposal which was afterwards modified; but probably it is a mistake for 'four'.

From a letter from George Stephenson to Timothy Hackworth[1] dated a week later than the above quotation it appears that the former claimed to have originated the idea, but that it had been introduced in consequence of a suggestion of Brandreth's. The latter, it will be remembered, entered a horse-machine for the competition at Rainhill the following year.

The use of dandy carts on the Ballochney Railway was mentioned by George Buchanan in his 'Account of the Lanarkshire Railways'.[2] There he ascribes the credit for the first introduction to the Mauch Chunk Railway in Pennsylvania, but Tomlinson considered the Stockton and Darlington to have been the first. He says that the practice continued on the Throckley line until 1907.

An illustrated sheet of note paper was issued at Carnarvon (undated), with a view of Portmadoc, showing the railway and a train of trucks, with the horse in a dandy cart.

From using a stationary engine to haul waggons up an incline, to doing so on the flat, is but a short step. The high priest of this system was Benjamin Thompson, whose patent was enrolled December 14th, 1821. A copy of the specification was published at Newcastle in the following year with 'Remarks thereon by the PATENTEE, and the Result of a Trial of the Invention, &c. &c.'. It is dated January 3rd, 1822.

In the preamble he says

that there are various modes in use by which animal and mechanical powers are made available for the purpose of conveying carriages upon rail and tramways, where the trade, or carriage, is principally, or altogether, in one direction. Fixed engines are employed to draw loaded carriages up inclined planes, the empty carriages being enabled by their gravity, and the declination of such planes, to run down the same and take out the rope, from the engine, along with them. Self acting planes are made use of where it is expedient to pass loaded carriages down declivities sufficiently great to allow their pulling upward an empty set of carriages at the same time. And where neither the acclivity nor the declination of a road is such, as to admit of one, or the other, of these methods being adopted, then horses are used for the purpose of drawing the carriages, and in some, altho' very few instances, locomotive engines.

He did not, of course, attempt to claim for the application of fixed engines to tractive purposes, but described a system of arranging a line in stages, with engines distributed at intervals along it, each pulling a train, which drew a rope behind it, ready for attaching to the next returning one. Where convenient he used the weight of a descending train to help the engine behind it, a device which he said was quite new, and had

---

[1] Cited by Tomlinson, p. 154.   [2] p. 128, *ante*.

never been used before,[1] but he did not claim it as any part of his invention. The latter he sums up in these words:

the reciprocal action of two engines, standing at the extremities of a stage, or portion of road to be travelled over, one engine drawing the carriages forward in a direction towards itself, and along with them a rope from the other engine, which rope, in its turn, pulls the same, or other waggons, by means of the other engine, back again, and also a rope therewith—thus by the alternatively active and passive agency of two ropes, are the powers of fixed engines made to act in opposite directions, thereby causing a road to be traversed, both ways, by loaden, or empty carriages, and at any desired speed.

For Stephenson and Locke's description, see p. 27, *ante*.

In the 'Remarks' which follow, he says:

Upon the waggon-way from Ouston Colliery, in the county of Durham, seven miles from Newcastle, leading to the river Tyne, four miles below that place, and in length seven miles and a quarter, the stage was selected upon which this new mode of conveyance has been put in force.

.   .   .   .

Six loaden waggons coupled together, carrying the same number of Newcastle chaldrons, or 15 tons 18 cwts. of coals, pass upwards at a speed of $10\frac{1}{2}$ feet per second, or 7 miles an hour, with the greatest ease and certainty, affording a dispatch by no means derived previously from the use of animal power. The two extremities being visible to each other, are furnished with flags, to give alternate signals of the readiness of the waggons to proceed. When the atmosphere is hazy and the flags cannot be seen, signals are made by drawing forward the rope, three or four yards with the engine, at that end from which the waggons are intended to go, and which is instantly perceived at the other end. And in the dark (for the work is daily prosecuted during five or six hours absence of light, at this period of the year) signals are given by a fire kept at each end for lighting the workmen, which is shut from, or open to, the view of the opposite extremity, by means of a door. A person accompanies the waggons, constantly, seated in a chair, fixed securely upon the fore end of one of the soles of the leading waggon of the set, which is easily removed from one end to the other. The use of such attendant is to disengage the haulage rope from the waggons by means of a spring catch in the event of any sudden emergency, such as the breaking of a wheel or rail, or the hazard of running down any object, the stage in question, lying over a common. Friction wheels, of cast iron, weighing 14 lb. each, having an axle of malleable iron, turned in a lathe, and weighing 1 lb., running upon

[1] The suggestion of novelty is rather subtle, because other people had used an engine to assist the descending weight!

a frame of oak, are placed eight yards asunder on the straight parts of the way, and five yards from each other along the curves.

Preparations are further making for carrying the same method into use . . . on the waggon-way from Fawdon Colliery.

BRAKES

The waggons had not only to be propelled on the level and uphill; it was equally important to control their speed on descending grades, especially as the loads were generally downhill.

The earliest publication dealing exclusively with the subject of brakes which is known to the author is one by Oswald D. Hedley, published at Newcastle in 1834; being a paper read before the Literary and Philosophical Society of Newcastle. The title is 'A Descriptive Account of the means used on the Tyne and Wear for effecting the safe Transit of Railway Carriages, in ascending and descending steep planes; together with a Historical sketch of the Brake, as applied to Railway Carriages'.

He begins by giving Desaguliers' account of the brakes on Allen's waggons, the hind wheels of which were retarded by brake-blocks pressing downwards upon them, and the front wheels by iron pins which were pushed between the spokes, and locked them. He mentions that for more than half a century later, the custom in other parts of the country was only to brake the rear wheels. He then gives the following description of brakes in the Newcastle district, taken from the *London Magazine* of 1764; with an illustration, reproduced in Fig. 79.

A coal waggon is drawn by a single horse, and guided by a single man. (See Fig. 1). It has four wheels; the two fore wheels are cast of metal for that purpose, and weigh several hundred weight, as represented at C and D; the two hind wheels are of wood. The extremities of the axles are fixed in the wheels, and turn round; the axles are of iron, as represented at *c c*. At F is a convoy, so called by the waggonmen but it is more properly a lever, for it is by this the waggon is guided when it comes down what the waggonmen call runs, or what may be called a precipice, or bank, or rising ground, where the waggon has to come down descendingly. Were it not for this convoy or lever, it would be impossible to guide the motion of the waggon down what are called as before runs, at such places of the waggon-way where they have to descend. This convoy or lever is taken out of a convoy band, as at G, and then the convoy or lever presses on the hind wheel, as at H. At I is a loyter pin, so called by the waggonmen, which pin is put into the end of the convoy or lever to hold it, so as it may not jump out of the iron ring at K. Sometimes they have pieces of wood, which they put into the ring to keep the convoy together, and which the waggonmen call scotches, and they lie in a scotch box, as is represented at L. The driver or waggonman has always the convoy in readiness against he comes to the top of these runs or banks, and then he instantly jumps upon the convoy or lever, by his weight and strength pressing upon the convoy or lever, so as to stop as he thinks

Fig. 1.

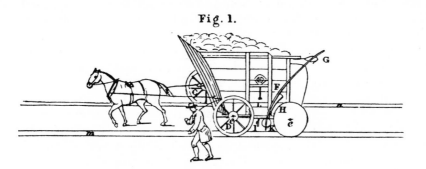

Fig. 2.

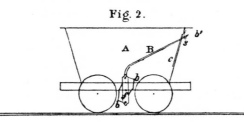

Fig. 3.

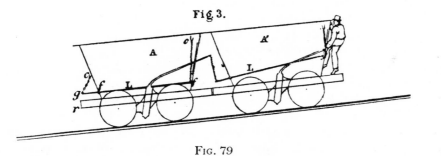

FIG. 79

proper, or to let it go fast or slow, till he gets down such places. They commonly unloose the horse when they come to the runs, and then put him to again when down. The reason of their taking him off at such places is, that were the convoy to break, it would be impossible to save the horse from being killed, or if the waggon-way rails, as at *m* and *n*, be wet, sometimes a man cannot stop the waggon with the convoy, and where the lever presses upon the wheel, it will fire and flame surprisingly. Many are the accidents that have happened as aforesaid; many hundred poor people and horses have lost their lives; for were there ever so many waggons before the one that breaks its convoy, and has not got quite clear of the runs, all are in great danger, both men and horses, of being killed. . . .

Inefficient as the brake in this state evidently was, it continued so until the year 1790, when its action was extended to the fore wheels of the carriages, rendering it thus a lever both of the first and second orders, and which forms an important era in its history. . . . This improvement, which is represented in Fig. 2, is stated to have taken place at Shield Row Colliery. B is the brake of the carriage A, which may be either of iron or wood; *f*, its fulcrum; *b b*, temporary pieces of wood, termed breasts, affixed to it, the design of which is to prevent its immediate contact with the wheels when applied. When wore, they are, without injury to the brake, replaced by others, and are generally made of birch or alder, these descriptions of wood being most suitable for the purpose, on account of their friction and durability. To prevent the lateral movement of the brake, a long iron *c*, is used; *s* is a small crook, to hold or support it when its action is not required; when circumstances render this necessary, it is taken out of the crook, and descends upon the wheels.

The brake under this form gave the rider complete control over the carriage to the limits of its friction upon the rails; but circumstances connected with the conveying of carriages along lines of railway shortly rendered the friction of more than one carriage essential to their safety. On railroads generally, anterior to the year 1793, each waggonman had charge of one horse and one waggon . . . but at the Western collieries, in that year, one man took charge of two horses, and consequently of two waggons. On the arrival of the carriages at the runs . . . one was occasionally left at the top until the other got down; but more frequently . . . the carriages were connected together by a coupling chain, the horses disengaged, and made to walk behind them. The brake of the first carriage was then put down, the waggonman taking his station at the brake of the last, the friction of which, to its limits on the rails, he could increase at his discretion. When the friction . . . was insufficient . . . it occasionally happened (probably the readiest means that presented itself) that a mouthpoke, filled with corn, was hung to the end of the brake of the first carriage, for the purpose of still further augmenting its friction; and this may be considered the first attempt at applying the brake in extension of one carriage—a humble one, certainly, yet, being the immediate precursor of that description of brake appropriately termed the long brake, it might with much probability originate the idea. The frequent occurrence of accidents under this precarious mode of descending the runs, forcibly directed the attention of an ingenious waggonman of the name of Hall, residing at Pontop Colliery, to the subject, the result of whose ingenuity was the invention of the long brake, in the year 1795 . . . the object in view was to enable the rider to have as much control over the first carriage as over the last, and which will readily appear on reference to Fig. 3.

It is unnecessary to give Hedley's lengthy description; the man applied
the brake on the rear waggon in the ordinary way, by pressing the lever
down; and by pulling up the chain, applied the brake on the forward one,
on which the lever L is shown out of action.

He then proceeds to describe an extension of the idea to an unlimited
number of waggons, beginning as follows:

So long as horses were the sole motive power on railroads, there
was nothing wanting in regard to the practical utility of the long brake;
but the opening out of a number of collieries in the interior, consequent
on the increasing demand for their valuable produce, and of the partially
wrought-out state of several in the vicinity of the two rivers; from the
steep, and in many parts, in regard to the application of horses, impracticable nature of the ground which intervened between them and their
places of shipment on the banks of the Tyne, and Wear, and over which
the transit of the carriages was to be effected; the consequent introduction
of the self-acting plane towards the close of the last, and of the steam
engine at the beginning of the present century, as a mechanical agent or
prime mover on railroads, when the transit of heavy trains of carriages
was to be effected, the action of two brakes on which, were obviously
insufficient to excite the requisite degree of friction consistent with their
safety; and further, as ropes were the communicating medium between
the power and the resistance, to obviate the effects generally consequent
on their breaking;—to these, with other causes, may be attributed the
still further extension of the brake which we now proceed to describe.

A train of waggons is then shown in which each has a chain connecting
the extremity of its brake lever to a point lower down, at the front of the
following waggon, the effect being, that if it ran forward to the extent of
the slack of the coupling chain, the brake would be put on. Thus the
action of applying the brake in the ordinary way on the last waggon
gradually brought them all into action. He says that this system makes
the use of the brakes on the drums of self-acting planes scarcely ever
necessary, and mentions a number of collieries where the brake-chains are
in use.

A description of what are now called 'catch points' follows, which he
believed were first introduced on the Stockton and Darlington Railway;
and ends with particulars of an apparatus called a 'cow', which was a kind
of double sprag with feet shod with iron, dragged up behind the last
waggon.

The primitive form of continuous brake described by Hedley appears
to have been used on the Liverpool and Manchester Railway, for George
Stephenson, when giving evidence on the G.W.R. Bill in 1835, said '40 or

50 waggons loaded with goods from Manchester frequently go down together, one Man managing the whole, there is a Brake to each, which by the chain to it he can tighten as he likes; they go by their own impetus at any rate the Man pleases'.

Hedley omitted to mention a brake invented in 1798 by a man named Le Caan, of Llanelly. This consisted of a shoe or shoes, attached to the shafts by a chain, and arranged to come into action if the horse fell and let the shafts down. As the latter were very seldom used on railways, it is not likely to have had any extensive application.

The paper by T. V. Simpson on the old Mining Records at Newcastle, from which quotations have been made in earlier chapters, contains a very interesting letter on the subject of brakes from William Brown[1] to Carlisle Spedding at Whitehaven, dated July 30th, 1754:

. . . As to the Runns in our Waggonways I know of none that exceeds 3 inches in a yard and very few that is so much, for we find that our Convoys will not hold a Large Waggon when the Runns is so much. Notwithstanding we lay Ashes and sometimes Cynders to Ruffen the Railes. Therefore in the Collieries where Sharp Run happens are forced to go with Lesser waggons than common tho knows of none so little as yours which as I Remember Contains only 18 Bools and the least of ours is 19 Do but most is 24 Bools. I think there is no Deficulty at all in getting your waggon Down tho your way be Streight as your greatest Descint? ye is no more than 3 foot in Ten yards; the Hard thing upon you will be your mettle wheels some of which indead is in our Country but these is used as fore wheels for we allways have wood for the Hind wheels which with a Convoy well Breasted will totally stop or Trail the Hind wheels and that is all that can be done by your Convoy. We have Lately contrived what we call a Long Convoy (i.e. Brake) which goes to the fore wheels & by the help of little Contrivance at the Hind End of the wagon the Same man Manages both so that now can trail all the four wheels.

Mathias Dunn ('View of Coal Trade'), speaking of the eighteenth century, when both rails and wheels were made of wood, says:

The waggons were regulated in their speed by convoys, bearing upon a single wheel; and in order to prevent the wear of the wheels (which were extremely expensive to maintain) they were studded thick with nails driven up to the heads; but the wear was proportionately great upon the breasts of the convoys, which was a source of great labour and expense. The braking of the waggons down the many rude steeps, was attended with continual loss of life, both to man and horse.

[1] This W. Brown obtained a lease of the Greenwich Hospital royalty at Throckley in 1745, after the estates of the Earl of Derwentwater had been sequestrated.

Wood gives the following interesting description of working on inclines:

Frequently where very steep descents occurred, for many days the work was laid off on account of the weather, a sudden shower of rain occurring when any of the waggons were on the declivity, set the whole away, and men were stationed to draw ropes, as booms across the line of road, to stop their progress. If the ropes could be drawn across before their momentum became very great, the damage was less; but if they broke the ropes then the most disastrous effects followed. . . . When the cast-iron wheels came into use, the hind-wheels of the waggons were still made of wood, that the brake might be enabled to take a better hold in regulating the descent. . . .[1]

After it [the brake] was prolonged beyond the fulcrum, and made to act on both wheels, the effect being doubled, I presume they found its action upon the cast-iron wheels sufficiently powerful . . . to secure the proper hold: the wooden wheels were therefore relinquished.

An unusual form of brake is described in Rees' 'Cyclopaedia', article Canal:

Some waggons which we have seen, had the convoy fixed to a move-able joint at the front of the waggon and had a large block of wood thereon, which when the convoy was let down, wedged in between the fore and hind wheels and acted most securely as a brake for stopping or regulating the velocity of descent.

The expression 'acted as a brake' shows that at that time (1819) Rees had not got quite so far as actually to call it one. Scott did so, in 1824.

In Chapter V it was recorded that Sir Humphry Mackworth made use of sails to propel his waggons. There is an interesting note on their employment for the opposite purpose in Lecount's 'Practical Treatise on Railways' (1839), where it says that 'on some of the American railways there are places so steep that sails are made use of in descending them to check the velocity'.

Brakes seemed to have originated on railways; they did not appear until quite late on horse-drawn road vehicles. The Commissioners of Post Office Inquiry, in their Seventh Report (1837), give drawings of 'improved mail coaches', but no brakes are shown. Thrupp's 'History of Coaches' (1877) says: 'The use of brake retarders to the hind wheels has now for some years superseded drag shoes.' Sir Walter Gilbey in 'Modern Carriages' (1905) says: 'Brakes in a practical form were first

---

[1] Obviously, the wooden wheels would not become so hot as iron ones.

fitted to private carriages about 1860–5; brakes of a kind were occasionally fitted earlier than 1860, but they were of little use.'

They were employed on the steam road coaches of the thirties, being
a necessity, to hold the vehicle still on an incline, apart from controlling
the speed.

SOME 'FREAK' SYSTEMS

Among the multitude of ideas which were put forward in the first
quarter of the nineteenth century in connexion with locomotion, and came
to nothing, there were one or two which were developed with a moderate
degree of success later on, and are therefore worthy of notice, especially
as from the originality of their character they are of considerable interest.

One of the agents which it was proposed to employ was the atmosphere;
and railways worked by this means were, to a certain extent, successfully
introduced in the forties; at which time they seemed to be quite formidable rivals to those on the normal principle, and had a number of
distinguished supporters, among whom were Farey, Field, Brunel,
Vignoles, and Cubitt. The author possesses a collection of books and
pamphlets on the subject which was formed by Samuda, to which he
has made considerable additions, and which now consists of about forty
volumes of all sizes, all bound uniformly.

The pioneer of this system was George Medhurst, who described
himself in a patent specification as a mathematical-instrument maker, but
whose principal business seems to have been the manufacture of weighing
machines of various kinds. It has been frequently said that he was a Dane.
This statement first appeared in a French report many years ago, and has
been often repeated, but the author has never found anything in Medhurst's own writings (of which he has a complete set), nor in any contemporary English publications, to support it, and feels sure it was due to
a foreigner's misunderstanding, based on the fact that Medhurst's address
was Denmark Street, Soho. It is curious how history is sometimes made.

His publications, which are now of great rarity, are as follows:

1. A New Method of conveying Letters and Goods with great certainty and rapidity
   by Air. 11 pp., 1810.
2. Calculations and Remarks, tending to prove the practicability, effects and advantages of a Plan for the rapid conveyance of Goods and Passengers upon an Iron
   Road through a Tube of 30 feet in area by the power and velocity of Air. 18 +
   (1) pp., 1812.
3. On the Properties, Power and Application of the Aeolian Engine . . . 23 pp., no
   date.
4. A New System of Inland Conveyance for Goods and Passengers, capable of being
   applied and extended throughout the country; and of conveying all kinds of Goods,

Cattle and Passengers, with the velocity of sixty miles in an hour, at an expense that will not exceed the one-fourth part of the present mode of travelling, without the aid of horses or any animal power. 34 pp., 5 plates. Followed by a four-page catalogue of weighing machines made and sold by Medhurst; and two pages describing a patent canal lock and lock gate. 1827.

He took out the following patents:

2299 of 1799. Condensing Wind Engine (i.e. a windmill working a pump to compress air. This was the 'Aeolian Engine').

2431 of 1800. Driving carriages without the use of horses (by compressed air stored in a reservoir, or, alternatively, by an internal-combustion engine with 'flint' ignition!).

2467 of 1801. A 'compound crank'.

2525 of 1801. A washing machine (he seems to have been the pioneer of the mechanical laundry).

4164 of 1817. A 'hydraulic balance' (lift for raising or weighing boats, &c., on the principle of the Bramah press).

Returning to his publications; the 'New Method' described the system of sending letters through a pneumatic tube, which was afterwards successfully carried out and widely applied; going on to propose it for goods and passengers in a tunnel of 12 feet area, the air to be impelled by a steam engine.

In 'Calculations and Remarks' he develops the idea, promising the conveyance of passengers at a mile a minute at a farthing per mile, and goods at a penny per ton per mile.

The 'Aeolian Engine' book proposes air compressed by windmills as a substitute for steam. The following quotation is interesting:

The late attempt to drive a carriage by strong steam,[1] though imperfect in itself, affords an abundant proof of the practicability of performing the same thing by condensed air; as this principle is entirely free from all those imperfections found in the application of steam to the purpose, namely, the cumbrous machinery, the weight of the furnace, fuel and water, the constant attendance of the fire, with the heat, smoke, and expense of fuel, all of which are unnecessary upon the Aeolian principle; moreover the condensed air may be conducted to great distances by tubes, so as to renew the charge of the magazine in motion every half hour, if required, and will continue its force unabated when it is not in action, which steam will not do; it is also ready the instant required, and may be magnified to a degree of strength, by artificial means, approaching to infinity.

The 'New System' describes more fully a pneumatic railway in a tunnel, now to be 6 feet high and 5 wide. He includes the principle of driving

[1] Probably referring to Blenkinsop, but we do not know exactly when he was writing.

the carriage by means of a vacuum; making the engine exhaust, instead of compressing. He then goes on to describe the system under which the carriages are outside the tube and are driven by a connexion through a longitudinal slot to the piston, which is that afterwards put into practice. The weak point, never satisfactorily dealt with, is of course the longitudinal valve, for which his design was hopeless. He preferred the other way of working, thus:

the greatest objection to this mode, and of the dimensions, is, that it is exposed to the wind, which would not only vary its velocity, but, the power being so feeble, it would entirely stop it, when any strength of wind was against it; while the carriage within the aerial canal cannot be affected by the winds nor the weather, by the frost or the snow, but might continue its course, under all the vicissitudes of nature, from one end of the kingdom to the other, so that a man might breakfast in London, dine at Edinburgh, and return to London within twelve or fourteen hours of his departure; and his travelling expenses, for this transit of 800 miles, would be paid with one sovereign.

The next projector of atmospheric railways was John Vallance of Brighton, who put the whole train in a tunnel, and constructed a short experimental line in 1826. His bibliography is as follows:

1824. On Facility of Intercourse. (Inst.C.E.)
1825. Considerations on the Expediency of sinking capital in Railways.
1825. Journal of Arts and Sciences No. LVIII, contains extracts from Vallance's specification (sealed February 19th, 1824).*
1827. A Letter to M. Ricardo Esq. in reply to his letter to Dr. Yates, on the proposed method of pneumatic transmission, or conveyance by atmospheric pressure.*
1833. A Letter to the Kensington Canal Company, on the substitution of the Pneumatic Railway for the common Railway.*

* Author's collection.

He proposed to form his tunnels of iron cylinders about 6 feet in diameter and 12 feet long. The carriages were to be cylindrical in shape, and were to be propelled by exhausting the air.

Several atmospheric railways were constructed between 1840 and 1847, and worked more or less satisfactorily. One from Paris to St. Germain was operated until 1860. They were all on the principle of having the train outside the tube, and the cause of failure was the difficulty of keeping the longitudinal slot airtight.

In the author's opinion, Vallancé's idea is quite a sound one, except that it would only be suitable for cases where a tunnel was necessary in any case; and in *The Engineer* for May 13th, 1932, he outlined a scheme for the Solent, and showed that a full-sized express train could be driven across at high speed with the expenditure of half the power necessary by the usual systems, while that required for a specially designed tube train would of course be very much less.

In 1823 a 'Description of a Railway on a new Principle' appeared, by Henry R. Palmer (2nd edn., 1824). This was the first mono-rail proposal, afterwards being put into practice as the Lartigue system. The book contains a discussion of railways from a general point of view, and

FIG. 80

gives some figures of resistance, which were frequently quoted by succeeding writers. Palmer was prominent in connexion with the London and Brighton schemes, and was the principal founder of the Institution of Civil Engineers. He wrote a paper in the *Journal of the Franklin Institute* in 1828, advocating the use of sails on railways. An illustration is given of his railway with that method of propulsion, from Hebert's 'Practical Treatise on Rail Roads' (1837).

Two short lines were made on Palmer's principle, on which horses were used: one at the Victualling Yard, Deptford; and one from some lime-kilns and tile-works near Cheshunt to the Lea Canal.

The best account of these lines is given by von Oeynhausen and von Dechen, in 'Ueber Schienenwege in England, 1826–27'. The following is a translation:

Palmer Railway in the Royal Victualling Yard, Deptford, near London.

This railway leads from the Thames through the Yard to the warehouses and serves for the transport of stores from there to the ships or vice versa. The railway consists of cast iron columns which project 3 to 4 feet above the ground, provided with forked pieces at the upper end and distant 10 feet apart. In these forks rest 9 by 3 inch planks on folding wooden wedges so that they can easily be adjusted to the right level. On the upper edge of these planks are nailed rolled iron rails, $3\frac{1}{2}$ inches broad of slightly convex shape, $\frac{1}{2}$ an inch thick in the middle. The ends of these rails are not square but end in a broken line and do not rest directly on the planks, but on a small iron plate let into the plank.

The road is very nearly horizontal and has only a fall to the river of about $\frac{1}{3}$ of a degree.

The wagons which run on these rails have three wheels of 18 inches diameter, one behind the other, which have two flanges and a rim shaped to the cross-section of the rail. These wheels are fixed fast in a wrought iron framing which consists of three stirrups going over the wheels and bound with one another; in these stirrups are fixed the axles of the wheels. These stirrups reach two or three feet below the railway and are provided on both sides with an inclined platform upon which the casks to be transported are laid. For loading the wagons, two upright frames serve; between them the wagon has just room and they are at the same height as the platform of the wagon. On each wagon ten casks can be loaded, the weight of each of which is about $4\frac{1}{2}$ centner, that is altogether 45 centner (4960 lb. or 2·21 tons). The wagon can be loaded up to 5 centner which makes the whole weight 50 centner, a load that can be moved upwards easily by four men.

Palmer Railway from the Limekilns and Brickkilns at Cheshunt to the Lea Canal.

From the lime and brick kilns on the highway at Cheshunt in Hertfordshire, about 20 miles north of London, a Palmer railway leads to the Lea Canal, along the quite flat and even Lea Valley. The railway had a fall of 1/6 to $\frac{1}{3}$ of a degree towards the canal. The length is 3 quarters of a mile; it serves for the transport of lime and bricks. The railway rests on wooden posts which project above the ground $3\frac{1}{2}$ feet on an average; in the direction of the lime kilns, the bottom of the road is in a cutting in the ground so that the posts stand in a kind of dry ditch 9 feet wide at the bottom. The wooden posts are at a distance of 10 feet from one another, and are 4 inches thick by $7\frac{1}{2}$ inches wide; above they are cut fork-shaped 3 inches broad and 16 inches deep. In the bottom of this fork lies a block 12 to 15 inches long of different heights; the block is carried by a pair of . . . angle pieces 14 inches high and 2 inches thick. On these rest two folding wedges 2 feet long such that the plank lying on them presents always a horizontal base. The planks are $10\frac{1}{4}$ inches high and 3 inches thick, 30 feet long, and the joint is in the middle of the post; through these posts pass iron bolts with nuts in order to hold together the forked end of the post; in the plank are oblong holes through which pass the posts in order that the wedges lying below can be driven when it is necessary.

These planks are overlaid with rolled iron rails, 4 inches wide, convex on the top, $\frac{1}{4}$ inch thick at the edges and $\frac{1}{2}$ inch thick in the middle. The individual rails are 20 feet long, cut off slanting at the ends and fastened with not more than two or three spikes $\frac{1}{2}$ an inch diameter, their heads being countersunk in the rails. Apart from this, the rails have reserve spike holes which can be used if one or other of the spike-heads breaks off.

Some of the posts are composed of three parts; the pieces are 6 inches wide, the middle one 3 inches thick and the two side pieces $2\frac{1}{4}$ inches thick, fastened together with three screw bolts; the wedges rest on blocks bolted together, which are 1 foot long on the top. Although the planks are very thick, they have been, on account of the great distance of the posts apart, bent in some places and have been brought back by supports inserted below at a later date.

In the vicinity of the canal there is a siding in the railway. The latter is doubled for a length of about 30 feet, and between the double parts and the single track, a strong door 10 feet wide is applied; this door is hung on the single track and can be fastened to either of the two tracks. On the upper edge of this door lies the railway, and directly over the hanging part a little piece of rail capable of being drawn aside in order to break the great angle which the door makes with the track. With a door like this, the railway crosses an ordinary highway.

The wagons which run on these roads have only two cast iron wheels 26 inches diameter provided with two flanges; the wheels inclusive of the $\frac{1}{2}$ inch thick and $1\frac{1}{4}$ inch projecting flanges, are $5\frac{1}{4}$ inches broad, have six spokes and a nave 6 inches long and 2 inches diameter. The wheel revolves about a hollow cast iron axle, 2 inches thick and $12\frac{1}{2}$ inches long, which at both ends rests in round brass bearings. The latter measure inside $1\frac{5}{6}$ of an inch and outside $2\frac{1}{2}$ inches and are $3\frac{3}{8}$ inches long internally. The bearings rest in plummer blocks which are situated in the wrought iron stirrups which constitute the principal framework of the wagon. Through the hollow cast iron axle and the brass bearings goes a wrought iron axle 26 inches long and 1 inch diameter which at its ends is connected with the stirrup and contributes to the more secure fastenings of the wagon framing. The two axle boxes are 46 inches apart. The platforms on which the wagon container is placed are situated 40 inches below the axle and 17 inches apart inside. The wagon containers, of which there is one on either side of the wagon, have a capacity of 20 cubic feet. Such a container is loaded with about 20 centner of lime or bricks and therefore a wagon load altogether is 40 centner. One horse draws two such wagons or 80 centner, exclusive of the containers and the wagons.

There was a short description of the Cheshunt line in the *Mechanics' Magazine* for August 6th, 1825, concluding thus:

One carriage, which has been constructed for the purpose of trying the application of the plan to the conveyance of passengers, differs from the others. Its boxes partake partly of the shape of a gig, and partly that of a balloon-car; in each are two cushioned seats *vis-à-vis*, with a little dickey behind, the whole carriage being covered with an awning.

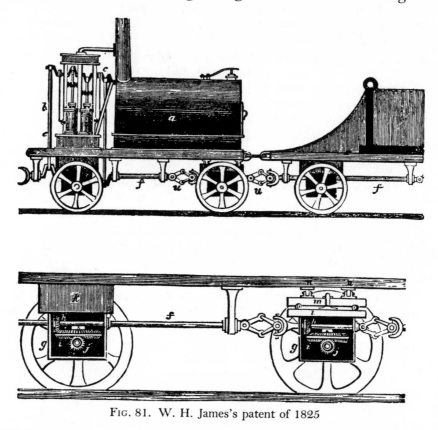

FIG. 81. W. H. James's patent of 1825

One more scheme may be noticed, as, although there is no record of its having been put into practice at the time, it was a foreshadowing of the Renard train, being a system by which all the axles on every vehicle were driven. It was patented by W. H. James in 1825, and is illustrated here from Hebert.

CHAPTER IX

THE AWAKENING OF PUBLIC INTEREST IN THE NINETEENTH CENTURY

Pʀɪᴏʀ to the year 1800, railways had been very short affairs and, with a few exceptions, intended entirely for private use.

In the first few years of the nineteenth century, a number of far-seeing individuals, who had realized their possibilities to a greater or less extent, published essays on the subject; and this chapter is devoted to a collection of some of the more interesting passages which are contained in their works.

On February 11th, 1800, William Thomas, of Denton Hall, Northumberland, read a paper before the Literary and Philosophical Society, entitled 'Observations on Canals and Rail-ways, illustrative of the agricultural and commercial advantages to be derived from an Iron Rail-way, *adapted to common Carriages*, between Newcastle, Hexham, and Carlisle; with Estimates of the presumed expense, tonnage and revenue'.

The paper was not printed until 1825, when it appeared in the form of a pamphlet published at Newcastle-on-Tyne, together with the second edition of a report on a proposed navigable canal between Newcastle and Hexham, by Barrodall Robert Dodd, civil engineer; and an appendix advocating a more extensive canal.

It appears from an 'Introduction' that by 1825 both Thomas and Dodd had died, as they are called 'the late'. Thomas's paper is stated to have been read in 1805, but there is a manuscript slip of paper in the copy belonging to the Society (which has been kindly lent to the author), giving February 11th, 1800, as the actual date. It has been confirmed by the Secretary, who has referred to the original minutes.

Thomas, therefore, is entitled to head the procession of prophets with whom we are dealing. Although his paper was written with a view of advocating the Newcastle and Carlisle Railway—which had to wait thirty-five years before it was made—the opening remarks are of quite general application. They are as follows:

In a country where commerce occupies so much of the attention, and constitutes so great a portion of the comforts and conveniences of its inhabitants, every measure that has a probable tendency to give additional vigour and expedition to general intercourse, merits the peculiar support and countenance of the public. The means of facilitating the carriage of heavy articles through the country, in the least expensive way, has long and deservedly been considered an object of great national importance, of which the multiplied introduction of canals bears strong evidence; and certainly no object of commercial speculation has a higher claim to un-qualified approbation, or which has, in various instances, so essentially answered the end proposed; yet there is a variety of objects unfriendly to the establishment of canals, so generally as the state of the country demands; such as natural impediments, individual prejudices, or local derangement of pleasure grounds, or forest scenery, and above all, the uncertainty of the expense which the execution may incur, and which the most judicious calculation is found unable to remove. There appears, therefore, a necessity for a middle line, embracing some of the advantages of a canal, divested of most of the objections above enumerated,[1] and possessing so great a superiority over the present mode of conveyance upon the public roads, as to render a plan advantageous to the adventurer as well as the public. To delineate the general outlines of such a plan, shall be the object of these observations.

When the mode of conveyance, established by many individuals in this country, for the carriage of coals from the pits to the vessels on the river, is considered, it may readily be conjectured that the plan proposed has a reference to that kind of conveyance, where the power of a horse is equal to two tons and a half, exclusive of the weight of the carriage, which is somewhat more than one ton, and which he draws with ease about three miles an hour. Hence we find a facility of conveyance, con-sidering the weight, very superior indeed to that at present practised on the common roads, where the weight drawn, by a single horse, is seldom more than twelve hundredweight, exclusive of the carriage, and that at little more than two miles an hour. This principle is, therefore, con-sidered perfectly applicable to the proposed plan, with some little varia-tion, which the increased quantity of carriage, and the more permanent nature of the road, seem to point out. The disposition of the road is in-tended to be as nearly horizontal as the nature of the ground, over which it passes, will permit; but in no part to ascend, or descend, more rapidly than at the rate of about one inch and a quarter in each yard [1 in 29].

It is proposed that no horse shall convey less than two tons, exclu-sive of the carriage, which including this inequality in the road, he can easily do. Though this may occasion a more circuitous route for the article to be conveyed, yet the superior quantity carried with more ease and expedition, are considerations which must overbalance the incon-venience arising from an increased length of the road. By the road ad-mitting of this inequality, some of the objections which attach to the line of a canal, where the preservation of a level is so essentially necessary, may be avoided. Commencing the ascent, or descent, in any given situa-tion, the line of the road may be so far diverted as to pass undisturbed

---

[1] It is curious that he did not perceive that every one of the objections mentioned applied also to railways.

those favored spots which the prejudices of individuals hold in estimation; or those great and almost insurmountable barriers which nature places in the way of a canal.

Instead of the common wood rail used in collieries, it is proposed to form this way of cast metal plates, applicable to the passage of the common carriage wheels, with a tread-way of five inches for each plate, and a ledge or margin three inches high, to prevent the carriage slipping off the road. Each plate to be about five-eighths of an inch thick, and four feet six inches long, to be laid at the joints on oak sleepers, and the middle of the plate to be supported by blocks of stone, twelve inches square in which shall be cut a grove to receive the thickness of the plate, and an oak plug in the centre, to which all the plates are proposed to be nailed. Where the way crosses common roads, small concave plates are intended to be fixed, to admit carriages to pass over it without obstruction from the ledge of the plate, as well as to allow their going off, or coming on, to the way without inconvenience. By the adoption of metal plate ways, in preference to the common wood rail-way, a great part of the friction of the latter will be avoided, the facility of conveyance increased, and the road rendered much more durable. In every half mile of the road, sideways of about sixty or seventy yards long, are proposed to be laid to admit carriages passing each other.

After a few further remarks of a descriptive nature, he gives an estimate of the cost, of which the total is £1,500 per mile on one section and £1,600 on another. The rest of the paper is taken up with estimates of the probable traffic and revenue. He also discusses the advisability of having two roads, and the accommodation of light traffic, such as the mail coach and post-chaises.

The next work of the kind with which we are dealing appeared in 1801, in Dr. James Anderson's 'Recreations in Agriculture, Natural-History, Arts, and Miscellaneous Literature,' vol. iv, from which the following are extracts:

Rail-ways, a mode of forwarding weighty articles that has long been in use under certain local peculiarities, but which has not yet been introduced into general practice. At the first, these were employed solely for transporting coals, chiefly for a moderate distance, from the coal pit to the place of shipping, and were universally made of wood. Long had they been applied to this use, without any idea having been entertained that they could be employed for more general purposes. By degrees they were carried to a farther extent; the scarcity of wood and the expence of their repairs suggested the idea of employing iron for the purpose of improving these roads. At the first rods of bar iron were nailed upon the original wooden rails, or, as they are technically called, *sleepers*, and this, though an expensive process, was found to be a great improvement. But the wood on which these rested being liable to rot and give way, some imperfect attempts were made to make them of cast iron, but these were found to be liable to many objections, until the business was taken in hand by Mr. Outram, engineer, at Butterley Hall, Derbyshire, who contrived at the same time so far to diminish the expence and improve the state of the road as to bring them to a degree of perfection that no one who has not seen these can easily conceive could have been done.

Railways of this kind may be seen leading from Derby to the Collieries, in that neighbourhood,—five miles. 2nd. Crick[1] rail-way,—one mile and a half, from the lime rocks to the Cranford[2] Canal. 3d. Messrs. Barber and Walker's rail-way from Biggarlee[3] Colliery to the Cranford Canal—one mile and a half. 4th. The Peak Forest rail-way from the limeworks near Boston to the canal near Whaley bridge—six miles. 5th. The Marple rail-way, on the Peak Forest canal—one mile and a half. 6th. Railways over Blisworth hill near Nottingham, on the Grand Junction Canal—three miles and a half long, double, just finished. 7th. The Ashby-de-la-Zouche rail-way—four miles of double and eight miles single rails, not yet completed, but will be finished about Midsummer next. These rail-ways were executed nearly in the order stated, and those last mentioned are of course the most perfect. All, I believe, in Derbyshire.

Topography was not the Doctor's strong suit, nor was he good at spelling names. Nos. 6 and 7 were not in Derbyshire. Blisworth is of course near Northampton, not Nottingham. The railways there were only temporary, for use while the tunnel was being made on the canal. All the above-mentioned lines have been dealt with before, in their appropriate places.

Anderson suggested the use of something very like 'containers'; i.e. waggons with bodies which could be lifted by a crane from the frames carrying the railway wheels, and placed on similar frames with road wheels and shafts.[4] He proposed railways 'from London to Bath, and any other part of the country'. A single line to cost about £1,000 per mile; double, about £2,000;[5] in the neighbourhood of London, £3,000. The cost of turnpike roads he states is £1,000 to £2,000. The annual repairs of the road from Hyde Park Corner to Hounslow came to considerably above £1,000 per mile. He expressed a hope that railways would never become 'a source of gambling traffic, similar to that which has taken place to such a vast extent with regard to navigable canals'. To guard against these evils, railways, he said, must never be private property, but must be on the same footing as public roads, under a set of Commissioners.

To equalize the labour of drawing loaded waggons downhill and the

---

[1] Crich.   [2] Cromford.   [3] Beggarlee.
[4] This suggestion rather leads one to infer that he had edge-rails in mind; but it was not so, as appears later.
[5] A double line of course does not cost twice as much as a single one, for a number of reasons.

empty ones up, the gradient should be about 1 in 100; or 'if the rail-way and carriages be of the very best construction', 1 in 150. On steep inclines iron slippers are to be used under the wheels:

where the descent is very great, steep inclined planes, with machinery, may be adopted, so as to render the other parts of the railway easy. On such inclined planes the descending loaded waggons being applied to raise the ascending empty, or partly loaded ones, the necessity of sledging the wheels is avoided; and the labour of the horse greatly reduced.

He recommended stone blocks for sleepers:

rails of the stoutest cast iron, one yard in length each, formed with a flanch on the inner edge about two and a half inches high at the ends, and three and a half in the centre; and shaped in the best manner to give strength to the rails, and keep the wheels in their track. The soles of the rails, for general purposes should not be less than four inches broad; and the thickness proportional to the work they are intended for. On rail-ways for heavy trades, great use, and long duration, the rails should be very stout, weighing 40 lbs. or, in some cases, nearly half a hundred-weight each.

The best width of road for general purposes is 4 feet 2 inches between the flanches of the rails; the wheels of the carriages running in tracts about 4 feet 6 inches asunder. Rails of particular form are necessary where roads branch out from, or intersect each other; and when carriage roads cross the rail-ways; and at turnings of the rail-ways, great care is required to make them perfectly easy. The rails of that side forming the inner part of the curve should be fixed a little lower than the other; and the rails should be set a little under the gauge, so as to bring the sides nearer together than in the straight parts: those deviations in level and width to be in proportion to the sharpness of the curve.

So he proposed super-elevation; and the suggested narrowing of the gauge on a plate-rail corresponds to the present practice of widening it slightly on our edge-rails, in order to ease the passage of the curve.

In Nicholson's *Journal of National Philosophy, Chemistry and the Arts* (New Series, vol. i, 1802) another essay appeared, which was the first to suggest the application of power to railways.[1] It was headed 'On the Practicability and Advantages of a general system of Rail Roads and the Means of carrying the same into effect. In a Letter from Richard Lovell Edgeworth, Esq.'. The following are extracts:

Many years ago I formed the project of laying iron rail-ways for baggage waggons on the great roads of England, but having consulted several of my friends, who were eminent mechanics, so many objections

[1] The first actual application was Trevithick's locomotive, on February 13th, 1804. The first use of a stationary engine for haulage was on the Bewicke Main waggon-way on May 17th, 1809 (see p. 19, *ante*).

were started, that I for some time despaired of success. One great objection arose from the vast expence of massive rail-ways, and the continued cost of repairs. To obviate this difficulty, it occurred to me to divide the weight that is usually carried on a single waggon into four or five portions and to place them on four or five small carriages; these carriages linked together would be as easily drawn as the same load upon one waggon. In pursuance of this idea, about 1768 I presented models of three such carriages to the Society for the Encouragement of Arts and Manufacturers, who for this and other inventions in mechanics, honoured me with their gold medal; the date of which and the journal of the Society may ascertain the early claim which I have to this invention. In 1788 I constructed four carriages with cast iron wheels, truly turned and supported on friction rollers; these were shown to several eminent persons and were employed upon a temporary moveable wooden railway for a considerable time, in carrying limestone for the improvement of land. . . .

I propose, that by way of experiment, iron rail-ways should be laid on one of the great roads to the distance of ten or twelve miles from the metropolis, upon something like the following plan: four rail-ways should be laid on the road, raised on sleepers of stone, so that their upper surface should stand about four inches above the road. They should be made hollow from the bottom upwards, for strength and to save expense, broad at bottom, and rounded at the top, to prevent the lodgment of dirt and dust. On these should run light waggons, each containing not more than one tun and a half weight.

I have mentioned four railways. The two inside roads should be appropriated for waggons and the two external rail-ways for coaches and chaises, &c. . . .

Now to accommodate coaches and chaises, &c. to these rail-ways, I would have them carried wheels and all in cradles or platforms, *which should have wheels adapted to the rail-ways* . . .

It is not impossible by *slight circulating* chains, like those of a jack running on rollers, to communicate motion between small steam-engines, placed at a considerable distance from each other; to these carriages might be connected at will, and when necessary they might be instantly detached. What a prodigious saving of expense might thus be effected? If the freedom and facility of intercourse, which has been obtained by good roads and canals, be, as Adam Smith asserts, one of the great causes of our national wealth, how far might the freedom and facility of intercourse be extended by the perfection of the scheme, whose outlines I thus lay before the public.

The above proposals were repeated, much condensed, in a book which Edgeworth published in 1813 (2nd edn., 1817), entitled 'An Essay on the Construction of Roads and Carriages'.

In 1770 he had taken out a patent (no. 953) for 'caterpillar' traction. Smiles states that sailing waggons were also covered,[1] but this is not so.

[1] 'Life of G. and R. Stephenson', edition of 1862, p. 74.

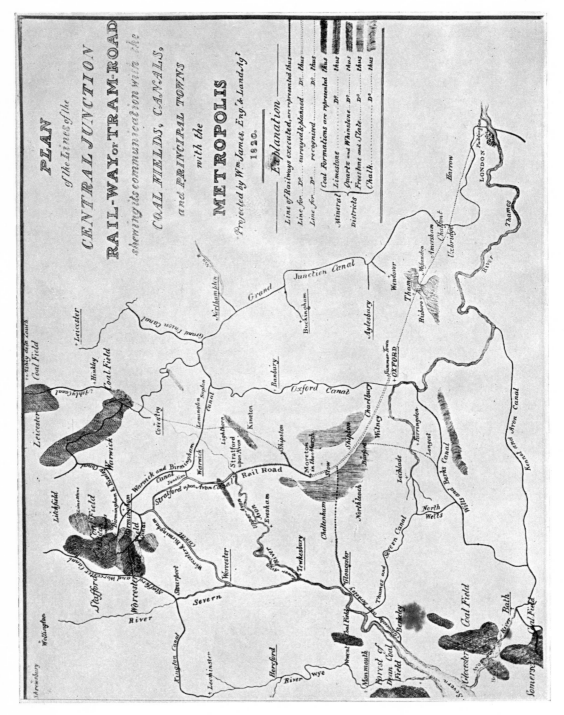

Fig. 82.   One of James's railway schemes, 1820

The patent (which is the only one on record in his name) was for a 'Portable Railway or Artificial Road, to move along with any carriage to which it is applied'. The invention is only vaguely described, without any drawings, thus:

Several pieces of wood are connected to the carriage, which it moves in regular succession in such a manner that a sufficient length of railing is constantly at rest for the wheels to roll upon, and that when the wheels have nearly approached the extremity of this part of the railway their motion shall lay down a fresh length of rail in front, the weight of which in its descent shall assist in raising such part of the rail as the wheels have already passed over, and thus the pieces of wood which are taken up in the rear are in succession laid in the front, so as to furnish constantly a railway for the wheels to roll upon.

The greatest of all these early projectors was William James (1771–1837), particulars of whose life will be found in a little book entitled 'The Two James's and the Two Stephensons', published in 1861. There is also a small pamphlet, anonymous and undated, in the British Museum, called 'Biographical Notice of William James, Esq. Projector of the Railway system in England'. Some account of him will also be found in Chapter III of the 'Centenary History of the Liverpool and Manchester Railway'.[1] In the early years of the nineteenth century he projected a number of lines, the best known of which is the Stratford and Moreton, opened in 1826. The following list is given in both of the first-mentioned publications:

Mr. James projected and surveyed the following lines of Railway, principally at his own expense—and many miles, during the latter part of his life, by his own labour:
1. Manchester and Liverpool, and adjacent lines to Warrington and Bolton.
2. Birmingham and Manchester, through Derbyshire.
3. Birmingham and Wolverhampton.
4. London and Birmingham, through Oxford.
5. Moreton-in-the-Marsh.
6. Canterbury and Whitstable.
7. Bishop's Stortford, Cambridge and Newmarket.
8. London and Brighton, Portsmouth and Chatham.
9. Bristol, Bath and Bradford on Avon.
10. Bristol, Salisbury and Southampton.
11. Padstow, Bodmin and Fowey.
12. Truro and St. Agnes.
13. Algavoar Moor.
    Other lines in Flintshire.

[1] See also an article 'William James, Railway Engineer', by Canon R. B. Fellows, *The Locomotive*, March 1937.

R

About 1808 he is said to have put forward a proposal for a 'General Railroad Company', with a capital of a million pounds, but there is no evidence that this scheme ever progressed beyond an entry in his diary. If it did so, all traces of it seem to have disappeared. A plan of his for a 'Central Junction Railway' is reproduced.

His Manchester and Liverpool scheme was the beginning of the campaign which was carried to victory in 1830.

In 1823 he published a pamphlet advocating lines from London to Brighton and Portsmouth to Rochester, the title-page of which is shown here, from the 'History of the Southern Railway'. He proposed to use Stephenson engines.

In that same year he also supplied the first plans for the Canterbury and Whitstable Railway, so that he stands out among the men whose work is dealt with in this chapter, in that he really produced something practical. Financial difficulties and impaired health caused him to fall out of the ranks just at the time an important advance was about to be made. He was one of the first to advocate the use of locomotives, although they were not actually employed on any of the lines which were made under his supervision, and was also the first to realize the vast possibilities of passenger traffic upon railways.

In passing, attention may be called to some remarks by Thomas Young, in his 'Course of Lectures on Natural Philosophy', 1807 (vol. i, p. 218); to the following effect:

> In mining countries, and in collieries, it is usual for facilitating the motion of the carriages employed in moving the ore or the coals, to lay wheel-ways of wood or iron along the road on which they are to pass; and this practice has of late been extended in some cases as a substitute for the construction of navigable canals. . . . It is possible that roads paved with iron may hereafter be employed for the purpose of expeditious travelling, since there is scarcely any resistance to be overcome, except that of the air, and such roads would allow the velocity to be increased almost without limit.

We now come to Thomas Gray (1787–1848), who devoted about twenty years of his life to advocating railways, becoming almost a monomaniac on the subject, reaping no satisfaction, falling into poverty, and dying, it is said, of a broken heart.

It is stated in a pamphlet of 1845, to be mentioned later, that Gray's attention was attracted to the possibilities of railways about the year 1816, and that for some years afterwards he pondered the subject carefully. 'He shut himself up in his room, secluded from his wife and rela-

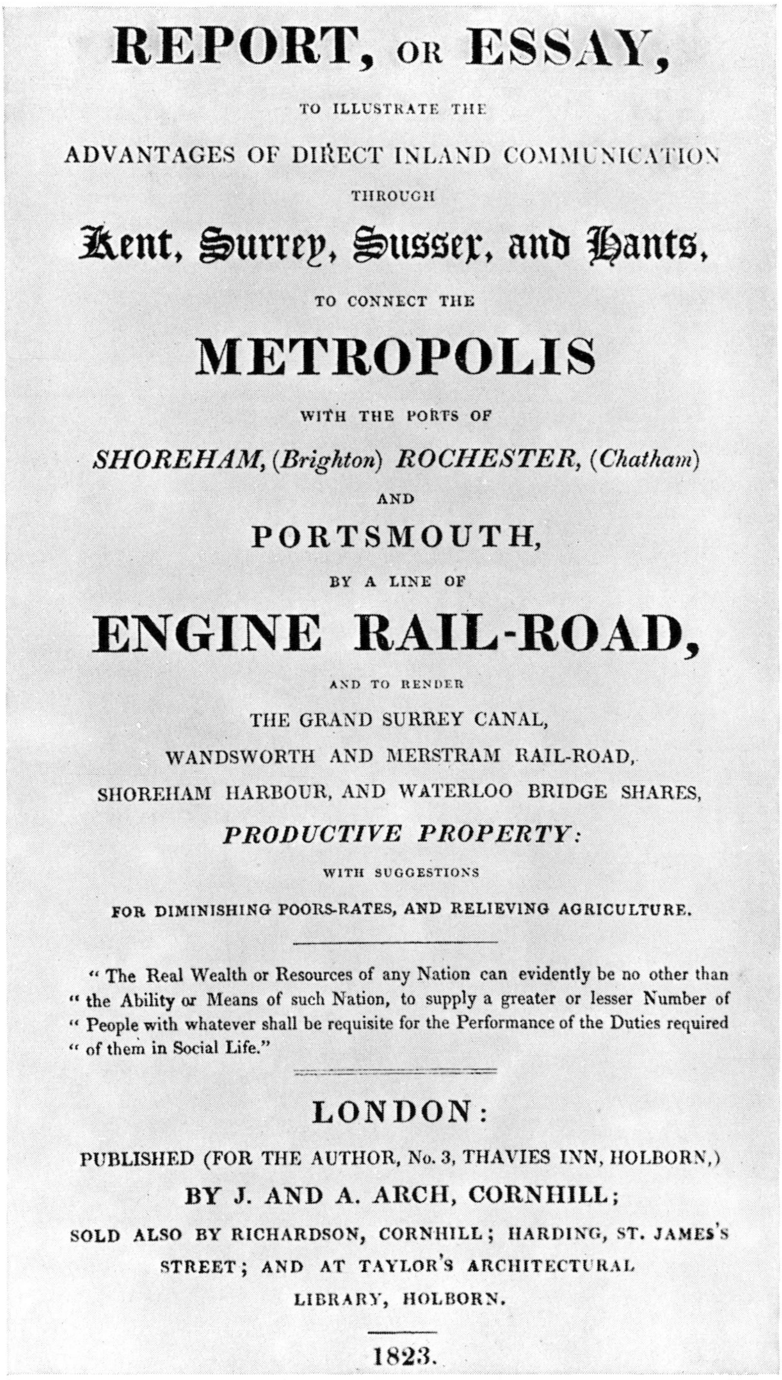

REPORT, OR ESSAY,

TO ILLUSTRATE THE

ADVANTAGES OF DIRECT INLAND COMMUNICATION

THROUGH

Kent, Surrey, Sussex, and Hants,

TO CONNECT THE

METROPOLIS

WITH THE PORTS OF

SHOREHAM, *(Brighton)* ROCHESTER, *(Chatham)*

AND

PORTSMOUTH,

BY A LINE OF

ENGINE RAIL-ROAD,

AND TO RENDER

THE GRAND SURREY CANAL,

WANDSWORTH AND MERSTRAM RAIL-ROAD,

SHOREHAM HARBOUR, AND WATERLOO BRIDGE SHARES,

PRODUCTIVE PROPERTY:

WITH SUGGESTIONS

FOR DIMINISHING POORS-RATES, AND RELIEVING AGRICULTURE.

" The Real Wealth or Resources of any Nation can evidently be no other than
" the Ability or Means of such Nation, to supply a greater or lesser Number of
" People with whatever shall be requisite for the Performance of the Duties required
" of them in Social Life."

LONDON:

PUBLISHED (FOR THE AUTHOR, No. 3, THAVIES INN, HOLBORN,)

BY J. AND A. ARCH, CORNHILL;

SOLD ALSO BY RICHARDSON, CORNHILL; HARDING, ST. JAMES'S
STREET; AND AT TAYLOR'S ARCHITECTURAL
LIBRARY, HOLBORN.

1823.

FIG. 83.   Title-page of James's pamphlet

tives, declining to give them any information on the subject of his mysterious studies, beyond the assurance that his scheme "would revolutionize the whole face of the material world, and of society".' The result was a pamphlet[1] which appeared in 1820, a second edition following in 1821. A third enlarged edition came out in 1822, with two folding plates, one showing three trains drawn by engines of the Blenkinsop type.

The other plate shows a plan of the lines at a junction with branches, which are at right angles to the main line. The latter has six tracks, the racks being laid in the middle, which, of course, is the correct place. Turntables permit the train either to go through or to be turned, vehicle by vehicle, on to a branch. In the centre there is a large traverser, which, by moving laterally, allows a vehicle to be transferred from one line to another. The explanation states that three tracks are for up traffic and three for down; 'the Rails on which the Vehicles are to run being CONVEX and the Rim of the Carriage-Wheel CONCAVE show at one view the Ease, Security and Velocity with which Vehicles can be impelled by Mechanic-power'. There are two maps: one showing a plan of railways for Great Britain, taking in Glasgow, Edinburgh, Newcastle, Scarborough, Norwich, Harwich, Dover, Portsmouth, Bristol, and Holyhead; the other being a scheme for Ireland.

One of Gray's principal objects was to relieve unemployment, which was very bad after the cessation of the Napoleonic wars. He proposed laying down railways on the beds of the canals. He condemned the cruelty inflicted on coach and post-chaise horses, quoting a statement from a newspaper that coach proprietors calculated on losing a horse every 200 miles; and that 'several horses, in endeavouring to keep time, according to the new post-office regulations, have had their legs snapped in two on the road, while others have dropped dead from the effect of a ruptured blood-vessel, or a heart broken in efforts to obey the whip'. These remarks bring out a great advantage of mechanical traction which has perhaps been rather lost sight of.

He suggested starting between Manchester and Liverpool, and expatiates on the advantages that would be attained thereby.

He then went on to enumerate, giving his reasons, the various interests that would derive benefit from a general system of railways; fishermen ('a steam fish-waggon would in one day convey fish enough to supply a town and the neighbouring villages, one or two hundred miles from any of the seaports'), farmers, builders, landowners, insurance companies, the Post Office, &c. He estimated the number of horses employed on the

---

[1] For a detailed bibliography thereof, see p. 214, *post*.

main turnpike roads as 500,000; the cost of which, including upkeep, he put at $173\frac{1}{2}$ millions over a space of twelve years. These were to be replaced by 10,000 steam-engines, at a cost, inclusive of interest and fuel, of about $35\frac{1}{2}$ millions, showing a saving of 138 millions, or $11\frac{1}{2}$ per annum.

There was no alteration in the fourth edition (1823), but the fifth and last, which appeared in 1825, was further enlarged. It contains copies of petitions which he had sent to various Ministers, the Board of Agriculture, and the Lord Mayor of London; also extracts from various works and reports.

Gray also contributed a number of articles and letters to the *Gentleman's Magazine* and *Mechanics' Magazine* on the subject. In a letter to the former (October 1825) he spoke of the 'manifest superiority of Blenkinsop's engines over all those at Newcastle'; going on:

it has been stated that the steam carriages at Newcastle work solely by friction, or by the adhesion of the wheels to the rails, and that Mr. Blenkinsop's rack-rail is quite unnecessary; this nonsense is, however, so completely exposed by the experimentalist who wrote it, that the "Practical Treatise on Rail-roads", recently published, must be put forth with motives I cannot comprehend. . . . The pretended ignorance of the Newcastle writer, of the superiority of Mr. Blenkinsop's rail-way, will meet with the contempt it deserves, and serve also to forewarn the public against his imbecile mis-statements, and plausible calculations.

He was rather down on Wood.

In 1845, a high-flown and strongly expressed pamphlet was published, pleading for recognition to be given to what Gray had done, and exalting him to the level of Watt, entitled 'The Railway System and its Author, Thomas Gray, now of Exeter. A Letter to the Rt. Hon. Sir Robert Peel. . . . By Thomas Wilson Esq. London, 1845'.

The first generally descriptive work was published at Denbigh in 1824 (re-issued in 1826). It is entitled:

Illustrations of the Origin and Progress of Rail and Tram Roads and Steam Carriages, or Loco-motive Engines: also, interesting descriptive particulars of the formation, construction, extent, and mode of working some of the principal rail-ways now in use within the United Kingdom: particularly those great and unequalled communications projected between Liverpool and Birmingham and Liverpool and Manchester, with a view to the more general employment of Steam Carriages, or Loco-motive Engines, for the conveyance of Passengers, as well as Merchandise. With remarks on the public advantages likely to accrue therefrom. To which is added, Observations on the comparative ease of draught, as regards the Work capable of being performed both on level Rail-ways and inclined Planes, as applicable to Steam as well as Horse Carriages. With an explanatory plate. By T. G. Cumming, Surveyor, &c.

He gives a description of the construction of railways, recommending inclined planes where the declivity is steep, either with power, or working by gravity. He says there is no prescribed distance between the rails, as in some cases a preference is given to long narrow waggons and in others to those of a short broad shape, consequently the distance between the rails varies from 3 to $4\frac{1}{2}$ feet; recommends stone blocks as sleepers; describes both tram-plates and edge-rails. There are notices of a number of railways, some of which are quoted elsewhere in the present work; also a long dissertation on the advantages likely to be derived from the Liverpool and Manchester line, the estimated cost of which, at the time he wrote, was only £300,000.

Another section deals with the Liverpool and Birmingham Railway, a scheme originally contemporaneous with the L. & M.R., but which failed to obtain parliamentary sanction. George Stephenson was employed to examine and report upon the route. The company were 'fully persuaded that . . . they will be enabled to carry passengers with perfect security, and at a speed of at least twelve miles an hour'.

He concludes with a discussion of weights that can be hauled by horses and locomotives. There is a curious remark bearing on starting resistance, in which he says:

it has been proved that a body weighing sixteen hundred pounds weight, was moved with a force of sixty-four pounds when first laid upon its corresponding surface, but after the expiration of three seconds, it required nearly three times the force; and at the expiration of six days, a force of six hundred pounds would not move it.

The year 1825 saw the publication of two 'Practical Treatises on Railroads', one by Nicholas Wood, and the other by Thomas Tredgold. The former, which is infinitely the better of the two, is too well known to need any description here.

Tredgold's book contains information mostly gathered from previous writers, together with original calculations. His best suggestion is a long truck on two bogies, the drawing of which has a very modern appearance. He seems to prefer stationary engines on the whole, and thinks ten miles an hour about the limit that is desirable for carrying passengers. He gives the expense of a railway as £5,000 per mile. A second edition, identical with the exception of the correction of one or two errors, was produced in 1835, by which time most of it was hopelessly out of date.

A pamphlet entitled 'Observations on the comparative merits of Inland Communication by Navigation or Rail-road, with particular reference to those projected or existing between Bath, Bristol, and London' appeared in 1825. It was written by 'A Proprietor of Shares in the Kennet and Avon Canal', and is 'anti-railroad'.

The Reverend James Adamson, of Cupar, Fife, was responsible for an extremely interesting little pamphlet. It originally appeared in the *Edinburgh New Philosophical Journal* for October 1825 and April 1826. In the latter year it was issued as a separate publication, at Newcastle, with additions, thus: 'State of our Information as to Rail-roads. Also an Account of the Stockton and Darlington Rail-way, with Observations on Rail-ways &c. &c. (extracted from the Caledonian Mercury)'. The 'Observations' include the discussion of a railway between Edinburgh and Glasgow, and an essay on the 'Conveyance of Passengers and light Goods'. Sixty pages in all.

The first part was reprinted and bound up with the 1827 edition of Longridge's 'Remarks on the comparative merits of Cast Metal and Malleable Iron Rail-ways'.

The 1826 edition contains a folding plate of the opening of the Stockton and Darlington Railway, which is the same as in the 1827 Longridge, except that the latter is lettered at the foot 'Train of Waggons drawn by a Loco-motive Engine'.

Adamson discusses the calculations and results given by Wood and Tredgold. He considers the proper load for an engine on the level is eight times its own weight; and that two engines will be required on an up grade of 1 in 250. Boiler explosions he did not fear, saying: 'The locomotive engines must certainly be high-pressure engines, but, from their size and treatment, are far more likely to be deficient in the power of raising steam, than able to spare any for explosions.'

Another, less known, writer was Maclaren. In *The Pamphleteer*, vol. xxvi (1826), the following article appeared: 'Railways compared with canals and common roads and their uses and advantages explained: being the substance of a series of papers published in The Scotsman in December 1824 and now republished with additions and corrections. By Charles Maclaren, Esq. London, 1825'.

It was also published separately at Edinburgh in 1825; a pamphlet of 68 pages, without the author's name, but signed 'C.M.'.

This paper contains a very early discussion of the air resistance on railways; which, he said, should be reduced first by making the vehicle long and narrow, rather than broad and short, and secondly by giving the front a round or hemispherical form. He concluded:

We see however, that the resistance of the air, which in vulgar apprehension, passes for nothing, comes to be the greatest impediment to the motion of the vehicles, and may in some cases absorb five parts in six of the whole power. Let it be remembered, at the same time, that this aerial resistance rises into consequence solely because the high perfection of the machinery—the vehicle and the road—almost annihilates any other. The atmosphere equally opposes the progress of the stage-coach, the track-boat, and the steam boat; but the motion of these vehicles is comparatively so slow, and the power of impulsion required to overcome the other impediments to their progress is so great, that the resistance of the air is disregarded.

It is extraordinary that any one could have adopted such views at a time when the world's record for railway speed was about 10 or 12 miles an hour.

He proposed elevated places for stopping, to facilitate pulling up and restarting; a regenerative arrangement which has been adopted on some of the modern tube railways. For passenger trains he suggested 'a form analogous to the steam-boat and track-boat'; proceeding:

It might . . . consist of a gallery seven feet high, eight wide, and 100 feet in length, formed into ten separate chambers ten feet long each, connected with each other by joints working horizontally, to allow the train to bend where the road turned. A narrow covered footway, suspended on the outside over the wheels on one side, would serve as a common means of communication for the whole. On the other side might be outside seats, to be used in fair weather. The top surrounded with a rail, might also be a sitting-place or promenade, like the deck of a track-boat. Two of the ten rooms might be set aside for cooking, stores, and various accommodations, the other eight would lodge a hundred passengers, whose weight with that of their luggage, might be twelve tons. The coach itself might be twelve tons more, and that of the locomotive-machine eight tons, added to these, would make the whole thirty-two tons. Each of the short galleries would rest on four wheels, and the whole would form one continuous vehicle.

Here we have what appears to be the first suggestion of the corridor train and the dining-car, but Chapman ran him very close, as he proposed 'long carriages, resting on eight wheels containing the means of providing the passengers with breakfast, dinner, &c., whilst the carriages are moving', in 1825.[1]

---

[1] 'Diaries of Edward Pease', p. 85.

Maclaren mentions that the price of coal in London was £2 a ton.

In 1827 a pamphlet was issued at Leeds, the title of which, as printed on the cover, was as follows:

HILL, upon *Railroads Generally*, including the Leeds, Selby & Hull, *Stockton and Darlington*; Manchester and Liverpool; The Northern, from London to Leeds and Manchester; Surrey & Croydon; and the Norfolk, from London to Watton. Also, a Sketch of the Patent Carriages that will run upon the streets and common Roads; also upon the Rail-roads. Leeds, 1827.

The title on the title-page is quite different, viz.:

A Treatise, upon the utility of a Rail-way from Leeds to Selby and Hull, with observations and estimates upon Rail-ways generally. As being pre-eminent to all other modes of conveyance for dispatch and convoy.
By Thomas Hill, Leeds.

There is not much information which cannot be found elsewhere, in more accessible publications. It is interesting to note that the Northern Railroad, which was evidently a subject of contemplation at that time, was to follow more or less the route of the G.N.R., and go 'to Edinburgh, perhaps'.

Watton was proposed for the terminus of the Norfolk Railroad on account of its central position.

Hill was in favour of horse-traction, as appears on the title of a 'Supplement' dated 1829, bound up with the author's copy, which professes to 'show that HORSE-POWER is *Cheaper*, *Preferable*, and *more Expeditious* than LOCOMOTIVE ENGINES'.

Even now, he was advocating horses for the Liverpool and Manchester Railway, also for the Leeds and Selby.

For steep ascents, he would have a self-acting arrangement, by virtue of which the horses drawing loads downhill are made to assist those going up, by means of a rope round a pulley fixed at the summit.

He concludes with a mention of the 'intended East London Rail-road, near White Chapel, London'; which was to run to the Docks.[1] He gives a plate showing his 'patent Carriages for Rail-ways, &c.', and states that they can be used either on rails or on the road without unloading, but does not say how it was to be done. The patent (no. 5160 of 1825) of course does. There were to be detachable flanges on the wheels, attached by bolts.

[1] See Fig. 51, facing p. 80.

A much more practical idea, though not a new one, had just been patented by Brandling (5148 of the same year) under which the thickness of the flanges was to be increased sufficiently for them to be able to carry the weight when travelling on the road.

An interesting pamphlet was published at Glasgow in 1828, by David Rankine, the scope of which is shown in the title, 'A popular Description of the effect of forces applied to Draught. With illustrations of the principles of action, and tables of the performance of Horses and of Locomotive Engines on Railways. And an Appendix, containing the results of some experiments on friction'. The author was the father of Professor Rankine, and was for some time Superintendent of the Edinburgh and Dalkeith Railway.

He discusses the question of increasing the size of locomotive driving wheels to 7 feet, from which he ventures to anticipate as much as $11\frac{1}{2}$ miles an hour, but points out that 'when we arrive at such a speed as the above, the resistance of the atmosphere comes to be of some importance'.

Locomotives he considers as being 'little beyond their infancy, and the public advantages that will one day be derived from them, as probably greater than have yet been conceived'.

Numerous reports, some very elaborate, on schemes for railways, were made by the engineers of the day. As such, they are outside the scope of this chapter, but the Report of Robert Stevenson on Edinburgh railways, dated December 27th, 1818, and published in the following year, is worthy of mention, for the sake of its historical section, which was considered authoritative, and has been quoted by many writers. Some extracts from it relative to Scottish lines have been given in Chapter VI; others in Chapter VII, in connexion with the introduction of iron. The following are of general interest.

The cast-iron tracks of the earlier Railways were made flat, or about four inches in breadth, with a projecting ridge or *flange* upon the outer verge, and are technically called *Plate Rails*. But the Reporter is led from his own observation, and the opinion of the following professional gentlemen obligingly communicated to him, viz. Mr. WILSON OF Troon, Mr. BALD of Alloa, Mr. LANDALE of Charlestown, Mr. GRIEVE of Sheriff Hall, and Mr. BUDDLE of Newcastle, who are not only scientifically but practically conversant with this matter, to conclude that the Plate Rail not only induces greater friction, but is more exposed to have the wheels clogged and interrupted with gravel or small stones, than that called the *Edge Rail*, which in its best construction of cast-iron, consists of a bar of about $1\frac{1}{2}$ inch in thickness or breadth, for the *seat* of the wheel, and of a depth corresponding to the weight to be carried. This bar is set on edge, instead of being laid flat. In this manner the edge rail presents less friction, and, weight for weight, is much stronger for the load than the plate rail; upon the same principle as, in modern carpentry, the beam is now set on edge, instead of being laid flat on its side as formerly. The Reporter is therefore to recommend an edge rail warranted to work with 2 tons, including the waggon, of the weight of 140 lb. per lineal yard of finished double Railway.

. . . .

A method has been adopted of making the cross fixtures under ground, with bars wholly of cast-iron, to which the rails are attached with iron pins. Much, however, depends upon the nature and tenacity of the ground to be passed over. At the works of Lord Elgin and the Carron Company the use of the sleeper or cross iron bar is laid aside, and other alterations are daily suggested as improvements, in the method of laying and fixing the rails, and also in the construction of the wheels and waggons. With regard to the construction of *Cast-iron Rails*, they are, in general, made in the lengths of from 3 to 4 feet; but the Reporter is inclined to think, that the perfection of the cast-iron Railway will be found to consist rather in shortening the rails very considerably, than adopting even the shortest of these lengths; but this and similar matters will fall more properly to be matured in the practical details of the business.

The passage given on p. 151, *ante*, then follows.

Two important articles on railways appeared in the *Quarterly Review*, both anonymous. The first, which was in the number for March 1825, was a review of Cumming's book, Sylvester's Report addressed to the Chairman and Committee of the L. & M.R., and Sandars' letter *re* the latter. After an eloquent and diverting description of the 'frenzy of speculation' which was spread throughout the land, partly due to the 'unparalleled prosperity of the country, the great amount of surplus capital, and the consequent low rate of interest', the writer scouts the idea of a *general* rail-road, as altogether impracticable. About a proposed railway from London to Woolwich, on which the speed was to be nearly 20 miles an hour, he was scathing to a degree; he would 'as soon expect the people of Woolwich to suffer themselves to be fired off upon one of Congreve's *ricochet* rockets, as to trust themselves to the mercy of such a machine going at such a rate', adding, in respect of heavy goods, 'we will back old father Thames against the Woolwich rail-way for any sum'.

The advantages of a railway over a canal are very fairly set forth. When speaking of the canal interests between Liverpool and Manchester, he quotes 'a writer against railroads' to the effect that

they scouted the very notion of the smallest reduction; they wallowed in their dividends with a confidence, that must always be impolite and presumptuous, when not perfectly secure; they engendered the elements of that opposition whose powers they at first ridiculed, but now respect; and they frittered away their concessions in a manner that excited the mirth of their opponents, and the pity of their friends.

He trusted that Parliament would, in all the rail-roads it might sanction, limit the speed to 8 or 9 miles an hour, which, he entirely agreed with Mr. Sylvester, was as great as could be ventured upon with safety.

One serious objection to the canals, which has turned out not to be *absolutely* unknown on railways, was the pilfering that went on. Wool, for instance, used to be stolen from bales, the weight being made up by pouring water on the remainder, which absorbed it easily.

Unlike the Woolwich Railway, the Liverpool and Manchester is approved of, so far as goods are concerned, but the question of conveying passengers should be postponed 'until the roads and the engines have acquired that degree of perfection of which they are capable, and such as will remove all apprehension of danger'.

The second article, which appeared in March 1830, was a review of Nicholas Wood's book, and of the accounts of the Rainhill Competition which had appeared in the *Mechanics' Magazine*, and other papers. Ideas with regard to speed were changed, e.g.:

It is now proved, that by the action of steam on the railway carriage we can advance with a facility and speed never before equalled, either on land or water, and to which indeed, we can hardly assign any limits, except in so far as the safety of the carriage and passengers may be concerned.

The opinion expressed by the former article as to a 'general' railway is also reversed, thus:

Could such perfect means of intercourse, indeed, be established generally throughout the country, it would give rise to a revolution in our internal trade and resources, such as no thinking man can contemplate without being lost in wonder!

Later on, speaking of speed, the writer says:

It would be still imprudent, however, to adopt the utmost limit of thirty miles, because such an unusual rate of velocity, surpassing that of the swiftest horse, would be alarming if it were not dangerous . . . at the rate of twenty miles an hour, however, it would, we think, be perfectly practicable to travel with the utmost safety and comfort.

He adds that before the Stockton and Darlington Railway was made, there were no coaches between the two towns on either of the roads running parallel with the railway, yet in less than a twelvemonth, the company was drawing four or five hundred a year from passengers; 'an intercourse and trade seemed to arise out of nothing, and no one knew how'. He concludes by hailing 'with unspeakable delight the occurrence of the first demonstration of its practicability [i.e. of the railway], at a moment when the national energy has so much need of a stimulus, owing to the depressed condition of industry in almost all its branches'.

Some very valuable information on the subject of early railways has been contributed by foreign engineers who came over to this country to see what had been done.

The visit of de Gallois, described by him in the *Annales des Mines* for 1818, is of interest in connexion with locomotive history.

In March 1825 'The Pennsylvania Society for the Promotion of Internal Improvement', which had been formed four months previously, sent over William Strickland, 'a native citizen', to collect information. The result appeared in a fine series of reports on canals, railways, &c., which was published in Philadelphia in 1826. It is an oblong folio volume, $17\frac{1}{2}$ by $10\frac{1}{4}$ inches, now of considerable rarity, containing 59 plates, one or two of which appear in part, in their appropriate places, among the preceding pages.

Another account is contained in 'Ueber Schienenwege in England: Bemerkungen gesammelt auf eine Reise in den Jahren 1826 und 1827. Von C. v. Oeynhausen und H. v. Dechen'. The authors were two Prussian mining engineers. The book is a reprint from *Archiv für Bergbau und Hüttenwesen*, and has seven plates. There is a long description of the Stockton and Darlington Railway, occupying 64 pages (a quarter of the book), followed by 21 pages on the Hetton line (this being the most detailed account in existence). The description of the locomotives of the former is one of the best there is; substantial extracts from it are given (translated) in 'A Century of Locomotive Building'. After another 20 pages on the Liverpool and Manchester, and Bolton and Leigh, there are some valuable 'short descriptions of other railways in England', divided under the heads:

A. With cast iron edge-rails (5).
B. With rolled iron rails (5).
C. Tram-roads (11).
D. Surrey Iron Railway, and about a dozen others, one or two of which do not seem to be otherwise known.

It concludes with 'General Observations on Railways in England' (74 pages), most of which is taken from Wood and Tredgold. There was also a French translation by Perdonnet, 1830.

Two French engineers, Coste and Perdonnet, came over in 1828, and visited Newcastle and the neighbourhood; recording their impressions in the *Annales des Mines* for 1829, which were reprinted separately with additions describing the Rainhill trials, as a 'Mémoire sur les Chemins à Ornières', Paris, 1830. They gave the best description extant of the Lancashire Witch, most of which is given (translated) in 'A Century'.

CHAPTER X

THE STOCKTON AND DARLINGTON RAILWAY

THE history of this line has been very fully written, and is to be found in the following works:

Smiles, 'Lives of George and Robert Stephenson'.
Jeans, 'Jubilee Memorial of the Railway System', 1875.
Heavisides, 'History of the First Public Railway', 1912.
Tomlinson, 'The North Eastern Railway', 1914.
Davies, 'The Railway Centenary', 1925.
'Centenary of Public Railways', published at Stockton, 1925.

There is consequently little more to add, as the ground has been so thoroughly explored.

In a note-book of Rastrick's belonging to the University of London, there are some interesting entries.

1829, 19th Jan.

Brusselton Incline. The cylinders are each 30 in. diameter and work a 5 ft. stroke made as Packet engines with Air Pumps and Condensers, steam 5 lbs. per square inch on the Boiler Safety Valve and was working 25 strokes per Mt. These engines J. Hackworth called 30 Horse Power each so that the two engines are equal to 60 Horse Power.

The Rope supplied by Mr. Grimshaw which lasted 21 months . . . was 932 Fathoms or 1864 Yards . . . it soon stretched 40 fathoms and . . . ultimately 100 fathoms.

The [three] Engine Men at the Incline Plane have one shilling for every twenty tons of coal that pass over this Incline; they having a guarantee of 18 sets of waggons . . . finding Coal Oil Tallow, &c.

At this Incline Plane there is One Man employed who is called a Bankrider, his Business is first to ride up and down the Incline Planes alternately with the loaded and empty waggons, he finds Oil for all the Pullies Sheaves and Rollers upon each side of the Incline Plane, and oils them, this he generally does once every Day, for this and riding with the Waggons he has fourpence halfpenny for every twenty tons of coals that pass on this Incline. The Company guarantee to him sixteen sets of Waggons per Day each set being 8 waggons of 53 cwt. each.

At Etherly two 15 h.p. Boulton and Watt engines as packet engines 21 inch steam cylinder 3 feet 2 inches stroke.

There has been two Accidents on the Stockton and Darlington Rail Road by the Bursting of the Tubes of the Boiler over the fire. The first was occationed by the Safety Valve being fastened down—while the Engine was standing upon one of the Embankments between Shildon and

FIG. 84. Portion of disused Brusselton incline, Stockton and Darlington Railway

FIG. 85. Stone blocks, Etherley north incline, Stockton and Darlington Railway

FIGS. 86 & 87. Ivory pass, Stockton and Darlington Railway. (Author's collection)

RAPID, SAFE, AND CHEAP TRAVELLING
By the Elegant *NEW RAILWAY COACH,*

THE UNION,

Which will COMMENCE RUNNING on the STOCKTON and DARLINGTON RAILWAY, on MONDAY the 16th day of October, 1826,

And will call at Yarm, and pass within a mile of Middleton Spa, on its way from Stockton to Darlington, and *vice versa.*

FARES.   Inside 1¾d.—Outside, 1d. per Mile.   Parcels in proportion.

No gratuities expected by the Guard or Coachman.

N. B. The Proprietors will not be accountable for any Parcel of more than £5. value, unless entered and paid for accordingly.

The UNION will run from the Black Lion Hotel and New Inn, Stockton, to the New Inn, Yarm, and to the Black Swan Inn, near the Croft Branch, Darlington; at each of which Inns passengers and parcels are booked, and the times of starting may be ascertained, as also at the Union Inn, Yarm, and Talbot Inn, Darlington.

On the 19th and 20th of October, the Fair Days at Yarm, the Union will leave Darlington at six in the morning for Yarm, and will leave Yarm for Darlington again at six in the evening; in the intermediate time, each day, it will ply constantly between Stockton and Yarm, leaving each place every half hour

Fig. 88. Passenger traffic on the Stockton and Darlington Railway

(From the *Durham County Advertiser,* October 14th, 1826)

Darlington, during which time there was a strong wind blowing in direction of the Tube by which the fire increased so violently that the Tube was forced down on the Fire Bars, the fire and fire bars were blown out and One Man was killed and another had his thigh broken.

The second accident happened at a Station where the Engine was waiting to take in water, the Engine Man had fastened down the valve and having waited longer than was necessary, the Steam had become verry strong he was just starting the Engine again when the Tube was forced down on the Fire Bars and bursting open blew out the fire bars and also the Water Steam and fire—the Engine Man was killed and the Man who had been pumping water to fill the Tender Cistern was scalded.

Fig. 91. Seal of the Stockton and Darlington Railway

The following passage from David Rankine's 'Popular description of the forces applied to Draught' (1828) with reference to passengers is interesting:

A railway coach I have not yet seen, nor have I heard of one that had been built expressly for the purpose. Those on the Stockton and Darlington railway are common heavy stage coaches slightly altered; they contain 6 persons inside, and 16 or more outside, and must weigh with their complement of passengers, considerably more than two tons. In one of these a friend of mine travelled between Stockton and Darlington, a distance of 12 miles, in 70 minutes; this was at the rate of fully $10\frac{1}{4}$ miles an hour: the same horse took the coach back again, making this his daily work 24 miles, or 2 hours 20 minutes, at $10\frac{1}{4}$ miles an hour. Although the coach had no springs, its motion was more easy than that of a coach with springs on a Macadam road. By this smoothness of movement, tear and wear must of course be diminished, and railway coaches may be proportionately lighter than others; they do not need to be fitted for

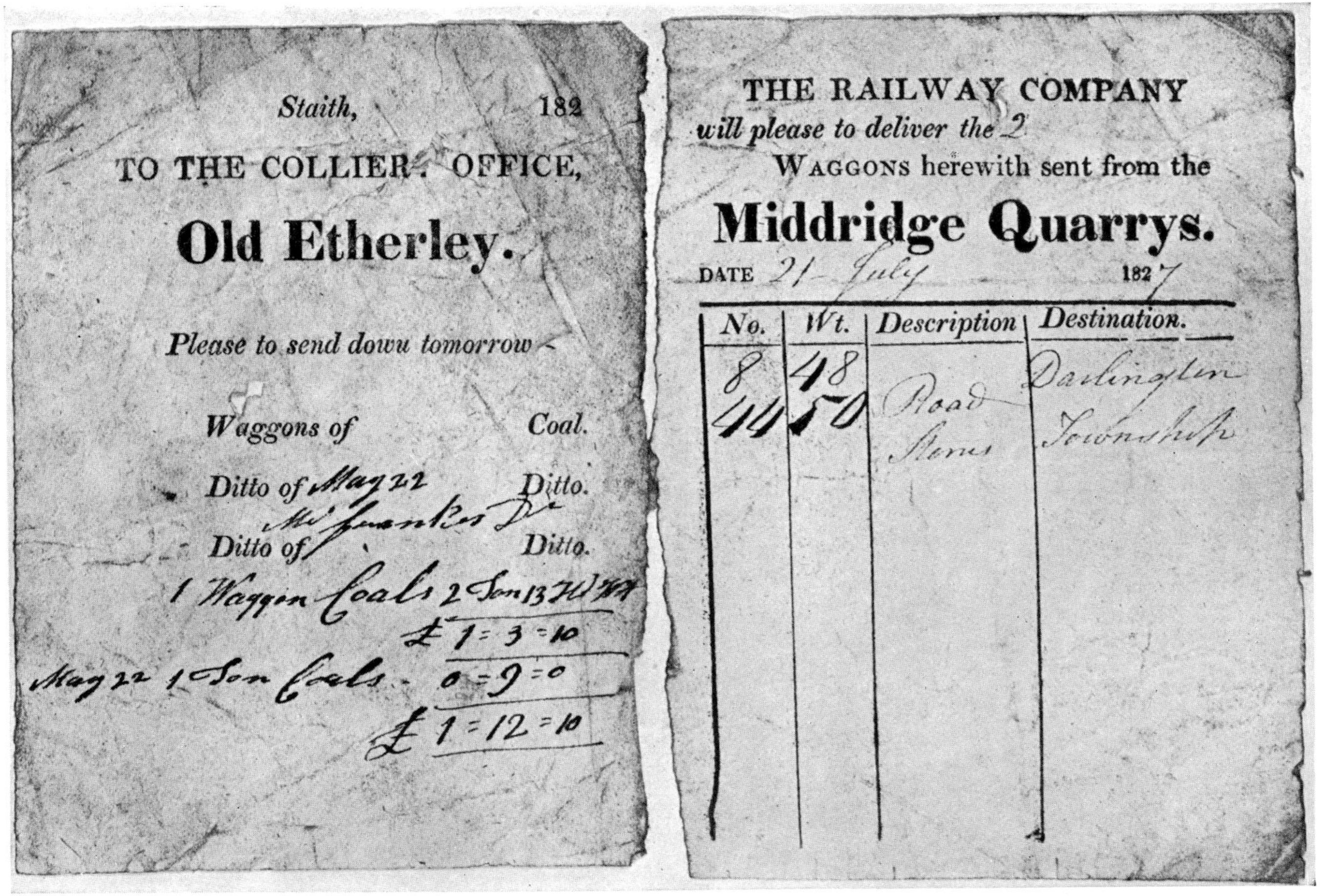

THE RAILWAY COMPANY

will please to deliver the 2

WAGGONS *herewith sent from the*

Middridge Quarrys.

DATE 21 July 182

No.	Wt.	Description	Destination.
8	48	Road Stones	Darlington Township

Staith, 182

TO THE COLLIERY OFFICE,

Old Etherley.

Please to send down tomorrow

Waggons of Coal.

Ditto of May 22 Ditto.

Ditto of Ditto.

1 Waggon Coals 2 Jan 13 Feb

£ 1 = 3 = 10
0 = 9 = 0
£ 1 = 12 = 10

May 22 1 Ton Coals

FIGS. 89 & 90. Old Stockton and Darlington 'bills of lading'. (Author's collection)

turning, but may be drawn indifferently by either end; and their wheels may, by having the edges of their flanches made of sufficient breadth, be adapted for running on upon a common road or street; this would, however, render springs necessary.

There is an excellent little description of the line in a small book called 'A Guide to Croft, Dinsdale, Middleton, Darlington, &c.', published at the latter town in 1834. At that time there were seven coaches plying regularly, 'drawn (until very lately) by a single horse'. The speed was given as 12 miles an hour, and on market days there were sometimes upwards of 40 persons on one coach. The description tallies with that just given from Rankine, adding, after the remark that they had no springs, 'by which they avoid the payment of duty'. It concludes by saying:

The mind certainly receives a very curious sensation when a person glides for the first time on the top of the coach along the raised parts of the road, and the stranger will find it an agreeable and novel diversity to his amusements to take an outside trip along the Stockton and Darlington Railway.

Horses, however, are now almost banished from the railway; and all the coaches, as well as most of the waggons, are drawn by the locomotive engines.

In a 'Report to the Committee of Proprietors' for 1832–3, the following passage occurs

The Committee found great inconvenience by Carriages travelling on the Railway at different speeds, and being convinced of the necessity of adopting one uniform rate of travelling, have had several interviews with the Merchandise Carriers for the purpose of inducing them to adopt the leading of Merchandise by LOCOMOTIVE ENGINES, instead of HORSES as heretofore.

Heavisides, it may be remarked, says that so late as 1856 a horse and railway coach ran from Stockton to Middlesborough and back every Sunday.[1]

The author's collection contains a large poster, dated August 1833, setting forth the penalties to be paid by persons violating the rules of the company (10 under the Act of Parliament and 27 under their by-laws) ranging from £5 down to 5 shillings.

Drivers were not to exceed 8 miles an hour, and were responsible for having with the waggons 'proper Breaks to regulate the speed'; and were

---

[1] 'History of the First Public Railway', Stockton-on-Tees, 1912.

to ring their bells one hundred yards previous to passing any Public Road.

No waggons were to pass earlier than one hour before sunrise, or later than one hour after sunset, without leave in writing.

A good and sufficient light was to be provided half an hour after sunset.

Every driver or owner of any waggon, the gauge of the wheels, of which, not being at the distance of 4 feet $5\frac{1}{2}$ inches from the outside of the flange of each wheel; not having the tread of any wheels less than 3 inches, or the axles more than four feet apart, from centre to centre, shall forfeit a Sum not exceeding £1.

Elaborate directions are given for the dimensions of the component parts of waggons.

Trains drawn by horses are always to take the sidings when meeting locomotives. The use of the latter for drawing passenger coaches is mentioned. This practice, according to Tomlinson, commenced on September 7th, 1833.

FIG. 92. Henry Booth (1788–1869)

CHAPTER XI

THE LIVERPOOL AND MANCHESTER RAILWAY

THE metamorphosis which the railway underwent from the Stockton and Darlington, as it was then, to the Liverpool and Manchester, is somewhat analogous to that between a grub and a butterfly.

The former was the highest development of the old colliery railways; its locomotion being effected partly by horses and partly by primitive engines of the Killingworth type; the latter, a fresh departure altogether, and the prototype of the evolution during the following century. It is only comparatively recently that new variations have appeared, some of which, at all events, are likely to be permanent.

This epoch-making line was described very fully in the author's 'Centenary History', and he will confine himself here to setting down additions and corrections.

The statement on p. 11 of that work, that locomotives are only mentioned once in the first prospectus, is inaccurate; as a matter of fact the word occurs twice, once in the remark 'Application has been made, on behalf of the Emperor of Russia, for models of the Locomotive Engine'; it also appears previously, when giving the estimate of the cost, 'including the charge for Locomotive Engines'. But those are the only references to them, so fearful were the promoters of arousing prejudice. On p. 14, the first paragraph conveys the impression that locomotives are only mentioned once in the Act, in the clause (XIX) prohibiting smoke; there is also another (XI), which forbids their use in the town of Liverpool.

The two buildings shown on the share certificates are the Exchanges at Liverpool and Manchester. On p. 16, footnotes 2 and 3, the pages to which reference is made should be 239 and 238 respectively.

The author has obtained an interesting little book entitled 'Frederick Swanwick, a Sketch', by J. Frederick Smith; printed for private circulation in 1888. It gives a tabular statement of Swanwick's engineering work, the more important entries being as follows:

In 1832 he surveyed the Whitby and Pickering Railway, afterwards superintending the construction. He was assistant engineer to George Stephenson on about six railways and in 1836 was Engineer to the Sheffield and Rotherham Railway; in 1841–4, Resident Engineer to the North Midland. During 1845–50 he had about a dozen appointments on various lines, including that of joint engineer with Robert Stephenson to the Eastern Counties.

The spot depicted in Plate XIV, namely Clayton's 'View of the Liverpool and Manchester Railway at the point where it crosses the Bridgwater Canal', is just where the Bridgewater Foundry stands, at Patricroft. Nasmyth saw the importance of this strategic point where railway and canal met, and established his works there, in 1836. In his 'Autobiography', on p. 203, the site is thus described:

> The Bridgewater Canal, which lay along one side of the foundry, communicated with every waterway and port in England, whilst the railway alongside enabled a communication to be kept up by rail with every part of the country. The Worsley coal-boats came alongside the wharf, and a cheap and abundant supply of fuel was thus ensured. The railway station was near at hand, and afforded every opportunity for travelling to and from the works, while I was at the same time placed within twenty minutes of Manchester.
> Another important point has to be mentioned. A fine bed of brick-clay lay below the surface of the ground, which supplied the material for bricks. Thus the entire works may be truly said to have "risen out of the ground", for the whole of the buildings rested upon the land from which the clay below was dug and burned into bricks. Then, below the clay lay a bed of new red sandstone rock, which yielded a solid foundation for any superstructure however lofty or ponderous.

Three or four more locomotives built by 1829, beyond those given at the beginning of Chapter VI, have come to light, namely at Whitehaven, Orrell, and Heaton.

It is recorded in the *Railway Times* (vol. i, p. 668) that the boiler of the Patentee burst on November 12th, 1838, when ascending the Whiston incline; killing the driver and fireman. The engine broke away from the tender and 'proceeded at a flying pace for three or four hundred yards along the line'. It was suggested that the safety-valves were overloaded. The train consisted of forty-three waggons and was propelled by four engines, two in front and two behind.

The Manchester, which on p. 89 is given the credit of having been the first to be built in the city, was built by Galloway, Bowman, and Glasgow at their Great Bridgewater Street Foundry, Manchester.[1]

It is worthy of note that the rails on the L. & M.R. were laid with cant. Under date January 13th, 1829, in a note-book of Rastrick's belonging to the University of London, it is recorded that 'the Rails are laid in a

---

[1] P. C. Dewhurst and S. H. Pearce-Higgins, 'Galloway, Bowman, and Glasgow, Caledonian Foundry, Great Bridgewater Street, Manchester', *Journal of the Stephenson Locomotive Society*, vol. xxix, November 1953, pp. 327–9.

slanting direction towards each other, the Inclination being about 3/16 of an inch in 4 inches so as to fit to the conical Rim of the Wheels'.

There is an interesting account of the accident to Huskisson in the 'Creevey Papers', under date September 19th, 1830.

Jack Calcraft has been at the opening of the Liverpool railroad, and was an eye-witness of Huskisson's horrible death. About nine or ten of the passengers in the Duke's car had got out to look about them, while the car stopt. Calcraft was one, Huskisson another, Esterhazy, Billy Holmes, Birch and others. When the other locomotive was seen coming up to pass them, there was a general shout from those within the Duke's car to those without it, to get in. Both Holmes and Birch were unable to get up in time but they stuck fast to its sides, and the other engine did not touch them. Esterhazy, being light, was pulled in by force. Huskisson was feeble in his legs, and appears to have lost his head, as he did his life. Calcraft tells me that Huskisson's long confinement in St. George's Chapel at the King's funeral brought on a complaint that Taylor is so afraid of, and that made some severe surgical operation necessary, the effect of which had been, according to what he told Calcraft, to paralyse, as it were, his leg and thigh. This, no doubt, must have increased, if it did not create, his danger and [caused him] to lose his life. He had written to say his health would not let him come, and his arrival was unexpected. Calcraft saw the meeting between him and the Duke, and saw them shake hands a very short time before Huskisson's death. The latter event must be followed by important political consequences.

Creevey's informant was John Calcraft, a well-known politician of the day; M.P. for Wareham most of the time from 1786 to 1831, except for ten years 1790–1800, when he was out of Parliament, and 1806–18, when he represented Rochester. He committed suicide in 1831.

The following passage relating to the Liverpool and Manchester Railway occurs in 'A Letter to a Friend, containing observations on the comparative merits of Canals and Railways', by F. P., 1832 (second edition). Whether true or not, it is sufficiently amusing to be worth repeating, and the mere fact that such a statement could be seriously made throws a curious light on the railway travelling of the day:

There have been occasions when the Railway was so slippery, that there was no adhesion of the wheels to the rails, and the passengers were obliged to alight, and assist in pushing the carriages up the inclined plane.

It has been pretty generally supposed that the Liverpool and Manchester engines did not carry numbers. They are always referred to by name in contemporary documents, both official and otherwise. But it is evident that they did so, high up on the front of the chimney. The statement on p. 51 of 'Two Essays', that none are shown, on any contemporary representations, is incorrect, as the Fury in the second of the long prints drawn by Shaw has 21 (the right number) in the position indicated. The location accounts for their being usually omitted from side elevations. The same position was adopted on the London and Birmingham engines (which had no names); it is shown in the drawing of the engine-house at Camden Town in Bourne's 'London and Birmingham Railway'.

There is a card in the Lawrence collection (which has now been acquired by Mr. Phillimore) headed 'Names and Numbers of all the Locomotive Engines on the Liverpool and Manchester Railway from the commencement to the present time March 1st 1836'.

The following interesting extract from a paper read before the Society of Arts for Scotland on February 20th, 1835, by David Stevenson[1] is enough to settle the matter alone:

> The Railway Company have had thirty-two locomotive carriages made, five or six of which are now out of use, and many of those at present on the road have been almost totally renewed. These engines are all numbered and named. No. 1 is called the 'Rocket'. This engine was made by Messrs. Stephenson, the engineers, and is that which did them so much honour in carrying off the prize of L. 500, given by the Directors of the Liverpool and Manchester Railway for the best locomotive carriage. It has been little used, and is still in good repair.

The date at the end of the first paragraph of p. 104 should be May 17th, 1831.

For a reference to the 'Asa' locomotive mentioned on p. 108, see Index.

The opening paragraph of Chapter XII requires amendment. The proposed route of the L. & M. of 1824 and that actually adopted were very near one another in the neighbourhood of Leigh, so that the Kenyon extension of the Bolton line would have been necessary to join up, in any case. In a lecture, entitled 'Lancashire; or our own county', delivered in 1879 (published at Bolton in 1891) by W. W. B. Hulton, whose grandfather had been the prime mover in the Bolton Railway, the reason given for the line stopping short at Leigh is that the canal authorities were successful in opposing its being crossed by the railway.

The lecture is very interesting. The original estimate for the line, in George Stephenson's writing, was shown, also one of the name-plates of the Lancashire Witch, together with other important relics belonging to

---

[1] Son of Robert Stevenson. He had been employed professionally on the L. & M.R.

the Hulton family. Two letters from Benjamin Hick were quoted, to the following effect:

I

Stephenson made "The Lancashire Witch". I have ridden upon it with the driver (Matthew Kirtley), long since dead. William Gowland afterwards drove it. Your grandmother presented a wreath of flowers to the engine driver, who, for want of a more convenient place, put the wreath on the chimney, the heat of which soon caused awful mischief to the flowers.

II

The Sans Pareil was one of the engines which competed for the prize of £500 in the year 1829. It ran for many years on the Bolton and Leigh line, and was bought by W. Hargreaves, who placed it over one of his coal pits at Coppul, to wind coal or pump—I am not sure which. It then worked for years, until nearly worked out, and the great bulk of it was thrown into the scrap heap of Mr. Hargreaves's yard at Bolton. I took the pieces, which I collected with some trouble, from Mr. Hargreaves, and had it put together and restored, as they now saw it at Kensington. The wheels are the only part not original.

It is just possible that there may have been another engine on the Warrington and Newton line, as in an old manuscript book dated 1836, the source of which is unknown, the three engines mentioned are given, together with no. 4 'Shrigley'; Planet type, same dimensions as the others. But inquiries have failed to produce any other evidence of the existence of this engine. The other three are claimed for Tayleur & Co. in the Vulcan Foundry's Centenary book, which is no doubt correct.

The statement on p. 118 that an Act was obtained for amalgamating the North Union with the Grand Junction, although taken from Tuck's 'Railway Shareholders' Manual', is inaccurate. A Bill was promoted for that purpose, but the North Union shareholders refused to approve it. An Act of 1845 consolidated the Liverpool and Manchester, Grand Junction, Bolton and Leigh, and Leigh and Kenyon, but the North Union was vested by an Act of 1846 in the Grand Junction and Manchester and Leeds; consequently it became the joint property of the L. & N.W.R. and the L. & Y.R.

One of the original engines on the Wigan branch was named Wigan; built by Mather, Dixon & Co. (their no. 22).

The four Grand Junction engines mentioned in the third paragraph on p. 126 as having been taken back by Jones, Turner & Evans, were nos. 28, 34, 35, and 36. No. 73 was originally named Prince Albert, and altered to Prince after his death.

THE EARLY VIEWS OF THE LINE

A good deal of fresh information has come to hand on the subject of the engravings. The word 'London' was accidentally omitted after 'A' in the first entry in the list of 'Publication lines' on p. 128.

There is a state of the first Ackermann plate intermediate between those given as 1 and 2 on p. 129; a copy of which is in the Science Museum. The operation of camouflaging the locomotive as a truck was at first only partly successful, as they merely removed the upper part of the chimney and squared up the boiler, the round front of which was left plainly visible, as were also the large leading wheels. The accompanying reproduction is given by permission of the Director of the Museum.

The description in the 'Centenary History' should therefore have been:

State 2. As last, but hauling ropes added. The upper part of the chimney of the locomotive has been erased, but the circular front of the boiler still remains, also the large leading wheels. Steam shows faintly.

State 3. The locomotive has been transformed completely into a truck, with rectangular front, as in Plate V, *supra*.

State 4. Spanish, &c.

The author's collection has been enriched by the exceptionally lucky 'find' of a pair of sepia drawings by T. T. Bury. One represents the bridge over Water Street, Manchester, and is very similar to no. 6 in the Ackermann set, except that it shows the whole of the bridge, without any buildings on the right side, being drawn at a slightly different angle. The other, which is illustrated here, is extremely interesting. It depicts the station at Edge Hill (in 1831), but is taken from the far side of the Moorish arch, thus showing the relationship of plates 2 and 10[1] to one another, which might not otherwise be realized. The deep shadow running across the extreme foreground of plate 2 is, of course, that thrown by the arch. Traces of the spiral lines round the chimneys, which are so prominent in the second plate by Hughes, can be seen; but as yet there was no balustrade to the stairs.

The author has now a beautiful copy of the aquatint of 1834 mentioned at the top of p. 134, with the four smaller trains, which is $16\frac{1}{2}$ inches square. It is a delightful production, the landscapes in the backgrounds being much more attractive than those in the 'long prints'. The first train is shown leaving Manchester, with warehouses and other buildings, all of which are much changed now, but there is a church steeple which is still identifiable.

---

[1] Plates IX and VIII of the 'Centenary History'.

FIG. 93. Ackermann's Plate I, second state

FIG. 94. Edge Hill station. (From a sepia drawing by T. T. Bury)

The pair of long chromolithographs produced by Raphael Tuck in 1894, mentioned in the middle of p. 134, were copied from the 1831 state of the originals, not 1833. They have detailed information about the engines, &c., in the margins. Another somewhat similar pair, which are very likely older, was copied from the 1833 state, but there are no particulars, publisher's name, nor date.

The lithographs mentioned in the last paragraph of p. 134 are those given at the foot of p. 136, with the exception of the last one, which is a line-engraving, and does not belong to this set. They are believed to be by Crane, and it is probable that the coloured copies which appear from time to time have been embellished since publication.

Mr. John Phillimore has acquired an example of Shaw's 'Opening' (illustrated on p. 59 of the 'Centenary History') in an earlier state than the usual specimens, which came as a surprise to the author, also to the Liverpool Library authorities, who possess untold wealth in the shape of L. & M.R. engravings. It is on india paper. There is no shading on the underside of the arch, nor any smoke. The title is quite different, namely 'Opening of the Railway Septr. 1830'. The publication line is 'Published Novr. 15th 1830, by I. Shaw, Liverpool, and Grundy & Fox, Manchester'.

The date of the ordinary copies is January 1st, 1831. It is just possible that the print in question is the first issue, but until another copy turns up, it must be assumed to be a rejected trial proof.

It now appears that the copies of the Shaw etchings on paper measuring about 12 by $9\frac{1}{2}$ inches are not necessarily proofs, as stated on p. 136 of the 'Centenary History', since there were two issues (of Part I, at all events). The first edition—the large one—had part of the title in ornamental capitals, with the words 'Royal Quarto 5s.' on the cover. In the smaller issue the type was reset all through, with a page of financial statistics added.

Some of the later reprints of the Havell aquatint described at the top of p. 137 have had the date 1825 added on the plate. The author has at last obtained an original (uncoloured), unfortunately with the publication line cut off.

There is now a copy of the portrait of George Stephenson by Moses Haughton in the Phillimore collection. He is holding a sheet of paper with a drawing of the Rocket on it. The name is misspelt 'Stevenson'.

Mr. Phillimore also has a coloured etching of two trains, 11 by $4\frac{7}{8}$ inches, 'drawn by Henry Austen, March 1832: printed by George Smith: published by Thomas Taylor, Castle Street' [Liverpool]. The engines are Planet and Venus.

He has also acquired a set of the three Clayton views, in the original cover, issued with descriptive letterpress.   The latter contains the following interesting remark about the chimneys:

The column which is seen under the arch is the chimney of one of the stationary engines, and is ingeniously constructed of brickwork wrought spirally, so that although 90 feet in height, it is composed of one course of brickwork only.

The author has obtained a charming and unchronicled set of nine views of the line, being small lithographs all on one sheet about 16 inches by 11 inches.   Eight of them are copied very closely from Ackermann's, in the 1833 state; the other being a view of Newton Viaduct.   The title is 'Panorama of the Liverpool and Manchester Railway', publisher not known.

The print described at the foot of p. 138 has for publication line 'Published July 16th, 1894, by the Leadenhall Press Ltd., London'.   It occurs low down, and is, more often than not, discreetly cut off by vendors, or masked in the framing.

THE BIBLIOGRAPHY

There were five editions of Sandars' 'Letter', as follows:

I.	1824	32 pp.	
II.	„	„	differently set.
III.	1825	46 pp.	
IV.	„	„	
V.	„	„	

Copies of the first and third are in the author's collection; a second is at the Institution of Civil Engineers; Mr. Elton has a fourth, and the British Museum a fifth edition.

The Minutes of Evidence taken before the House of Lords Committee were 'Ordered to be printed 18th April 1826'.   Folio, 3231+34 pp. (Phillimore collection.)

Besides a fine map, to be mentioned presently, another important item for 1829 was omitted.   Before the Exchequer Loan Commissioners would advance the £100,000 mentioned on p. 15, they employed Telford to report as to the progress that had been made.   The Report was published with 'Observations in reply by the Directors' on the pages facing his remarks, 16 pages altogether, with two folding lithographed plates showing work done in colour at the Sankey Valley and Newton Bridge, and on the Broad Green embankment.   The author's copy is bound up with a first edition of Walker's and Rastrick's Reports.

There were two impressions of the first edition of Scott Walker's 'Accurate Description'. In the second the word 'object' is omitted from the second paragraph of the Preface and the word 'laterally' in the Errata is corrected to 'Latterly'.

There was a second edition of Kirwan's 'Descriptive and Historical Account' (p. 143); also dated 1831, which only differs by having 'Second Edition' on the title-page.

At the end of the first paragraph of p. 144, the date should be 1831. In the middle of the last paragraph, for 'probably 4th edition' read 'fifth edition'. Add 'There was a sixth edition in 1838'.

The author has had the great good fortune to acquire George Stephenson's own set of maps of the railway. There are seven, fitting into a case which bears his autographed signature.

No. 1 is the map of 1824, forming the second entry on p. 140. It measures 38 by $26\frac{1}{2}$ inches, and represents the line shown in the small illustration on p. 12 ('Centenary History').

The second is a companion one dated 1829, produced by the same publishers, showing the line as made. The rest are as follows (lithographed):

3. 'Plan and Section of an Intended Branch Railway from the Liverpool and Manchester Railway in Roby to the Regent's Road in Liverpool and of another Branch therefrom terminating near the Borough Gaol in Liverpool all in the County Palatine of Lancaster. November 25th, 1830. (Signed) Geo. Stephenson, Engineer'. 32 by $16\frac{3}{4}$ inches. (The scheme was abandoned.)

4. 'Plan and Section of the alterations proposed in the Line of the Railway from Liverpool to Manchester in the County Palatine of Lancaster'. 18 by 11 inches.

Shows the line between Rainhill and Culcheth, a distance of about 12 miles; the 'Parliamentary line' being in red, and the revised route, which is more direct, in blue.

5. The same title as no. 4. 14 by 11 inches. This is a most interesting one, as it gives the alteration made at Manchester; the line crossing the Irwell and Water Street, instead of, as originally planned, bending round in a north-easterly direction, and terminating at Irwell Street in Salford, without crossing the river.

6. A map of the country between Liverpool and Manchester, which appears to have been cut out of a larger one, as there are no lines bounding it. Three railways are indicated; the lowest being 'Present Liverpool and Manchester Railway'; above that, the 'Former Line from which the Liverpool and Manchester Railway Company were driven by Opposition in

1825'; above that again, a dotted line entitled 'Proposed Leeds & Liverpool Railway' (not continued to the east beyond Manchester). It is never farther from the actual L. & M. line than $3\frac{1}{2}$ miles. $19\frac{1}{4}$ by $16\frac{1}{2}$ inches. A meeting of the Leeds and Liverpool subscribers is known to have been held on January 17th, 1831. No Act was obtained. It was also called North Liverpool Railway. The author has reports on it by Vignoles and Locke, which were ordered by the L. & M. directors; also one by Walker and Burges, who were the promoters.

7. 'Plan showing the mode of effecting the Junction of the Liverpool and Manchester Railway with such other Railways as branch from the North side thereof'. 39 by $9\frac{1}{2}$ inches.

Shows a most clumsy arrangement. Trains from the north to Liverpool have a straight run, of course crossing the other line; but those proceeding from Liverpool to the north have to reverse twice.

Two small books on the subject of Huskisson may be added to the bibliography:

> 'Huskisson und die Eisenbahnen', von Joseph Ritter von Baader; München, 1830.
> 'Huskisson and Liverpool', by George S. Veitch, M.A.; Liverpool, 1929.

The last-named author also produced a most valuable addition to the history of the line in the shape of 'The struggle for the Liverpool and Manchester Railway'; Liverpool, 1930.

The date of Sekon's book should be 1899, not 1894.

In 1930 the author wrote a little book for the London, Midland and Scottish Railway Company, which they published at a shilling, entitled 'One Hundred Years of Railways'. The first half of it deals with the Liverpool and Manchester Railway, and gives some information supplementing the 'Centenary History', also some illustrations of the line at the time of writing, taken from the same points as the Ackermann prints, and the comparisons will be found of interest. In that book, the author's intention was to have given both the two 'long prints' in their 1833 state, but by some mistake the lower one was taken from one of 1831.

To the information given at the end of the Bibliography on p. 151 of the 'Centenary History', the following may be added:

The subject of a mythical Rocket no. 2, which was discussed in *The Engineer* during 1884 and 1885, also in the *English Mechanic* of that period, was revived in correspondence in the former, beginning in the issue for December 19th, 1930, and continuing in the first two months of

FIG. 95. Mug showing the Rocket. (Liverpool Museum)

FIG. 96. Jug with the Novelty. (Author's collection)

1931. The author does not believe in it. The extract from David Stevenson's paper, given on p. 202, *ante*, has some slight bearing on the matter.

Weale's *Quarterly Papers on Engineering*, vol. ii (1844), contains 'A Review of the circumstances which have affected the consumption of fuel in the Locomotive Engines of the Liverpool and Manchester Railway, from the opening to the present time; being a paper read before the Liverpool Polytechnic Society: by Edward Woods, C.E. Liverpool'.

A good deal of the above is reproduced in the longer paper in 'Tredgold', mentioned on p. 99 of the 'Centenary History'.

MEDALS, ETC.

The following interesting paragraph appeared in the *Liverpool Courier* for September 15th, 1830, the day of the opening.

THE RAIL-WAY MEDAL.—We were highly gratified yesterday with a sight of the very superb medal just published by Thomas Woolfield, Fancy Bazaar, to commemorate the opening of the rail-way. As a work of art, it is a beautiful and highly-finished production and leaves its competitors far behind, and, being the production of one who is so constantly exerting himself to place before our fair townswomen and townsmen every elegant novelty in his business, we trust it will meet with the patronage so splendid a production deserves. A copy in gold was last evening forwarded to his Grace the Duke of Wellington, Sir Robert Peel and Mr. Huskisson, and we suppose they will be generally worn by those who attend the ceremony this day.

The medal in question was no doubt no. 2 on p. 152.

It may be mentioned here that the *Courier* for September 22nd contained a long and very interesting account of the opening, with a piece of information we did not possess before, namely that Huskisson was taken to Eccles on the band-truck.

Two dies exist of the obverse of medal no. 3. In the first, the fifth line is 'undertaking had', and it is signed 'Ottley' at the foot; in die II, 'undertaking' stands alone in the fifth line, and the signature is 'Ottley Birm.' There is also a slight difference in the arrangement of the leaves at the top of the left palm-branch.

It may be of interest to note that there are also two dies of the reverse of the Stephenson Centenary medal with the Rocket. In die I, the final E of George is level with the centre of the driving wheel and 'THE ROCKET' is 17 mm. long; in die II, the second G is in the position indicated, and 'THE ROCKET' is only 12½ mm.

There are one or two inaccuracies in the lower paragraph of p. 154. A very fine 'frog' mug showing the Rocket is in the possession of the Liverpool Museum, and is illustrated here. The name 'Jaco' as appearing on engines on mugs was a misprint; it should have been Jago. He was a civil engineer, employed on the Brighton Railway under Rastrick, but the author has never heard of his having attained any special eminence in his profession, and is unable to understand why he should have been immortalized in this fashion.

The Leeds and Selby Railway had an engine named Express in 1839. It was apparently only a four-wheeler (see Whishaw, pp. 181, 182).

Another jug showing the Novelty is also illustrated. The man in uniform is probably meant for the Duke of Wellington, but whether he ever rode behind the Novelty is not known. Other examples (one each) of the Northumbrian and William IV pieces are now known.

The marks 'E.U. & M.', 'R.L. & B.', and 'B. & T.' can be added.

Several more examples of the two handkerchiefs illustrated have been reported. Three have been added to the author's collection, one of which is illustrated here; showing the opening procession. It measures $23\frac{1}{2}$ by 20 inches, and is printed in a rich blue. Another, in red, 29 by $26\frac{1}{2}$ inches, depicts the Sankey Viaduct, with trains round the edge, drawn by the Rocket, Novelty, and Sans Pareil.

The above are in fine condition, but the third is unfortunately very pale and faded, probably from injudicious cleaning. It is, however, exceptionally interesting, as it bears five vignettes copied from the Crane lithographs. The trains round the edge are drawn by the Novelty. It is silk, 34 by 38 inches, printed in brown. No other example is known.

A further interesting acquisition is a papier-mâché tray, shown in Fig. 98. The representation of the opening, which is painted, is copied very closely from Shaw's etching.

An illustration is also given of a 'peep-show', belonging to Mr. C. L. Winey, of New York, evidently made in Germany. When extended like a concertina, a longitudinal view of the railway appears inside. The author has a similar one, probably French, as the inscription on the left tower is in that language, and on the right, in English.

The following two newspaper cuttings, which have been pasted in a volume of pamphlets of 1830–2 in the author's collection, are interesting. The sources and dates are not given.

I

STEAM CARRIAGES.—The machinery for arresting the progress of these pleasant and dangerous vehicles, appears to be still extremely de-

FIG. 97. Handkerchief showing the opening procession of the Liverpool and Manchester Railway

FIG. 98. Tray depicting the opening of the Liverpool and Manchester Railway

Fig. 99. Liverpool and Manchester Railway 'peep-show'

ficient. On Wednesday evening the 29th ult., while some men were attempting to take a stone waggon across the Liverpool rail-road, they saw the Meteor coming on at the rate of twenty miles an hour. The watchman made the usual signal to stop the engine; the engineer immediately shut off the steam, and the guards of the different carriages applied the breaks to the wheels; notwithstanding which, the engine came in contact with the waggon, passed over it, and was itself thrown off the rail-road.

II

On Thursday morning the carriages on the railway from Manchester were nearly five hours before they arrived at Liverpool, in consequence of the ice and sleet on the rails; and we are sorry to find report states that a gentleman on one of the carriages had both his legs broken by one carriage coming in contact with another.

CHAPTER XII

BIBLIOGRAPHICAL NOTES

For short details of the bibliography of railways down to the end of 1830, one must refer readers to the excellent results of much research in Mr. R. A. Peddie's 'Railway Literature 1556–1830', published in 1931. The following notes indicate a few omissions and mistakes—inevitable in a pioneer work of the kind—and give fuller particulars of some of the more interesting items. Editions marked * are in the author's collection.

1530? Haselberger (J.). Der Ursprung . . . (The origin of common mining Law). (Illustration of a truck on rails. See Fig. 1.)

1550. Münster (S.). Cosmographia Universalis. (Illustration of a truck on rails. See Fig. 2.)

1556. Agricola (G.). De Re Metallica. Has been translated into English by H. C. and L. H. Hoover. London, 1912.*

*1649. Gray (W.). Chorographia. (See p. 6, *ante.*) Besides the reprint of 1818 recorded by Mr. Peddie, it was reprinted in 1884 by Joseph Crawhall, (*a*) large-paper edition with numerous rough woodcuts coloured by hand,* (*b*) small-paper, illustrations not coloured (Newcastle); and in 1892 at South Shields* (twenty copies, privately printed).

1698. Waller (W.). An Essay on the Mines late of Sir Carbery Price. (See p. 82, *ante.*)

1701. Yalden (T.). Poem on the Mines late of Sir Carbery Price. 2nd edition. (See p. 84, *ante.*)

*1770. Young (A.). A Six Months' Tour through the North of England. In the 1st edition all four volumes are dated 1770.

1778. Hutchinson (W.). A View of Northumberland, vol. ii. (Describes waggon-ways.)

1787. Plan of the Collieries on the Rivers Tyne and Wear. Also Blyth, Bedlington, and Hartley. With the country 11 miles round Newcastle. Taken from actual surveys by John Gibson 1787. 39 by 25 inches. (All the waggon-ways are clearly marked in red. With a vignette showing a coal-staith and waggon-way, for which see frontispiece.) Copy in Newcastle Public Library.

*1788. Reissue of above, with date altered.

1795. Holt (J.). General View of the Agriculture of the County of Lancaster. (Describes railways used in draining Trafford and Chat Mosses.) B.M.

*1796. Curr (J.). The Coal Viewer. First issue. Sheffield, 1796. (See p. 145, *ante.*)

*1801. Outram (B.). Report and Estimate of the Proposed Rail-ways from the Collieries in the Forest of Dean to the Rivers Severn and Wye. Hereford, 1801.

1803. Marshall (R.). An Examination into the respective merits of the proposed Canal and Iron Railway from London to Portsmouth. Pat. Off. L.

*1807. The correct title of the plan in the second paragraph on p. 20 (P.) is 'Plan of a Proposed Line of Rail Way or Tram Road from Kilmarnock to Troon on the West Coast of Ayrshire, 1807'. (See Fig. 66.)

1810. Rennie (J.). Report respecting the proposed Rail-way from Kelso to Berwick. (Phillimore coll.)

1813. Edgeworth (R. L.). An Essay on the Construction of Roads and Carriages (contains proposals for railways with stationary engines; the first suggestion of the use of steam power).

1814. Sinclair (Sir J.). General Report of the Agricultural State and Political Circumstances of Scotland, vol. iii. (Note on iron railways.) B.M.

*1817. Edgeworth (R.L.). An Essay on the Construction of Roads and Carriages. 2nd edn., London, 1817.

1818. Stevenson. The 5th par. on p. 28 should be deleted. There was only one edition (recorded by Peddie on p. 29). It is dated on the title-page 1819; the date on the first page of the Report being December 28th, 1818, it is frequently quoted as 1818. The author's copy is complete, but the one in the Newcastle Literary and Philosophical Society's Library lacks the title-page, and so was entered in their catalogue under the year 1818.

*1819. Dupin (C.). Two Excursions to the Ports of England, Scotland and Ireland in 1816, 1817 and 1818. Translated from the French of C. Dupin. (Description of railway at Plymouth Breakwater.) London, 1819.

1820. P. 29. Omit last paragraph. This entry was made on the strength of a supposed copy in the Barclay Parsons collection, but the author has been informed by the Director of the New York Public

Library that the earliest one in the Parsons collection is dated 1821. (The patent was not obtained until December 1820.)

1824. Jessop (W.). High Peak Steam Railway. Second Report. Derby, 1824.

1825. P. 41. First paragraph should read M(ACLAREN) C. and P.O.L. instead of B.M. The second paragraph should be deleted.

1826. P. 44, seventh paragraph. For 'Gap' read 'Cap'. This is the Hereford Ry.

1826. P. 44, last paragraph but one. Adamson's 'Sketches' appeared in two articles in the *Edinburgh New Philosophical Journal* for October 1825 and April 1826.

1826. P. 46. Sixth paragraph. Add *The Pamphleteer* 1826, and after L.C., B.M.

1828. P. 52. The entry 'Adamson' should come out; it was wrongly entered as 1828 in the Birmingham Library Catalogue.

The following notes give fuller details of some of the most important items, for the benefit of collectors:

Observations on a General Iron Rail-way (by Thomas Gray).

(First edition) 1820: 22 pp.: no illustrations. (Copy in the Inst. C.E. Library.)

Second edition: 1821: 60 pp.: no illustrations. (Copy in British Museum.)

*Third edition, 'revised and considerably enlarged': 1822: xii + 131 pp.: 2 folding plates: 2 maps: one other plate.

*Fourth edition, 'considerably improved': 1823. Identical with the third, except for the title-page. A few small irregularities (though it is extremely well printed) show that the type is the same.

*Fifth edition: 1825: xxiv + 233 pp.: illustrations as 3rd. The first to give the author's name.

All the editions were published by Baldwin, Cradock, & Joy, Paternoster Row, London. For further details see pp. 183, 184, *ante*.

A French translation appeared in the *Bulletin des Sciences Technologiques* in 1827.

The following publication is a fascinating one to collectors, but its bibliography is difficult to make out with certainty, as none of the editions is numbered.

Specification of J. Birkinshaw's Improvement in Malleable Iron Rails to be used in Rail Roads. (See p. 152, *ante*.)

(First edition): Newcastle, 1821. 10 + (2) pp.: 1 folding plate show-ing a coal train drawn by a horse. (Reproduced, reduced, in Fig. 74.) (Copy in British Museum, also in Swan collection.)

(Second edition): 1822. As last. (Copy in University of London Library.)

*(Third edition): Specification of John Birkinshaw's Patent for an improvement in the construction of Malleable Iron Rails, to be used in Rail Roads; with Remarks on the comparative merits of Cast Metal and Malleable Iron Rail-Ways. Newcastle, 1824. 14 + 8 + (2) pp. The folding plate shows the train drawn by a Stephenson engine of 1816 (reproduced in part in Fig. 75). The eight pages separately numbered contain correspondence.

*(Fourth edition): Remarks on the comparative merits of Cast Metal and Malleable Iron Rail-Ways; and an account of the Stockton and Darlington Rail-Way, &c., &c. Newcastle, 1827. 22 + 39 + 26 pp. 3 folding plates, two showing views of the Bedlington Iron Works, and the other the opening of the S. & D. Railway. The plate illustrating the patent is omitted. The third section is a reprint of the Rev. J. Adamson's 'Sketches of our information as to Rail-Roads'.

*(Fifth edition): the title has the addition 'and the Liverpool and Manchester Rail-way'. Newcastle, 1832. 26 + 39 + 38 + (2) + 32 pp. Illustrations as those in the previous edition, together with a very fine folding plate of a Planet-type engine; the best ever published. (Repro-duced on p. 83 of the 'Centenary History of the L. & M.R.'.) The last item in the author's copy is the 'Answer of the Directors' (L. & M.R.) to an article in the *Edinburgh Review*, but Mr. Phillimore has also one with Adamson's 'Sketches' instead; as in the 1827 edition.

(Sixth edition): 'By Michael Longridge' on the title-page, which is otherwise as last. Newcastle, 1838. 32 + 40 + 40 pp. Two plates, one of Bedlington Iron Works, smaller than those in the previous editions, and one of a locomotive named Bedlington (and built there). Also two folding plates containing reports on rails. (Copy in Phillimore collection.)

An important contribution to the history of railways is given in the *Transactions of the Highland Society*, vol. vi (1824).

In the year 1818 'A piece of Plate of Fifty Guineas value' was offered by the Society for the best essay on the construction of railroads for the conveyance of ordinary commodities. The value of the prize was divided between several candidates. Precisely the same thing happened on a second occasion. Some selected essays, edited by Robert Stevenson, were published in the volume mentioned above. They are quite a mine of information, and have been utilized in many places in the present work, either by direct quotation, or by way of check.

In an introduction, Stevenson made the following interesting remarks:

> The wealth of England enables her to stand unrivalled in the formation of her Water-ways or numerous Canals. By these the horse-load has been much extended, and the conveyance of merchandise greatly facilitated. In Scotland and Wales, her less wealthy neighbours have endeavoured to supply this want by the construction of numerous Rail-ways which are perhaps better adapted than canals to the undulating surface of their respective countries; while they are more economical and more generally applicable to the ordinary purposes of commercial traffic.

The best essay is the first one, by Alexander Scott of Ormiston.

A Practical Treatise on Rail-Roads and Interior Communication in general, with original Experiments and Tables of the comparative value of Canals and Rail-Roads. By Nicholas Wood.

*(First edition): London, 1825: (4) + 314 pp.: 6 folding plates. The frontispiece shows an engine with steam springs and chain coupling (Killingworth no. 3?) under the 1816 patent, resembling the Hetton engine illustrated by Strickland exactly. Plate VI shows one of the Wylam engines, which is omitted from the other editions.

*(Second edition): London, 1831 (Hurst, Chance & Co.): xxiii + (5) + 530 pp.: 8 folding plates. The frontispiece is a lithograph of a Planet-type engine, with a fluted chimney like a classical pillar. Plate VII shows one of the Killingworth engines (no. 4?), with plate springs and outside coupling rods. This edition contains an account of the Rainhill trials (at which Wood was one of the three judges) and the competing engines.

Second edition (second issue). Similar to the above, but dated 1832 and published by Longmans. 'Second Edition' on title-page.

*Third edition: London, 1838: xxvii + (1) + 760 pp.: 13 folding plates. The frontispiece is an absurd geared engine built for the G.W.R. in 1838. Small drawings of a Killingworth engine are given on pp. 292 and 293, which are copied from Plate VII of the second edition and may therefore be taken as the most improved form. French and American railways are mentioned; also, at considerable length, the G.W.R.

American edition: Philadelphia, 1832. From the second English one, with additions.

French translation: Paris, 1834. 14 plates. This was based on the second edition and is in two volumes, I, text; II, plates. It contains notes and additions. Possibly there was another French edition.

A Practical Treatise on Railroads and Carriages, showing the Principles of estimating their strength, proportions, expense, and Annual Produce, and the conditions which render them effective, economical and durable; with the theory, effect, and expense of steam carriages, stationary engines, and gas machines. By Thomas Tredgold. London, 1825. 4 plates. For description, see p. 185, *ante*.

Second edition, 1835.

American edition: New York, 1825.

French edition: Paris, 1826.

Report to the Directors on the comparative merits of Loco-motion and fixed engines. By Jas. Walker and J. V. Rastrick.

Mr. Peddie has not recorded the editions quite correctly. The bibliography on p. 141 of the 'Centenary History of the L. and M.R.' has been carefully verified, and is quite right, as far as it goes.

It follows that on p. 62 of Peddie's book, paragraph 5 should be deleted: in paragraph 6 the words 'and Walker (J.)' should also come out. On p. 63 it would be better to transpose paragraphs 9 and 10.

It may be remarked that the above reports, also the Birkinshaw pamphlets, have sometimes been bound up at an early date with other papers, although not originally published in that state. On the other hand, undated copies of Adamson's 'Remarks', which are sometimes found, are believed by the author to have been removed from later editions of 'Birkinshaw'.

Some fine maps appeared in 1829 and 1830:

1. Bradshaw's Map of Canals, Navigable Rivers, Railroads, &c., in the Midland Counties. Published February 12th, 1829. 50 by 54 inches. (L.M. & S.R.)

The author has a second edition, with additions, dated February 12th, 1830. It is accompanied by an 'Appendix' of letterpress giving details, which is dated 1829.

2. Bradshaw's Map of Canals situated in the counties of Lancaster, York, Derby, and Chester. No date. Shows Liverpool and Manchester and five connecting lines. (L.M. & S.R.)

3. *Map of the Inland Navigation, Canals and Railroads, with the situation of the various mineral productions throughout Great Britain. J. Walker, Wakefield. To accompany Priestley's Historical Account of Canals, &c. Published by Richard Nichols, Wakefield. Also Longman & Co., London. January 1st, 1830. $61\frac{1}{2}$ by 75 inches.

The following is a list of the principal books, published since 1830, which contain information concerning the railways previous to that year.

A. WORKS RELATING TO THE RAILWAYS THEMSELVES

1831. Historical Account of the Navigable Rivers, Canals, and Railways of Great Britain, as a reference to Nichols, Priestley, and Walker's New Map of Inland Navigation, derived from original and parliamentary documents in the possession of Joseph Priestley, Esq. First edition $10\frac{3}{4}$ inches high, with preface dated October 1st, 1830. (Phillimore coll.)

*1831. Second edition of the above; 9 inches high, the preface dated April 1831.

Though mainly taken up with canals, this is a most valuable book for the student of early railways; it is, however, confined to those constructed under Acts of Parliament.

*1837. A Practical Treatise on Rail-Roads and Locomotive Engines for the use of Engineers, Mechanics and others; in which the mechanical construction of Edge, Tram, Suspension, and all other railways, and the various Locomotive Carriages, designed for rail and common roads, are described in chronological order, accompanied by an analysis of the whole; including an explanation of every patent that has hitherto been granted in England for improvements in the Mechanism of Locomotion. By Luke Hebert. (London, T. Kelly.)

This book formed, or was founded upon, the article Railway in the 'Engineer's and Mechanic's Encyclopaedia' (of which Hebert was the editor). It contains much of interest, but cannot be implicitly relied upon. There only seems to have been one edition.

*1839. A Practical Treatise on Railways, explaining their construction and management. By Lieut. Peter Lecount. (Edinburgh, A. & C. Black.)

This book was based on the article Railways in the seventh edition of the 'Encyclopaedia Britannica'. It is really a guide to the making and running of a railway, and contains no history, except for a chapter on that of the locomotive, perhaps partly founded on Hebert. It was reissued, in rather an attractive binding, in 1851, in the same type; with errata uncorrected.

1839. The Railways of England; containing an account of their origin, progress and present state; a description of the several parts of a railway, and a history of their invention; together with a Map; with all the lines carefully laid down, both of those already constructed, and those which are projected, or in course of execution. (London, E. Grattan.) There is no author's name, but an 'Advertisement' says: 'The present little Treatise has been compiled by the Author of the "ZOOLOGICAL

GARDENS" to illustrate Mr. Gilbert's excellent *Map of the Railways of England and Wales*.' In the book mentioned, 'The Zoological Gardens' (1st edn. 1838; 2nd 1841), the author's name is not given.

The title stamped on the cover is 'Gilbert's Railway Map of England and Wales'. By way of frontispiece, there is a very clear and interesting folding map, 12 by 15 inches, being a reduced form of the one just to be mentioned. The book itself is small, and of little importance, except that it is interesting to a collector as having a claim to being the first history of railways.

We now come to some more maps, all published about the same time.

*1. Gilbert's New Map of England and Wales, drawn and engraved from the best authorities. London, published by Grattan & Gilbert, January 1st, 1840. 28 by 41 inches, folding into a cloth cover 5 by 7. (An advertisement in the last-mentioned book says it was to be published January 1st, 1839.)

*2. Map and Sections of the Railways of Great Britain. Dedicated by permission to James Walker, F.R.S., L. & E. President of the Institution of Civil Engineers. By George Bradshaw. Published 1st month, 14, 1839. 40 inches by 64½. Folding up into covers like a book, with silk 'tiers'. Also 29 pages of letterpress.

*3. A Geological Map of England, Wales, and part of Scotland, showing also the Inland Navigation by means of Rivers and Canals, with their elevation above the sea, together with the Rail Roads and principal Roads. By J. & C. Walker, No. 3, Burleigh Street, Strand, London. 39½ inches by 57, folding into leather case.

There is no date. It is possibly earlier than the other two. The 'London and Southampton Railroad' is shown as 'complete or in progress', without the branch to Gosport, which was authorized in 1839. The name was changed to L. & S.W.R. in June of that year; but that is no help in dating the map, as the G.W.R. is called 'London and Bristol', which title was not used officially after 1833.

A number of excellent maps were published by Cheffins.

*In 1840 the first bibliography of railways appeared, published in Brussels. It was issued as a 'sample,' with the prospectus of an ambitious work, entitled 'Épistémonomie,' intended to embrace the whole of science, which never appeared. There are over 300 entries, mostly Continental.

Whishaw's 'The Railways of Great Britain' (1840) contains no early history to speak of. There is some in a little book 'Railways; their rise, progress and construction' by Robert Ritchie (1846). It was translated into German; 1st edn. 1847, 2nd, 1853.

In 1851 an important work appeared: 'A History of the English Railway; its social relations and revelations, 1820–1845', by John Francis, 2 volumes. It is well written and full of interest, but is not of a technical nature. A still more popular book came out in the next year, 'Our Iron Roads, their History, Construction and Administration', by F. S. Williams, which ran into at least four editions, but it does not contain any information prior to 1830 which is first-hand.

In 1857 both the first and second editions of Smiles' 'Life of George Stephenson' appeared. He was a ready writer, and his principles were of the highest. Moreover, he took great pains in gathering his material. But he failed to make a study of the subject generally, and discover what others had contributed to it, the result being that he wrote in an 'Eclipse first, the rest nowhere' style, which provoked a good deal of acrimonious controversy. In fact, Oswald Hedley was almost justified in writing: 'Everything connected with locomotion, its invention and subsequent improvements, is ascribed by Mr. Smiles to Mr. Stephenson, to the exclusion of the claims and merits of other scientific men.' The author has the editions of 1857 (2nd), 1862, and 1868, and it is amusing to see how Smiles trimmed his sails from time to time to meet the blasts that assailed him. The 1862 edition, which was the first to incorporate a life of Robert, and to be called 'The Lives of George and Robert Stephenson', contains an appendix entitled 'Narrative of George Stephenson's inventions and improvements in connection with the Locomotive Engine and Railways, by his son, Robert Stephenson' followed by a dissertation written by Smiles himself, endeavouring to justify the claim of Stephenson to the invention of the blast-pipe. But by the time the edition of 1868 appeared, apparently even this line of defence had been rendered untenable, as the appendix was omitted.

Though marred by the faults that have been mentioned, and containing other errors which have not been particularized, this book is one of the great biographies of the world.

A most interesting and valuable epitome of the lives of the Stephensons is contained in an 'Address on the two late Eminent Engineers, the Messrs. Stephenson, Father and Son' delivered to the North of England Institute of Mining Engineers by Nicholas Wood, and published at Newcastle in 1860.

In that year a pamphlet was published at Windermere entitled 'Recollections of Edward Bury by his Widow'. It contains some information about the productions of the Clarence Foundry not given elsewhere, but adds nothing to our knowledge of their locomotives.

During the next thirty years a few books dealing with British railways came out, but none bearing on their early history, except the 'Jubilee Memorial of the Railway System. A History of the Stockton and Darlington Railway', by J. S. Jeans, in 1875.

In 1893 Mr. Edward Baker, a bookseller of Birmingham, issued a 'Handbook to various Publications, Documents and Charts connected with the Rise and Development of the Railway System chiefly in Great Britain and Ireland', which is quite a little mine of bibliographical information.

The year 1896[1] saw the publication, in New York, of a most attractive book measuring 14 by 11 inches, 'The World's Railway,' by J. G. Pangborn. On every page there is a tinted sketch of some form of locomotive. In several cases, however, these are rather imaginative; and the text, so far as European history is concerned, contains a number of inaccuracies derived from earlier writers.

A popular work in two volumes, called 'Our Railways,' by J. Pendleton, which contains a little sketchy history at the beginning, was issued by Cassell & Co. in 1896.

An interesting and valuable résumé of early railway history is contained in an address to the Newcastle-on-Tyne Association of Students of the Inst. C.E. given by J. R. Fletcher in November 1901 and published at Newcastle in 1902. The title is 'The Development of the Railway System in Northumberland and Durham'. Unfortunately, no references are given for the statements and dates. There is a useful plan of the collieries and waggon-ways, copied from one of 1801.

In 1906 a 'Bibliographie des Chemins de Fer' was published in Paris, covering the period 1771 to 1846.

A 'Catalogue of Books on Railway Economics' was brought out at Chicago in 1912. Though containing an immense number of entries, it is confined to the contents of fourteen libraries in the U.S.A.

In 1914 a good little book appeared, 'The British Railway System: outlines of its early development to the year 1844', by H. G. Lewin; it is, however, overshadowed by a rather larger one produced by the same writer eleven years later.

In 1921 an interesting book was published under the title 'A Story of Railway Pioneers, being an account of the invention and works of Isaac Dodds and his son Thomas Weatherburn Dodds', by Major S. Snell. It contains a number of inaccuracies, claims much more for Dodds than he is entitled to, and gives no references.

The centenary of the Stockton and Darlington Railway in 1925 called

[1] The date on the title-page is 1894.

forth a delightful book by Randall Davies called 'The Railway Centenary, a Retrospect', together with another, 'The Centenary of Public Railways', which was published at Stockton. There also appeared a book by H. G. Lewin, 'Early British Railways: A short history of their origin and development, 1801–1844', which gives condensed but valuable information about all the lines constructed under Acts of Parliament during the period laid down in the title. An interesting little pamphlet was issued that year, which has some nice illustrations, entitled 'Intimate Story of the Origin of Railways', by W. D. (i.e. Wayman Dixon).

In 1928 a life of Matthew Murray was published, edited by E. Kilburn Scott, which gives some details of the Blenkinsop railway and engines.

An excellent pamphlet by F. G. Bing on 'The Grand Surrey Iron Railway' came out in 1931. There is a fairly full bibliography, but it appears to be confined to works in the Croydon Library. It is far from correct to say, as the preface does, that it 'embraces all the known literature on the subject'.

A truly magnificent book was published in 1935 by *L'Illustration*, Paris, the historical section of which was written by Mr. C. Dollfus. As it comes down to the present day, only a small part falls within our period. It is one of the finest books on railways which has ever appeared.

In 1937 an admirable little book appeared, called 'The Evolution of Railways', by Charles E. Lee. The very close correspondence between the early records it contains with those comprised in Chapter I of the present work is surprising, in view of the fact that both researches were completely independent of one another, and encourages the hope that the material available has been thoroughly sifted.

B. WORKS DEALING WITH LOCOMOTIVE HISTORY

The books mentioned below are mostly on the steam-engine, including some before 1830. Much of the information about early locomotives contained in them is inaccurate; the same mistakes cropping up again and again, owing to 'the blind leading the blind'.

The first to take in locomotives was Partington's, of which there were two editions, 1822 and 1826.

The second was by Stuart (pseudonym for Robert Stuart Meikleham), of which two (identical) editions appeared in 1824 and a third (also unchanged) in 1825. Further editions came out in 1829 and 1831.

The third was Galloway; first edition, 1826; reissued, 1827; 'second edition', 1828. A third edition came out in 1829, with an appendix by Luke Hebert, and a fourth in 1836.

Lardner's book on the steam-engine ran into many editions, but they contain nothing first-hand on the early history. The same remark applies to Tredgold's, and a host of smaller books. Thurston's (1878) contains a little, also R. L. Galloway's 'The Steam Engine and its Inventors' (1881). Both these last two books are excellent small histories of the steam-engine.

A book with some very interesting drawings of early locomotives, not, however, all accurate, was published at Paris in 1886, called 'Origine de la Locomotive', by Deghilage.

A paper was read before the Cleveland Institution of Engineers in 1886: 'An outline History of the Locomotive Engine', by Theodore West. The author's copy is 'second edition', 1887.

Three popular books on locomotives followed: Stretton (1892, succeeded by several editions), Bowen Cooke (1893), and Sekon (1899).

In 1923 two important books were added to those dealing with the history of the locomotive, 'A Century of Locomotive Building', by J. G. H. Warren, and 'Timothy Hackworth and the Locomotive', by Robert Young.

The year 1927 saw the publication of the late E. L. Ahrons' fine volume 'The British Steam Railway Locomotive, 1825–1925', the first two chapters of which deal with engines before 1830.

The author's 'Two Essays in Early Locomotive History' appeared in 1928. A Supplement is in preparation, to be entitled 'Early British Locomotives'.

Bibliographical notes on the following have been given on previous pages:

Medhurst: Chapter VIII, pp. 168, 169.
Vallance: ,,   ,, p. 170.
S. & D.R.:   ,,   X, p. 194.
L. & M.R.   ,,   XI, pp. 206–9.

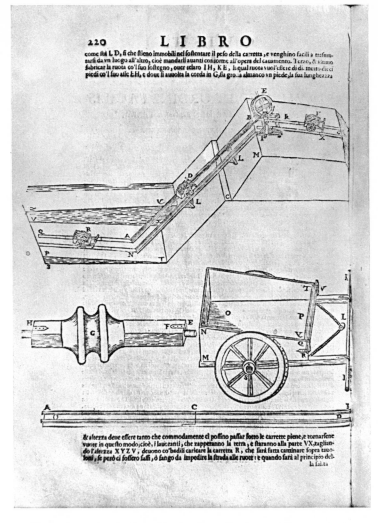

220 **LIBRO**

come ftà L D, fi che ftieno immobili nel foftentare il pefo della carretta, e venghino facili a trafmu-
tarfi da vn luogo all'altro, cioè mandarfi auanti conforme all'opera del cauamento. Terzo, & vltimo
fabricar la ruota co'l fuo foftegno, ouer fclaro I H, K E, la qual ruota vuol'effere di di. metro diici
piedi co'l fuo alfe E H, e doue fi auuolta la corda in G, fia groffa almanco vn piede, la fua lunghezza

& altezza deue effere tanto che commodamente el poffino paffar fotto le carrette piene, e tornarfene
vuote in quefto modo; cioè, i lauoranti, che zapperanno la terra, e ftaranno alla parte VX, taglian-
do l'altezza X Y Z V, deuono co' badili caricare la carretta R, che farà fatta caminare fopra tauo-
loni, fe però ci foffero faffi, ò fango da impedire la ftrada alle ruote; e quando farà al principio della falita

FIG. 100. An Italian illustration of 1609. (See p. 234)

FIG. 101. Relics of the Stondart Quarry Railway. (See p. 242)
From a photograph by A. Stanley Davies

INDEX AND GLOSSARY

A

D

E

    According to Willet, 'Memorials of Hawarden', 1822, a wooden tramway was built about 1770 to carry coals from the Ewloe hills. There are several references to railways in the Hawarden deeds in the National Library of Wales. A lease of 1751 gave the right to level ground and lay rails from coal-pits in Pentrobin and Benwell or from Ewloe (ref. no. 1327). Two acres of common land were granted by deed dated July 8th, 1818, for a church in the manor of Ewloe, which were bounded by a 'railway leading from the river Dee to the brickworks of Mr. Jonathan Catherall' (no. 1798).

F

    Author of 'General View of Agriculture and Minerals of the County of Derby', 1811–13.

—, John (1791–1851), engineer

    Son of the above. Author of 'A Treatise on the Steam Engine', 1827.

Fatfield Colliery, Durham

    Near Chester-le-Street. Used brake-chains in 1834. The railway is not in maps of 1788 and 1812, and may have been made after 1830.

Flange

    Applied (1) to the ledge of a plate-rail. 1818, R. Stevenson ('Report on Edinburgh Railways'), 'a projecting ridge or flange upon the outer verge'. Farey calls it flanch (1817); Cumming, flaunche (1824).

    (2) to that of a wheel. 1838, Simms ('Public Works of Great Britain'), 'the flange or rib on the tire shall not project more than an inch'.

Fodder, or Fother

    A measure for coal, about 19 cwt. *See* Chaldron.

    At first called Bullo Pill Ry.

G

    Sold to the Caledonian Ry. 1846.

Gate

    Sometimes used for an underground way in a mine.

    The following is an interesting quotation from Brees' 'Railway Glossary' (1839), s.v. Trackway: 'There is . . . a trackway at Glasgow, part of which is laid at 1 in 20, upon which a horse can drag 4 tons, and the amount of repairs on it is very trifling. The trams are 8 inches wide, 2 inches thick, and are made in 3 feet lengths.'

I

Q

R

S

T

Taunton Grand Western Railroad Co.
   Prospectus, 1825 (B.M.). 'To use locomotive steam engines, or other power for the convey-ance of passengers and merchandise.' Not made.

Tavistock Canal 70
Taylor, Messrs., of Ayr 135, 151
Team Colliery, Durham . . .· 9, 18
Telford, Thomas (1757–1834) 114, 130, 135
   See 'Life'; 'The Story of Telford'; D.N.B.; &c.
Tempest, Sir Richard 6
Temple, Simon, colliery owner 23
Tender
   Wood calls it the 'convoy carriage' in all three editions. The O.E.D. quotes Maclaren (1825) as saying, 'A small waggon bearing water and coals follows close behind the engine, and is called the Tender, i.e. the "Attender".'
Thanet Canal, Yorks.
   Act, 1773. Constructed by the Earl of Thanet from near Skipton Castle to the Leeds & Liver-pool Canal. The length was only ⅓ of a mile. Railways were laid from it to quarries about a mile above the Castle (Priestley).
Thomas, William, of Denton, Northumbd. . . . . 16, 175 *seq.*
Thompson, Benjamin, engineer . . . 17, 26 *seq.*, 150, 160 *seq.*
—, James, engineer 153
Thornhill, Elias, inventor 14
Thornley Colliery, Durham 18
Throckley Ry., Northumbd. 23, 160
Ticket
   A share certificate was so called about 1800.
Ticknall, Derbysh. 44, 47, 50
Tiller . . . . 12, &c.
   An old name for a brake. Originally used in the days before there was a separate block to take the wear. Called by Farey a 'clamp or logger'; 'convoy' by many writers.
Tindale Fell Ry., Cumbd. 34, 145, 151, 153, 154
Titchfield, Marquis of (1768–1854) 131
   Became 4th Duke of Portland in 1809.

Trackway
   The following is taken from Brees' 'Railway Glossary' (1839), s.v. Tram.
   'Trackways form the nearest approximation to railways, and were introduced into this country about the year 1600; they were originally constructed of timber, the transverse sleepers being of oak or fir, from 4 to 6 inches square, 5 or 6 feet long, and laid about 2 feet apart. The longitudinal beams or rails were generally of sycamore or larch, laid across the former, being secured thereto by pins, and were from 4 to 6 inches square, and laid in about 5 or 6 feet lengths; and this description of line formed what was called a *single way*. When two longitudinal beams were laid one upon the other, it was called a *double way*, the which constituted a great improvement on the former.'

Trafford Moss, Lancs. 37
Train
   The first instance of application to railway vehicles in the O.E.D. is a quotation from Scott's 'Highland' paper, 1824.
Tram
   The earliest meaning seems to have been the shaft or handle of a cart or barrow. There are very similar words with the same meaning in other languages. In coal-mining it was used to denote a truck; O.E.D. gives two xvith-century quotations and one of 1708.
   Also used for the track or the rails themselves: 'An improvement on the tram or wooden

Railway' (Stevenson's 'Report' of 1818). 'The Manchester and Liverpool railroad, in my opinion, is constructed too narrow both in the trams and the spaces between them' (N. W. Cundy, 'Inland Transport,' 1833). Cf. Latin *trames*, a path, road, or way.

Trammer

A man or boy who moves the coals in a tram (Ure, 'History of Arts', 1839).

Tram-plate

A plate-rail. (Le Caan, 'Improved Tram-plates for carriages on Rail Roads', *Trans. Soc. Arts*, 1807.)

Tramroad

An agreement of Dec. 18th, 1800, is quoted in J. Lloyd's 'Old South Wales Iron Works', 1906: 'The Monmouthshire Canal Company . . . shall make a good and sufficient tramroad, according to the plans of Benjamin Outram . . . from the Tredegar Iron Works to join their canal near Risca Church.' Here we have it in juxtaposition with the name of Outram, from which it has been falsely derived.

Simms, 'Public Works', 1838, uses the term 'tram road' for a road with stone sills for the wheels of carts.

Turn-out

'In single railways it is necessary to have places at certain intervals where the empty waggons in returning, may get off the road to allow the loaded ones to pass. A place of this kind is termed a *turn-out*; and the waggons are directed into it by a moveable rail termed a *pointer* . . . This contrivance is also used whenever one line of railway crosses another.' (Encyc. Brit., 1824; article Railways.)

U

Usk Tramroad, *see* Mamhilad Ry.

V

W

Further note on the Belvoir Castle Railway.

> In an article in the *Railway Magazine* for June 1938, Mr. Charles E. Lee
> has shown that the account given on p. 51, on the authority of C. E.
> Stretton, is utterly inaccurate. Documents at the Belvoir Castle Estate
> Office show that the railway was built in 1815, by the Butterley Iron-
> works Company.

Further note on Northampton.

> The author has just acquired a copy of a pamphlet entitled 'The Iron Roads
> of Northamptonshire' by Christopher A. Markham, F.S.A. (1904). It
> mentions a tramway from Gayton, on the Grand Junction Canal, to Nor-
> thampton (about 4 miles as the crow flies) which was made prior to 1806,
> and quotes the following resolution passed by the Corporation of Nor-
> thampton in October 1809 (from the Borough Records, vol. ii, p. 542):

> 'That this assembly has observed with regret a railway substituted for a
> canal by the Grand Junction Company, a mode of communication equally
> as injurious to this Town and Neighbourhood as to the Canal Company,
> experience having fully proved it to be inadequate for the purpose intended
> inasmuch as the articles that are conveyed along it are unavoidably subject
> to great waste breaking and Pilferage the communication is much more
> difficult and expensive than it would have been by water and nearly all
> perishable articles of Merchandise are prevented from passing along it.'

> The above is of interest in connexion with the attempt that has recently
> been made to refute the established tradition that the London and Birming-
> ham Railway was driven away from Northampton by local opposition
> ('Northampton Vindicated, or Why the Main Line missed the Town', by
> Joan Wake, 1935).